LITERACY INSTRUCTION WITH DISCIPLINARY TEXTS

Also from the Authors

Cracking the Common Core:
Choosing and Using Texts in Grades 6–12
*William E. Lewis, Sharon Walpole,
and Michael C. McKenna*

Differentiated Literacy Instruction in Grades 4 and 5,
Second Edition: Strategies and Resources
*Sharon Walpole, Michael C. McKenna,
Zoi A. Philippakos, and John Z. Strong*

Literacy Instruction
with Disciplinary Texts

STRATEGIES FOR GRADES 6–12

William E. Lewis
John Z. Strong

Foreword by Lyn Long and Bilinda Sikes

THE GUILFORD PRESS
New York   London

Library of Congress Cataloging-in-Publication Data

Names: Lewis, William E. (Associate professor of literacy education), author. |
  Strong, John Z., author.
Title: Literacy instruction with disciplinary texts : strategies for grades 6–12 /
  William E. Lewis and John Z. Strong ; foreword by Lyn Long and Bilinda Sikes.
Description: New York : The Guilford Press, [2021] | Includes bibliographical references
  and index.
Identifiers: LCCN 2020032814 | ISBN 9781462544684 (paperback) |
  ISBN 9781462544752 (hardcover)
Subjects: LCSH: Language arts—Correlation with content subjects. | Language arts
  (Secondary)
Classification: LCC LB1631 .L43 2021 | DDC 372.6—dc23
LC record available at *https://lccn.loc.gov/2020032814*

To the memory of Michael C. McKenna,
literacy leader, mentor, and friend

About the Authors

William E. Lewis, PhD, is Associate Professor of Literacy Education in the School of Education at the University of Delaware, where he teaches undergraduate and graduate courses in content-area literacy, English language arts (ELA) methods, and young adult literature. Dr. Lewis presents a range of professional development seminars on secondary content-area literacy and text-based writing. Before teaching at the University of Delaware, he taught high school ELA for 20 years in Pennsylvania public schools. His research has been published in leading journals. Dr. Lewis is a recipient of the Excellence in Teaching Award from the University of Delaware.

John Z. Strong, PhD, is Assistant Professor of Literacy Education in the Graduate School of Education at the University at Buffalo, State University of New York, where he teaches graduate courses in middle childhood/adolescent literacy methods and reading strategies instruction. Dr. Strong previously taught high school ELA in Delaware. His research interests include integrated reading and writing interventions for students in grades 4–12. He has published in leading journals and is a recipient of the Timothy and Cynthia Shanahan Outstanding Dissertation Award from the International Literacy Association.

Foreword

As educational professionals who are responsible for the literacy development of our students, we know that instructional decisions significantly impact adolescents and their ability to be successful in a world that demands robust literacy skills. Like many of you who are reading this book, we too have faced the challenges of implementing high-impact literacy initiatives in secondary schools and the confusion that often accompanies decisions about how to choose, introduce, and use evidence-based strategies that can improve students' learning. Before you begin this book, we offer up our own stories—one from an assistant principal (Lyn Long) and one from an instructional coach (Bilinda Sikes)—to help you see how we approached these challenges in a struggling middle school. We began slowly at first, choosing specific high-impact strategies with which our teachers could experience success. Then we worked together to increase our repertoire of strategies and expand their use across all content areas. Here are our experiences.

THE ASSISTANT PRINCIPAL

When I became an administrator in the Title I middle school where I taught, it was a challenge that was near and dear to my heart. Going into the new assignment, I already knew how hard the teachers worked and the obstacles that our students faced. I also knew that the state education department was making some changes that would be difficult for the school and teachers to weather (e.g., changes to the teacher evaluation system, state standards, and high-stakes assessments). We had an uphill battle.

Two of the three schools in the district serving the greatest number of economically disadvantaged students were the "feeder" schools for our middle school. Each year, 60–70% of our incoming sixth graders came to us reading below grade level. When the state adopted new, more rigorous English language arts (ELA) standards, our students were ill equipped to meet grade-level expectations. Students who had no trouble with previous standards experienced greater difficulty with the more challenging requirements, and their behavior in response to these challenges seemed more difficult to manage. Because of this, our teachers were exhausted, both mentally and physically. And this was just the beginning of the tidal waves we were about to experience in the next couple of years.

The state's accountability measure ranked our school the lowest in the district. With a failing grade, we had a large turnover of teachers and, perhaps even more devastating, a turnover in our principalship, with three different principals in 3 years. As a new administrator, I felt like my head was swimming with problems. Which problem should we address first? I kept picturing that cartoon of the kid who puts his finger in a hole in the wall to stop a leak, but when another leak appears he uses another finger to stop that one. Of course, in the cartoon as in reality, the leaks kept coming. We were running out of fingers, and I knew that none of us, neither the teachers nor the administrators, could work any harder.

I vividly remember holding a faculty meeting that first year in order to address some of the teachers' concerns. As the noise level grew, I asked what they wanted us to recognize as their chief concern. One of our beloved, veteran teachers vehemently yelled out in the faculty meeting, "They can't read! How can I help them if none of them can read?" The moment that this child-loving, guitar-playing, joke-telling, grandfatherly veteran teacher yelled this out in a faculty meeting was profound for all of us. It was at that moment that we knew the first thing that had to be done was to address the literacy problem in our school.

We formed a literacy team, and then we applied for and received a grant from our state education department. The principal (our second principal) and I attended a Striving Readers Comprehensive Literacy conference for administrators as part of the grant requirements. It was there that we were introduced to the Comprehensive Reading Solutions team. We listened as data were shared on other struggling middle schools and the strategies used to meet the needs of their learners. From that conference, we took away three things that were key to our plan for success.

First, the number of students with reading difficulties was too large to handle through Tier 2 intervention or Tier 3 remediation. We first had to support *all* learners, and that work had to be done in Tier 1 instruction by incorporating research-based strategies across the board. We didn't have time to experiment with what "might" work. We needed to implement strategies that would lead to results. Luckily, our instructional coach had previously worked in one of the schools that was highlighted by the state as making strong gains in achievement. They did that by incorporating Peer-Assisted Learning Strategies (PALS) in every content area at least 2 days per week. Because of its proven success, we decided that we would use our schoolwide flexible (flex) time to explicitly teach all of our students to use PALS as a during-reading strategy. The instructional coach and I worked together to design the instruction to model and practice the use of PALS. On Monday teachers used a prereading activity to build background knowledge. On Tuesday they taught students to read a content-area article using PALS. On Wednesday teachers assigned postreading, a text-based writing activity, and a prereading activity for a second article. On Thursday students practiced PALS with the second article. On Friday students completed a postreading activity to synthesize the information in both articles. We were able to use the grant money to pay teachers a stipend over the summer to write the curriculum for the next school year's literacy flex time. We also used the grant to flood our school with high-interest, grade-level texts in all content areas to use with the new curriculum.

Our second take-away was that if we attempted to solve everything, we would solve nothing. We were spreading our teachers too thin, and we ourselves were being spread too thin. As administrators, we had to clear the table of all other initiatives. Yes, behavior management is important, but we couldn't expect teachers to become experts in behavior management strategies and literacy strategies at the same time. We had to focus on our greatest need, and that was literacy. With our flex time being devoted to literacy, we had to go back and take a hard look at the *whys* and the *hows*. We had to revisit why we were using certain procedures and reevaluate how effective they were. We were moving a barge, and so that move had to be carefully planned, as it takes time and space. Each phase of that maneuver had to be carefully planned and supported. As I write this, there is a barge off the coast of Georgia that didn't make that turn successfully. It is now turned over on its side, divested of its crew and cargo, empty and failed. Every time I see it, I am reminded of how easily that empty barge could have been our school and its literacy goals. In order to be successful, we had to make sure that everyone in our school knew what we were doing, why we were doing it, and how we were doing it. Four years later, I can finally say that every teacher and administrator can articulate our literacy goals.

Third, and possibly most important, we found that ongoing professional learning would be paramount to our success. We had to implement this literacy initiative in phases so that we could provide adequate support for our teachers. We first focused our professional learning on before-, during-, and after-reading strategies, with a lot of coaching on implementation. We offered all of our teachers the chance to go to the Striving Readers Secondary Institutes to learn firsthand about research-based instructional strategies. We then contracted with Comprehensive Reading Solutions and Dr. William Lewis to come to the school and lead teachers in all content areas in creating our own *instructional brand* that utilized the reading strategies highlighted in this book. We later added text-based writing strategies to our brand. The strategies were welcomed with open arms by all of our teachers, especially those in math and science.

THE INSTRUCTIONAL COACH

As a classroom ELA teacher who was part of writing the initial literacy lessons for our flex time, I was all in when it came to providing a schoolwide focus on literacy across content areas in Tier 1. I knew firsthand the reading difficulties our students had, and I was both frustrated and overwhelmed by the magnitude of the problem. There was no way literacy instruction during one daily instructional block would produce any appreciable growth for students performing two, three, and even four grade levels below proficiency. We needed help, and we needed everyone to take on the mantle of responsibility for making sure our students received the help they needed, even if it meant stepping out of our comfort zones.

The initial summer professional learning days for our teachers went just about how I expected. Some teachers were enthusiastic participants who couldn't wait to implement the new strategies and help build our instructional brand. Others were a little slower to buy in to the idea. They did as they were asked, but they had more of a wait-and-see attitude because they weren't convinced this approach was going to work. Most of us had been through training like this before, sessions in which someone tries to convince you that their solution is the one you need. Teachers' initial skepticism was understandable. I, too, had been through professional learning that I felt lacked understanding of the realities I dealt with in my classroom. But this was different. It wasn't a packaged program someone was selling us. It was a set of research-based strategies handpicked to meet our students where they were and guide them to where we needed them to be.

Those summer work days when we developed the initial units for our literacy flex time forged a bond between those of us who were involved. We were going to be the ones to champion this cause and move the school forward. We set out to create high-interest, thematic units that teachers would want to teach and in which students would want to actively participate. The work was exhausting, but it was meaningful and worthwhile. The finished product was not perfect, but it reflected our best work based on what we knew at the time. We eagerly shared those lessons with our colleagues, looking forward to the difference we were all going to make together.

Then came the hard part: getting everyone on the same page at the same time. That year we welcomed a new principal, so we were adjusting to new leadership at the same time that we were rolling out this new initiative. Needless to say, the road was a little bumpier than I expected. Our teachers were struggling to implement the strategies consistently, and our students weren't exactly excited about an additional instructional period in which we asked them to read and write. Those of us who were so hopeful when we designed the units were discouraged at the lack of excitement over the fruits of our labors. I had no problem approaching the process with energy and passion in my classroom with my students. But teachers talk, and I knew not everyone had bought in to the idea. It was going to take more hard work to get us where we needed to be.

At the end of that first year, our school went through another transition as we welcomed another new principal and I took the position of instructional coach. At the time, I fully expected there to be a period of adjustment for everyone as I settled into my new role. What I wasn't prepared for was the isolation that exists in the in-between, when you're no longer strictly a colleague but you're not a person of authority either. I didn't have a plan in place for navigating the inevitable bumps in the road ahead, so I approached my new position with one goal in mind: remember why you're here. This school is my home, and the people in it are my family. It was going to take time to figure out the effect that a change in title would have on individual relationships, but nothing changed in our shared mission to serve "our kids."

How was I going to support our teachers in a way that would guarantee most—if not all—teachers would at least feel equipped to implement the strategies with fidelity? I reflected on what made it difficult even for someone like me who was convinced of the necessity of a schoolwide focus on literacy and who was completely on board with the plan. I ultimately settled on four things I would have to do to get everyone else on board with me.

The first thing I had to do was make it *easy*. Our teachers work hard. Adding "one more thing" for them to do was not an option, so my first task was to give them everything they needed. When they had a text to read, I made sure they had copies. When there was an activity to be done, I provided the supplies. When they couldn't access a resource, I resolved the issue.

The second thing I had to do was make it *personal*. It wasn't enough to tell our teachers the aggregated data that supported the need for our literacy plan. They needed to know that what they did during this time every day had a direct impact on the students who sat in their classrooms, played on their sports teams, and participated in their clubs. I posted data on the wall in our professional learning community (PLC) meeting room, I gave teachers updated reports on students' reading achievement when they were available, and I conducted regular walkthroughs with administrators to recognize and applaud the work that was being done.

The third thing I had to do was make it *flexible*. There's not a teacher anywhere who likes being told how to do his or her job. We're professionals and we want to be treated as such. So, teachers were asked to give feedback on the units. We began looking at the units critically to find places where we needed to make changes and places where we needed to start over. We spent another summer revising and improving the units based on teachers' feedback, and we began to incorporate additional research-based strategies that offered teachers more flexibility and choice.

Finally, I had to make it *safe*. No one wants to feel like a failure, so I had to make sure that teachers were encouraged to take risks and try some of these literacy strategies in their content-area classes and that they were given the necessary resources and support to do so. The point of our literacy flex time was not to create a single time and place for connected reading and writing to take place in the school day. Rather, it was designed to be a place where we practice reading and writing strategies so we could use them meaningfully and purposefully in every class, in every content area, and with every student. The professional development team's visits to our school—first to train teachers in the use of reading and writing strategies and then to provide feedback on their use—were the jumping-off point for providing ongoing, meaningful support to our teachers.

LOOKING BACK AND MOVING FORWARD

The authors of this book provided an invaluable comprehensive guide as we implemented new strategies and created an instructional brand in our school. We've reached a point where most of our teachers are confident in their ability to match texts and tasks with the reading and writing strategies that best assist students with meeting the demands of our state standards. Through targeted professional learning, we have expanded our repertoire of literacy strategies to include quad text sets, PALS, Reciprocal Teaching, Reading Guides, Magnet Summaries, CSET, and several others. Teachers who once felt, out of necessity, that they had to read the text to their students in order for them to understand the content now routinely utilize these strategies as a way to support students as they construct their own understanding of grade-level texts.

More importantly, our students are better equipped to be self-directed learners. They are increasingly able to choose the appropriate learning strategy from those that are embedded in the high-utility instructional frameworks found in this book in order to read and understand complex texts and produce original written work that meets and exceeds grade-level expectations.

Looking back, would we do this work again? It's hard, it's draining, it's slow-moving, and it's excruciatingly difficult, but it is also rewarding. It is difficult for teachers to look reflectively at their own practice. It is tough to balance the fierce urgency of now with the reality that if we don't take time to pause and ask ourselves the *whys* and *hows,* we find ourselves endlessly looking for solutions rather than truly fixing the root cause of the problem. But when you see the barge beginning to turn, and you know everyone is rowing in the same direction, you know it is worth it. Yes, we would do it all over again. Our children are worth the struggle.

LYN LONG, Assistant Principal
BILINDA SIKES, Instructional Coach
Effingham County Middle School
Guyton, Georgia

Contents

CHAPTER 1

Introduction to Adolescent Literacy

There is a common saying in the field of secondary education that you may have heard before: Every teacher is a teacher of reading. This expression has been echoed for decades (e.g., Bossone, 1962; Penhale, 1939). It suggests that teachers of all content areas should be responsible for teaching reading, not just teachers of English language arts (ELA). As we ourselves are former high school ELA teachers, we are familiar with the expectation that teaching students how to read has traditionally been considered to be within our purview. Yet many middle and high school ELA teachers are not adequately prepared to teach reading (Lovette, 2013). In fact, as a first-year teacher, John realized that although he felt prepared to teach his students about *literature,* he knew little about teaching *literacy,* the ability to read and write. Teachers of other content areas, including science, social studies, and mathematics, may also feel underprepared to teach reading and writing (Fang, 2014; Graham, Capizzi, Harris, Hebert, & Morphy, 2014; Kiuhara, Graham, & Hawken, 2009; Romine, McKenna, & Robinson, 1996).

In this book we offer up a different saying. Every teacher is *not* a teacher of reading, but every teacher should know how to use reading to teach their content. Instead of being responsible for the actual teaching of reading and writing, we argue that content-area teachers should know how to capitalize on reading and writing as a way to support learning (Fisher & Ivey, 2005). To paraphrase something that Bill regularly tells his preservice teachers, reading and writing are *vehicles* for teaching and learning of content. In order to maximize the efficiency of those vehicles, teachers need to select high-quality texts that will appropriately challenge their students, provide opportunities for a high volume of reading and writing across content areas, and teach reading and writing strategies that support learning from texts.

This book is an extension of an earlier book, *Cracking the Common Core: Choosing and Using Texts in Grades 6–12* (Lewis, Walpole, & McKenna, 2014), that we have used extensively in our work with middle and high school teachers across content areas. The primary audience of that book was school leaders, including administrators and instructional coaches, who were looking for guidance on meeting a challenging new set of standards. In the years since its publication, we have found that many teachers with whom we have worked have requested more guidance in implementing the instructional frameworks and recommendations within that book.

Our purpose in writing this book is to help teachers choose texts and use them to promote learning of content through reading and writing. We discuss considerations for selecting complex texts in Chapter 2, and then we present a framework for increasing reading volume by using sets of connected texts in Chapter 3. The next three chapters provide a menu of instructional strategies to support students' learning before, during, and after reading disciplinary texts. These are followed by three chapters on teaching writing, including brief written responses, extended writing, and inquiry projects that involve conducting research. We conclude the book with ideas for putting it all together to help content-area teachers integrate literacy in their daily instruction.

We begin the book with an introduction to adolescent literacy instruction that serves as a foundation on which the rest of the chapters are built. First we discuss adolescents' literacy achievement to set the stage. Next we provide an overview of literacy development and instruction, focusing on reading and writing skills and their role in next-generation learning standards and content-area instruction. We conclude with a preview of the book's chapters, which aim to help you get started using literacy to improve your content-area instruction.

ADOLESCENT LITERACY ACHIEVEMENT

Understanding the literacy needs of adolescents is critical to using reading and writing to support their content learning; these needs have changed rapidly in the past decade. With the adoption of college and career readiness (CCR) standards in many states, the presence of new technologies and multimodal texts in classrooms, shifts in diversity of the nation's adolescents, and growing interest in better preparing students for civic engagement (Baye, Inns, Lake, & Slavin, 2019), the goals for secondary instruction have changed dramatically.

Unfortunately, adolescent literacy achievement has remained largely unchanged over the past decade. By literacy achievement, we mean the reading and writing skills that are necessary to be successful in school, at work, and throughout life. These are skills that many adolescents have difficulty acquiring (Graham et al., 2018). Adolescents' reading and writing skills, along with their knowledge of subjects such as mathematics and science, are measured periodically through the National Assessment of Educational Progress (NAEP) in grades 4, 8, and 12. The most recent NAEP reading assessment was administered in grades 4 and 8 in 2019, and the most recent NAEP writing assessment was given in grades 8 and 12 in 2011. Three achievement levels—Basic, Proficient, and Advanced—are used to describe the knowledge and skills that readers and writers should possess within each grade (National Assessment Governing Board, 2017, 2019). The percentages of students who performed at each achievement level on the most recent NAEP reading and writing assessments are presented in Figure 1.1.

The most striking statistics are the percentages of students who score below the Proficient level in reading and in writing. Approximately two-thirds of fourth- and eighth-grade students do not possess the reading skills necessary to comprehend challenging academic subject matter (National Center for Education Statistics [NCES], 2019). The writing results are even more troubling. Nearly three-fourths of eighth- and twelfth-grade students do not possess the writing skills necessary to communicate effectively (NCES, 2012). Another way of interpreting these results is to look at how little they have changed over time. Figure 1.2 shows the percentage of students scoring at or above the proficient level on the NAEP reading assessment from 2002 to 2019. As you can see, adolescents' reading skills have hardly improved in 17 years. As a result, capitalizing on students' literacy abilities to support learning poses a significant challenge.

What these figures don't show you is also troubling—the disparities in literacy achievement for different subgroups of students. The percentages of Black/African American students, Hispanic/Latino students, Native Hawaiian/Other Pacific Islander students, and American Indian/Alaska Native students scoring at or above the proficient level in reading and writing are significantly lower than the national average, hovering around 20% (NCES, 2012, 2019). The percentages are around the same for students who are eligible for free or reduced-price lunch and worse for students with disabilities and English learners.

A similar picture of disparities in adolescent literacy achievement by race/ethnicity is evident in the most recent SAT results. The CCR benchmark for the Evidence-Based Reading and Writing (ERW) section, which includes a test of reading comprehension and a test of writing and language skills, is 480. Students

| | Reading | | Writing |
Achievement Level	Grade 4	Grade 8	Grade 12
Advanced	9	4	3	3
Proficient	26	29	24	24
Basic	31	39	54	52
Below Basic	34	27	20	21

FIGURE 1.1. NAEP reading and writing percentages by achievement level.

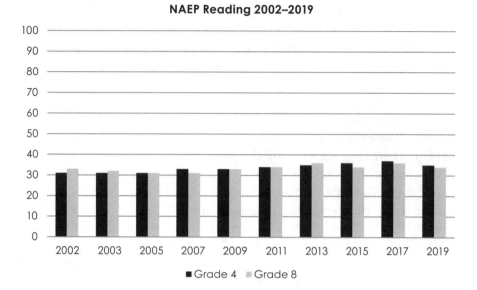

FIGURE 1.2. Percentage at or above proficient on NAEP reading assessment.

who meet the benchmark score have a 75% chance of earning a C or better in their first-semester history, literature, social science, or writing course in college (College Board, 2019). While 71% of students met the ERW benchmark overall, only 55% of Hispanic/Latino students, 51% of Native Hawaiian/Other Pacific Islander students, 46% of Black/African American students, and 39% of American Indian/Alaska Native students met this benchmark. This means that three out of ten high school students do not possess the reading and writing skills necessary to be successful in college, and students from racial/ethnic minority groups make up a greater percentage of those students who are likely to be unsuccessful.

To better understand why adolescents' literacy achievement is at such unacceptable levels on high-stakes assessments, it helps to know what is being assessed. In the section that follows, we aim to define the reading and writing skills that constitute adolescent literacy. Our goal is to provide you with the critical background knowledge about literacy processes and their development that will help you to leverage literacy instruction to support content-area learning.

ADOLESCENT LITERACY DEVELOPMENT

Before turning to adolescent literacy development, we must define the term *literacy* more broadly. The most basic definition of literacy is the ability to read and write. But what does it mean to read and write? The simple view of reading (Gough & Tunmer, 1986) states that reading is the product of two subprocesses:

decoding (recognizing words using knowledge of letters and sounds) and listening comprehension (understanding the meaning of words, sentences, and discourse). Therefore, reading requires at least some level of proficiency in both word recognition and comprehension. If either amounts to zero, the product will also be zero. For instance, imagine reading aloud a sentence in Italian or another language you studied in high school but have not spoken in many years. Would you be able to decode the words even if you don't know their meaning? If so, would you consider yourself a proficient reader in that language? It is likely that you said "no." At the very least, reading requires some skill with both decoding words and comprehending meaning. This relationship is shown visually in Figure 1.3.

A similar relationship between translating print and interpreting meaning holds for writing. Although writing contains complex subprocesses such as planning, revising, and editing (Hayes & Flower, 1980), the simple view of writing (Berninger et al., 2002; Juel, 1988) states that the two critical factors in writing are transcription (handwriting [or keyboarding] and spelling) and text generation (generating and organizing ideas). This simple view of writing is represented in Figure 1.4. For a student who has difficulty with writing, it is reasonable to expect that the challenge resides in either transcription, text generation, or both (Hebert, Kearns, Hayes, Bazis, & Cooper, 2018). Likewise, students with reading difficulties typically have problems with decoding, comprehension, or both (Catts, Tomblin, Compton, & Bridges, 2012). As Shanahan (2016) put it, reading and writing are like "two buildings built on a common foundation" (p. 195) of skills for interacting with print and for understanding meaning.

FIGURE 1.3. The simple view of reading.

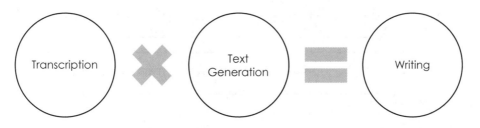

FIGURE 1.4. The simple view of writing.

Although they are different processes, reading and writing draw on shared knowledge and skills as they develop. Naturally, the knowledge and skills that adolescents use when reading and writing are different from those used by children who are just beginning to learn how to read and write. They are also different from those used by adults who have attained considerable proficiency with reading and writing. These differences are largely concerned with the way that readers and writers interact with text. Reading researcher Jeanne Chall (1996) proposed six stages of reading development that describe the ways that readers interact with text at different ages and grades from birth through adulthood. Fitzgerald and Shanahan (2000) proposed a developmental model based on Chall's stages that also describes the knowledge and skills associated with writing. These stages of literacy development are presented in Figure 1.5.

Much of literacy development occurs during childhood. Typically developing adolescent readers and writers will have first passed through the emergent literacy stage. By the end of kindergarten, many children have developed awareness of phonemes (individual speech sounds) and graphemes (individual letters and groups of letters representing phonemes). When children are in the initial literacy stage, typically in first and second grade, they learn to use letter-sound knowledge to decode and spell words. During the third stage they will have consolidated what was learned in the first two stages, developing the ability to read and

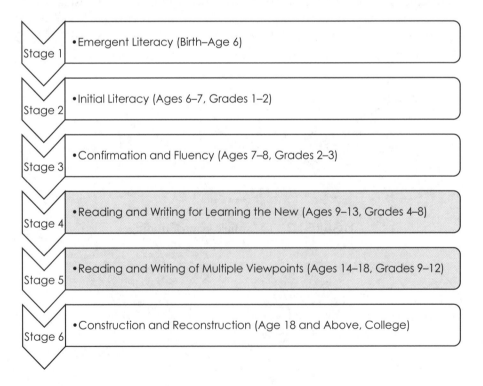

FIGURE 1.5. Stages of literacy development.

write words and sentences with fluency and automaticity (Chall, 1996; Fitzgerald & Shanahan, 2000). Children will have also gained a great deal of content knowledge during these stages, initially through oral language and read-alouds, which contribute to listening comprehension and text generation skills.

Adolescent literacy concerns the next two stages of literacy development. Adolescence is considered a distinct period in human development between childhood and adulthood, ranging from ages 12 to 18 and characterized by physical maturation, cognitive development, greater focus on social relationships, and changing school contexts (Alexander & Fox, 2011). Each of those changes experienced by adolescents also influences their literacy development.

As you can see in Figure 1.5, the ages associated with adolescence span across the fourth stage, reading and writing for learning the new, and the fifth stage, reading and writing of multiple viewpoints (Chall, 1996; Fitzgerald & Shanahan, 2000). In the beginning of the fourth stage, adolescents build on their knowledge of the relationship between speech and print to use reading and writing for learning new information in the upper elementary grades. This stage extends through middle school, when adolescents are expected to read and write in content-area classes as primary modes of learning. The main focus is on meaning as adolescents use literacy to build content knowledge and learn new vocabulary, as well as develop strategies to monitor their own understanding when reading and writing texts with more complex sentence and text structures. Put simply, much instructional attention should be devoted to reading comprehension and text generation, especially reading and writing of informational text.

This focus continues into high school, when many adolescents enter the fifth stage of literacy development. Consistent with their cognitive and social development, adolescents' literacy skills in this stage are marked by viewing the world from multiple viewpoints, with increased attention to critical reading and revision in writing focused on authorial intent and attending to audience. It is success with these skills that leads adolescents to the difficult work of constructing and reconstructing knowledge through reading and writing in college and careers.

Understanding literacy from a developmental perspective allows teachers to attend to the knowledge and skills necessary for reading and writing at the appropriate stages. For teachers of adolescents, this means an intense focus on comprehending and writing about literature and informational texts for the purpose of building knowledge, including background knowledge, vocabulary knowledge, and knowledge about text structures. In the following section, we provide a preview of adolescent literacy instruction that sets up the rest of this book's chapters.

ADOLESCENT LITERACY INSTRUCTION

When it comes to literacy instruction for adolescents, it's important for teachers to keep their eyes on the prize. We think most teachers would agree that the prize for middle and high school students is understanding the content that will enable them to engage with increasingly difficult material and be successful in college and careers. Understanding the content of texts, or reading comprehension, has been called the "end goal" of literacy instruction (Snow, Burns, & Griffin, 1998, p. 41). As a result, we find it useful for teachers to plan their literacy instruction using a research-based framework for meeting that goal.

The RAND Reading Study Group defined reading comprehension as "the process of simultaneously extracting and constructing meaning through interaction and involvement with written language" (Snow, 2002, p. 11). For comprehension to occur, there must be a *reader* to extract or construct meaning from a *text* on the basis of involvement in a particular reading *activity* or purpose for reading. These three elements of comprehension are also shaped by the sociocultural *context* in which they occur. This framework for thinking about comprehension is displayed in Figure 1.6. Beginning with context, we discuss considerations for planning effective literacy instruction according to each of these elements.

Context

Readers, the texts they read, and the reading activities in which they engage are influenced by context (Snow, 2002). Because this book is about literacy instruction, we focus on the context in which reading and writing skills are most likely to be taught—the classroom. The knowledge and skills that readers are expected to learn, the texts that are assigned, and the instructional activities that occur in classrooms are also undoubtedly shaped by a larger context.

In the United States, nothing has had as profound of an impact on classroom instruction over the past decade as the Common Core State Standards (CCSS). In 2010, the National Governors Association Center for Best Practices (NGA) and the Council of Chief State School Officers (CCSSO) released the CCSS as

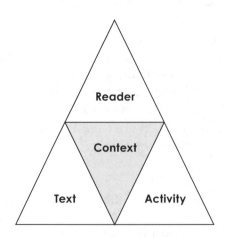

FIGURE 1.6. Essential elements of reading comprehension.

an option for individual states to adopt a common, more rigorous set of edu-cational standards. The CCSS were subsequently adopted by 43 states, which by some estimates means that 82% of American students received instruction aligned to these standards (Shanahan, 2015). And in many states that either did not initially adopt them or have since unadopted them due to political contro-versy, students are taught according to CCR standards that are nearly identical to the CCSS (Friedberg et al., 2018). Although you might have mixed feelings about the CCSS and the high-stakes tests used to measure student achievement, there is no denying that they have changed the nature of classroom instruction in schools across the nation.

There are two main sections of CCR standards that concern literacy in grades 6–12: the ELA Standards and the Standards for Literacy in History/Social Stud-ies, Science, and Technical Subjects. The introduction to the CCSS advocates that all secondary teachers use their "content area expertise to help students meet the particular challenges of reading, writing, speaking, listening, and language in their respective fields" (NGA & CCSSO, 2010, p. 3). For teachers of history/social studies, science, and technical subjects, the expectation is that the literacy standards supplement their state content standards. The division of the literacy standards into these two sections clearly indicates that teachers in all content areas have a "shared responsibility for students' literacy development" (NGA & CCSSO, 2010, p. 4).

When planning for classroom instruction, a logical starting point is to con-sider what the CCR standards for a particular grade and subject expect students to know and be able to do. The first place to look is the "anchor" standards that delineate the reading, writing, speaking and listening, and language skills that students should develop in ELA as well as history/social studies, science, and technical subjects. The anchor standards are consistent across grades and across content areas. However, the knowledge and skills in each anchor standard are also tailored by grade level from kindergarten through eighth grade and then by grade-level bands for grades 9–10 and 11–12. While we feel it is necessary for teachers to understand how the standards change across grades instead of just the grades they teach, we stick to a general discussion of the anchor standards in this section. We invite you to compare the specific requirements of the standards for different grade levels with colleagues in your school after reading this chapter. In this section, we present the anchor standards for reading, writing, speaking and listening, and language in ELA, as well as in history/social studies, science, and technical subjects.

The CCR anchor standards for reading emphasize comprehension and text complexity. The design of the reading standards suggests that four categories of skills are necessary for comprehension: attention to key ideas and details; recog-nition of craft and structure; integration of knowledge and ideas; and ability to read a range of texts of appropriate text complexity. In order to meet these four categories, a classroom context must be a print-rich environment with extensive opportunities to read and write about various types of texts. The CCR anchor standards for reading are presented in Figure 1.7, organized by categories of skills.

Although it may seem counterintuitive to begin at the end, we think it is most important for teachers to keep standard 10 in the back of their mind as they plan instruction. Standard 10 has received more attention from the research community than any other standard, with entire articles written to help teachers understand this "deceptively simple" standard (Fisher & Frey, 2014a, p. 237). Essentially, standard 10 says that students must read and be able to comprehend grade-level texts independently and proficiently, though there is room for scaffolding as needed within specific grade levels. Requiring students to read complex texts is one of the three key shifts from previous state standards to CCR standards. Although this requirement has been challenged for beginning readers (e.g., Hiebert & Mesmer, 2013), we believe it is appropriate to require adolescents

Key Ideas and Details

1. Read closely to determine what the text says explicitly and to make logical inferences from it; cite specific textual evidence when writing or speaking to support conclusions drawn from the text.

2. Determine central ideas or themes of a text and analyze their development; summarize the key supporting details and ideas.

3. Analyze how and why individuals, events, or ideas develop and interact over the course of a text.

Craft and Structure

4. Interpret words and phrases as they are used in a text, including determining technical, connotative, and figurative meanings, and analyze how specific word choices shape meaning or tone.

5. Analyze the structure of texts, including how specific sentences, paragraphs, and larger portions of the text (e.g., a section, chapter, scene, or stanza) relate to each other and the whole.

6. Assess how point of view or purpose shapes the content and style of a text.

Integration of Knowledge and Ideas

7. Integrate and evaluate content presented in diverse media and formats, including visually and quantitatively, as well as in words.

8. Delineate and evaluate the argument and specific claims in a text, including the validity of the reasoning as well as the relevance and sufficiency of the evidence.

9. Analyze how two or more texts address similar themes or topics in order to build knowledge or to compare the approaches the authors take.

Range of Reading and Text Complexity

10. Read and comprehend complex literary and informational texts independently and proficiently.

FIGURE 1.7. CCR anchor standards for reading.

to read texts that are sufficiently challenging for their grade. For example, as a former high school ELA teacher, one of John's colleagues attempted to teach the ninth-grade standards using the seventh-grade textbook for students who had difficulty comprehending grade-level texts. Although this decision was made in earnest, the end result was that students were being shortchanged by teaching them according to the seventh-grade text complexity standard. Thus, meeting the other reading standards requires that students read grade-level text.

Reading comprehension skills are addressed in the other three categories. In the first category, students are expected to read and understand texts at the literal and inferential level, cite evidence when communicating about the text, summarize the key ideas and details, and analyze the development of ideas within the text. The focus on using evidence from texts was the second key shift from previous state standards to CCR standards. In each content area students are generally required to use different types of evidence, such as direct quotations from literature in ELA, narrative accounts of historical events from primary-source documents in social studies, and descriptions of procedures from experiments in science (NGA & CCSSO, 2010).

The next category of standards requires students to critique the author's craft and structure, including the impact of word choice, text structure, and point of view. These are high-level comprehension skills that go beyond understanding the literal meaning of the text and are appropriate for adolescents. Knowledge of academic and discipline-specific vocabulary, text structures, and analysis of multiple viewpoints are expected to emerge during the fourth and fifth stages of literacy development (Fitzgerald & Shanahan, 2000). The final category of reading standards expands on comprehension of print texts to focus on integrating content from multiple print and digital texts, evaluating an author's argument within a text, and comparing content across texts. The impetus for achieving these standards is providing a wide range of texts about different topics in a variety of disciplines for the purpose of building knowledge, which was the third key shift associated with the adoption of CCR standards (NGA & CCSSO, 2010). To achieve this ambitious set of standards, every teacher need not be a reading teacher, but every teacher needs to create a classroom environment where reading is the norm every day.

The CCR anchor standards for writing emphasize composing different types of texts, the connection between reading and writing, and using writing to support research. They are displayed in Figure 1.8. We think it is wise to begin again with standard 10, which requires that students write both brief responses and extended compositions over longer periods of time (NGA & CCSSO, 2010). This will only be accomplished by providing students with frequent opportunities to write and effective writing instruction (Graham & Perin, 2007).

The first category of writing standards describes the skills associated with three types of writing—using reasoning and evidence in argumentative writing; selecting and organizing ideas in informative/explanatory writing; and choosing

Text Types and Purposes

1. Write arguments to support claims in an analysis of substantive topics or texts using valid reasoning and relevant and sufficient evidence.

2. Write informative/explanatory texts to examine and convey complex ideas and information clearly and accurately through the effective selection, organization, and analysis of content.

3. Write narratives to develop real or imagined experiences or events using effective technique, well-chosen details, and well-structured event sequences.

Production and Distribution of Writing

4. Produce clear and coherent writing in which the development, organization, and style are appropriate to task, purpose, and audience.

5. Develop and strengthen writing as needed by planning, revising, editing, rewriting, or trying a new approach.

6. Use technology, including the Internet, to produce and publish writing and to interact and collaborate with others.

Integration of Knowledge and Ideas

7. Conduct short as well as more sustained research projects based on focused questions, demonstrating understanding of the subject under investigation.

8. Gather relevant information from multiple print and digital sources, assess the credibility and accuracy of each source, and integrate the information while avoiding plagiarism.

9. Draw evidence from literary or informational texts to support analysis, reflection, and research.

Range of Reading and Text Complexity

10. Write routinely over extended time frames (time for research, reflection, and revision) and shorter time frames (a single sitting or a day or two) for a range of tasks, purposes, and audiences.

FIGURE 1.8. CCR anchor standards for writing.

details and structuring events in narrative writing. Students should be taught how to write in genres that are appropriate for different content areas within each type of writing. For instance, students should learn how to write historical arguments using evidence from primary and secondary sources in social studies, informational reports of experimental procedures and results in science, and personal narratives and arguments about literature in ELA. It should be noted that narrative writing is not explicitly required in the Standards for Literacy in History/Social Studies, Science, and Technical Subjects (NGA & CCSSO, 2010). As a result, most narrative writing instruction will likely occur in ELA.

The second and third categories of writing standards indicate that students should learn how to use the writing process and research skills to demonstrate understanding. The first two standards in the production and distribution category concern the cognitive processes associated with writing—generating and organizing text based on the writing task, audience, and purpose, as well as planning, revising, and editing to improve writing (Hayes & Flower, 1980). The third standard necessitates the availability of technology in the classroom for students to engage in collaborative writing and publish their work, both of which are features of effective writing instruction (Graham & Perin, 2007). The final category of writing standards states that students should learn to conduct research projects to build knowledge and demonstrate understanding, synthesizing information from print and digital sources including literary and informational texts. Inquiry activities that involve analysis of real data and that lead to writing tasks that promote content learning should also be part of effective writing instruction for adolescents (Graham & Perin, 2007). Standard 9 is also particularly important, as it highlights the need for integrating reading and writing across content areas, which can improve students' reading comprehension and writing skills, as well as their critical thinking and content knowledge (Graham et al., 2016).

There are two categories of CCR anchor standards for speaking and listening (see Figure 1.9). The first category focuses on using speaking and listening skills for comprehension and collaboration. The standards include participating in conversations as part of a whole class, in small groups, and with a partner in multiple domains; integrating information from multimedia sources; and evaluating a speaker's argument (NGA & CCSSO, 2010). There are clear connections to the reading standards, emphasizing the strong relationship that listening comprehension and oral language skills have with reading comprehension (Gough & Tunmer, 1986; Snow, 2002).

Comprehension and Collaboration
1. Prepare for and participate effectively in a range of conversations and collaborations with diverse partners, building on others' ideas and expressing their own clearly and persuasively.
2. Integrate and evaluate information presented in diverse media and formats, including visually, quantitatively, and orally.
3. Evaluate a speaker's point of view, reasoning, and use of evidence and rhetoric.
Presentation of Knowledge and Ideas
4. Present information, findings, and supporting evidence such that listeners can follow the line of reasoning and the organization, development, and style are appropriate to task, purpose, and audience.
5. Make strategic use of digital media and visual displays of data to express information and enhance understanding of presentations.
6. Adapt speech to a variety of contexts and communicative tasks, demonstrating command of formal English when indicated or appropriate.

FIGURE 1.9. CCR anchor standards for speaking and listening.

The second category is focused on the use of speaking and listening skills in formal presentations. Students are required to present research findings in a form that is appropriate to the task, purpose, and audience; employ digital media to share information; and communicate their ideas effectively across contexts. There are also clear connections between the writing standards and presentation skills, which are necessary for producing visual presentations from written documents in many academic fields and occupations (Graham & Perin, 2007).

The CCR anchor standards for language focus on conventions, knowledge of language, and vocabulary. They are displayed in Figure 1.10. The first two standards state that students should demonstrate command of standard English grammar, capitalization, punctuation, and spelling when writing. The third standard indicates that students should also be able to use their knowledge of language when reading, writing, speaking, and listening in different contexts. You may have noticed that the writing standards focused primarily on text generation skills with no attention to transcription, the other critical factor in the simple view of writing (Berninger et al., 2002). While the language standards cover spelling, students are simply expected to "spell correctly" beginning in sixth grade (NGA & CCSSO, 2010, p. 52). Handwriting, another transcription skill, is noticeably absent; however, students are also expected to "demonstrate sufficient command of keyboarding skills" by sixth grade (NGA & CCSSO, 2010, p. 43).

Conventions of Standard English
1. Demonstrate command of the conventions of standard English grammar and usage when writing or speaking.
2. Demonstrate command of the conventions of standard English capitalization, punctuation, and spelling when writing.
Knowledge of Language
3. Apply knowledge of language to understand how language functions in different contexts, to make effective choices for meaning or style, and to comprehend more fully when reading or listening.
Vocabulary Acquisition and Use
4. Determine or clarify the meaning of unknown and multiple-meaning words and phrases by using context clues, analyzing meaningful word parts, and consulting general and specialized reference materials, as appropriate.
5. Demonstrate understanding of figurative language, word relationships, and nuances in word meanings.
6. Acquire and use accurately a range of general academic and domain-specific words and phrases sufficient for reading, writing, speaking, and listening at the college and career readiness level; demonstrate independence in gathering vocabulary knowledge when encountering an unknown term important to comprehension or expression.

FIGURE 1.10. CCR anchor standards for language.

The standards for vocabulary acquisition and use focus on understanding the meaning of new or multiple meaning words through the use of context, morphology (word parts), and reference materials; interpreting figurative language; and using both academic language and discipline-specific vocabulary when reading, writing, speaking, and listening. To accomplish these vocabulary goals, decontextualized vocabulary instruction that includes memorizing a new set of words each week isn't going to cut it. Instead teachers must promote contextualized word learning to support comprehension, content learning, and writing about texts in all content areas.

If that sounds like a lot to accomplish, that's because it is! External reviewers agree that the CCR standards in place in many states are more challenging than previous state standards (e.g., Friedberg et al., 2018). But we urge you to remember the prize—knowledge. If adolescents are to build the content knowledge necessary to be successful in college and careers, they will need ample opportunities to read, write about, and discuss complex texts in all content-area classrooms.

Readers

Readers bring different abilities to the classroom that will impact their comprehension and learning (see Figure 1.11). These include various types of knowledge such as vocabulary, content knowledge, text structure knowledge, and knowledge of comprehension strategies; cognitive skills such as attention, memory, critical thinking, and inferencing; and motivation (NGA & CCSSO, 2010; Snow, 2002). Although the CCR standards give scant attention to motivation, we think that promoting motivation for reading should be front and center when planning

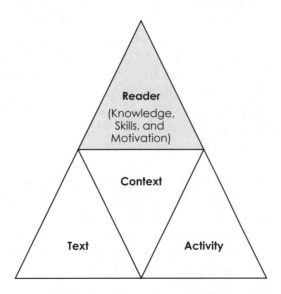

FIGURE 1.11. Reader characteristics in reading comprehension.

instruction. If you ask parents whether their teenager enjoys reading for school, there's a good chance you will hear a resounding "no." If you ask teachers of adolescents, they will likely tell you how many of their students won't read the texts they assign. We believe that motivating adolescent readers is an "attainable goal" (Conradi, Jang, Bryant, Craft, & McKenna, 2013, p. 565). And attaining that goal is a prerequisite to the extensive reading and writing of texts in all content areas that are required to meet the CCR standards.

Adolescents' lackluster predispositions toward reading are not a new phenomenon. In a national survey, McKenna, Kear, and Ellsworth (1995) found a steady decline in elementary-aged students' attitudes toward recreational and academic reading through sixth grade. Not surprisingly, females had more positive attitudes toward reading than males, and attitudes toward recreational reading were worse for students with lower reading achievement. However, attitudes toward academic reading were negative regardless of achievement. A more recent survey found that reading attitudes continued to worsen from sixth through eighth grade (McKenna, Conradi, Lawrence, Jang, & Meyer, 2012). Among middle school students, females had more positive attitudes toward academic reading with print and digital texts and recreational reading of print texts, and males had more positive attitudes toward recreational reading of digital texts. Attitudes toward academic reading were consistently negative throughout the middle grades.

There is a reciprocal relationship between motivation and reading achievement. Readers who are motivated to read are more likely to engage in reading activities, which leads to higher reading achievement (Afflerbach & Harrison, 2017; Guthrie & Wigfield, 2000; Toste, Didion, Peng, Filderman, & McClelland, 2020). But motivation is not as simple as either engaging in reading or not engaging in reading. Guthrie and Wigfield (2000) described many different types of motivation related to reading (see Figure 1.12). First, motivation itself is related to a student's mindset and *reading goals*. Students with a fixed mindset, or those who believe that intelligence is static, tend to be motivated by performance goals (Dweck, 1986). Their goals for reading are to receive positive evaluations of their abilities. In contrast, students with a growth mindset believe that intelligence is malleable and are more motivated by learning goals. These students are motivated to engage in reading to improve their content knowledge and reading skills.

Readers can also possess intrinsic (internal) and extrinsic (external) motivations for reading. *Intrinsic motivation* refers to whether someone chooses to engage in reading for the sake of reading during his or her own free time (Guthrie & Wigfield, 2000). Readers with high intrinsic motivation tend to experience a sense of excitement, interest, or enjoyment as an internal reward for engaging in reading activities. *Extrinsic motivation* refers to the external rewards for engaging in reading, whether that be recognition or an incentive such as a prize for reading the most books as part of the local library's summer reading program. We don't

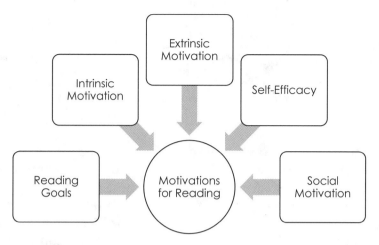

FIGURE 1.12. Different types of motivation for reading.

want you to get the impression that it is a teacher's responsibility to convince all of his or her students to be intrinsically motivated to read. There is nothing wrong with coaxing reluctant readers with external rewards. As a high school teacher, John awarded extra credit (and an occasional pizza party) for students who completed independent reading assignments outside of class. These short-term rewards might initially motivate students to engage in reading activities, but successful and positive reading experiences will keep them motivated in the long term (Afflerbach & Harrison, 2017).

Individual and social characteristics also influence reading motivation. As it applies to reading, the term *self-efficacy* refers to a reader's judgments of his or her own abilities as a reader (Guthrie & Wigfield, 2000). Whereas readers with high self-efficacy are motivated by challenging reading activities, readers with low self-efficacy tend to avoid them out of fear of failure (Afflerbach & Harrison, 2017). Reading, however, is not an entirely solitary activity. Especially in school, readers interact with others around reading activities. Thus, students may also have *social motivation* to read in order to discuss interesting books with their peers and be a functioning member of a community of learners (Guthrie & Wigfield, 2000). When there is strong social motivation and collaboration, readers are more likely to engage in reading.

Building motivation and engagement with reading is essential for planning effective adolescent literacy instruction (Biancarosa & Snow, 2006; Kamil et al., 2008). But how can teachers motivate adolescents to read? Guthrie and Davis (2003) identified six classroom practices to support engaged reading, which are presented in Figure 1.13. They argue that teachers should begin with rich *content goals*. Learning objectives that focus on teaching students something interesting about the world are likely to be motivating. *Real-world interactions* might take two forms: (1) hands-on inquiry activities and (2) authentic reading and writing

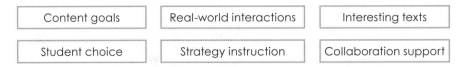

| Content goals | Real-world interactions | Interesting texts |
| Student choice | Strategy instruction | Collaboration support |

FIGURE 1.13. Motivating adolescents to read.

activities that are relevant to students' lives. They also suggest selecting *interesting texts*. Teachers should supplement textbook reading with diverse texts that are motivating for adolescent readers, such as magazine articles about popular culture, graphic novels, young-adult book series, and informational texts about sports or other topics that students find interesting (Ivey & Broaddus, 2001; Worthy, Moorman, & Turner, 1999). Guthrie and Davis (2003) also suggest promoting engagement through *student choice* in deciding which texts to read and which instructional activities to complete. For students with reading difficulties, *strategy instruction* is not only effective but also motivating. Teaching students how to use reading and writing strategies to support learning through modeling, guided practice, and independent practice can build self-efficacy by having positive experiences with texts. Finally, adolescents should be provided with *collaboration support*. Providing opportunities for students to interact with their peers in pairs and small groups can increase engagement with reading and writing activities.

Getting to know your students and their interests will go a long way toward motivating them to read and write. We suggest that teachers give their students a survey about their reading practices and what types of texts they find interesting during the first week of school. There are many examples of research-validated surveys that are appropriate for adolescents, including the Survey of Adolescent Reading Attitudes (Conradi et al., 2013) and the Adolescent Motivation to Read Profile (Pitcher et al., 2007). We cannot overstate the importance of motivating adolescents to read if they are going to engage in the challenging reading and writing activities in all content areas that are necessary to meet CCR standards and ensure their success beyond high school.

Texts

Readers will also have more or less difficulty comprehending texts depending on text type and text complexity (Snow, 2002; see Figure 1.14). You likely noticed that the CCR anchor standards mention reading different types of complex texts, including print and digital texts as well as literature and informational texts. They also call for students to write argumentative, informative/explanatory, and narrative texts in response to reading (NGA & CCSSO, 2010).

One of the biggest changes in classroom instruction since the release of the CCR standards is that teachers are assigning more informational texts than ever

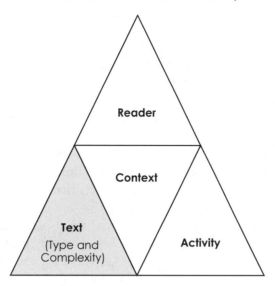

FIGURE 1.14. Text characteristics in reading comprehension.

before (Griffith & Duffett, 2018). That's because the CCR standards require it. Figure 1.15 shows the percentages of each text type that students are expected to read and write in fourth, eighth, and twelfth grade according to CCR standards. The equal balance between literary and informational text reading in elementary school gradually shifts to 70% informational texts in high school. Likewise, there is a greater emphasis on argumentative and informative writing than on narrative writing in twelfth grade. Unfortunately, students tend to have more difficulty reading and writing informational texts than narratives (Best, Floyd, & McNamara, 2008; Newkirk, 1987). As a result, most students will need an increased emphasis on informational texts across content areas.

The shared responsibility for reading and writing informational texts between ELA and other content areas is important. Some teachers and school leaders initially misinterpreted the percentages in the CCSS to mean that they applied only to ELA class (Shanahan, 2015). In fact, when John was a teacher, an instructional leader in his district argued that ELA teachers were required to exclusively assign

Grade	Reading		Writing		
	Literature	Informational	Argumentative	Informative	Narrative
Fourth	50%	50%	30%	35%	35%
Eighth	45%	55%	35%	35%	30%
Twelfth	30%	70%	40%	40%	20%

FIGURE 1.15. Distribution of reading and writing by text type.

informational texts in order to meet the demands of the CCSS. On the contrary, much of the literary reading and narrative writing students experience will occur in ELA. Therefore, students will have to read and write informational texts in their other content-area classes in order to meet the distributions outlined in the standards. In observations of middle and high school ELA and social studies classes, nearly three-fourths of students' time spent reading in ELA was narrative text or poetry compared to one-fourth informational text (Swanson et al., 2016). In contrast, all of students' time spent reading in social studies was informational text, including textbooks and primary-source documents. Not only is this distribution consistent with what we see in the schools that we work with, it is closer to what the CCR standards expect.

Providing access to diverse texts is essential when planning effective literacy instruction for adolescents (Biancarosa & Snow, 2006; International Reading Association, 2012). By diverse we mean that there is variety in the texts that students read in terms of genre and difficulty. According to CCR standards, students should read multiple genres of literature and informational texts (see Figure 1.16). The literature that students should read includes stories (e.g., realistic fiction, historical fiction, science fiction), drama (e.g., Shakespeare's tragedies, comedies, and histories), and poetry (e.g., sonnets, odes, ballads, and epics), representing both canonical and noncanonical works (NGA & CCSSO, 2010). The informational texts that students read should feature a wide range of literary nonfiction (e.g., personal essays, speeches, biographies, memoirs) as well as historical, scientific, and technical accounts written in expository, argumentative, and functional genres (NGA & CCSSO, 2010). Further, the texts that are assigned in 21st-century classrooms should not be exclusively print. Effective adolescent literacy instruction demands reading multiple texts, both print and multimodal digital texts.

The text reading that students experience should also be diverse in terms of difficulty. Although the CCSS clearly define the level of text complexity that students are expected to read at each grade level, literacy experts have argued that

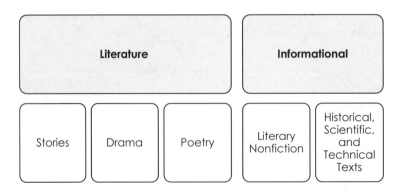

FIGURE 1.16. Range of text types for middle and high school.

students should not be required to *only* read texts within those levels. That is, they should have opportunities to read a variety of less and more difficult texts, with the average reading level falling within the ranges outlined in the standards (Shanahan, 2015). Providing access to a range of texts on the same topic but written at different reading levels may actually improve comprehension and content learning (Biancarosa & Snow, 2006). Because teachers often require more guidance for determining text complexity than is provided by state standards' documents (Friedberg et al., 2018; Griffith & Duffet, 2018), we devote Chapter 2 to describing a process for teachers to analyze text complexity and select appropriate texts for their students. In Chapter 3 we present a framework for using different types of texts on the same topic to support comprehension and learning across content areas.

Activities

Reading comprehension is also dependent on the difficulty of the prereading, reading, and postreading tasks in which readers engage as part of the reading activity (Snow, 2002; see Figure 1.17). Comprehending a relatively easy text might be more difficult if a teacher provides a complex purpose prior to reading or poses challenging questions as part of a postreading discussion (NGA & CCSSO, 2010; Valencia, Wixson, & Pearson, 2014). The tasks that students are asked to complete in secondary grades vary widely by discipline (Baye et al., 2019; Biancarosa & Snow, 2006; International Literacy Association, 2017). For example, students might make inferences about scientific processes by piecing together information from multiple texts; determine the causes of a historical

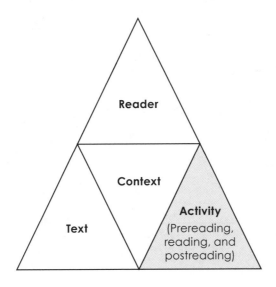

FIGURE 1.17. Characteristics of activities in reading comprehension.

event based on primary and secondary sources; or analyze literature by making judgments about an author's choices of rhetorical devices (Goldman & Lee, 2014). Thus, comprehension of content-area texts is not guaranteed if teachers select appropriate texts and motivate students to read them. What teachers ask students to do as part of the reading activity involving those texts also carries great importance.

Teachers should select instructional practices that aim to promote comprehension and learning throughout a reading activity and adapt them to meet the specific task demands in their discipline. In classroom contexts, a reading activity has three distinct phases: prereading, reading, and postreading (Snow, 2002). A preview of effective instructional practices to employ before, during, and after reading is shown in Figure 1.18. Before reading, the teacher should set a purpose for reading a text as well as build knowledge and interest that will lead to engaged reading. In addition, teachers should provide explicit instruction in vocabulary that they will encounter when they read the text (Baye et al., 2019; Kamil et al., 2008). We describe specific strategies for building vocabulary and background knowledge in Chapter 4.

During reading, readers focus on understanding the text according to their purpose for reading (Snow, 2002). To support readers in understanding the text, teachers should provide explicit instruction in comprehension strategies (Biancarosa & Snow, 2006; Kamil et al., 2008), as well as strategies for monitoring when comprehension breaks down and how to fix it (Boardman et al., 2008). Adolescent readers should also have opportunities to collaborate with peers in cooperative groups when constructing understanding of the text (Baye et al., 2019; Biancarosa & Snow, 2006). We present instructional strategies for supporting reading comprehension during reading in the context of collaborative learning in Chapter 5.

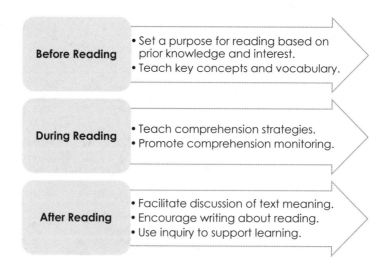

FIGURE 1.18. Prereading, reading, and postreading practices.

After reading, readers engage in activities for the purpose of building knowledge, application of knowledge, or engagement with content (Snow, 2002). Teachers should promote comprehension and support their students in building knowledge through extended discussion of the meaning and their interpretations of a text (Kamil et al., 2008). We offer suggestions for conducting classroom discussions in Chapter 6. Students should also write about what they read in order to build knowledge and comprehension (Baye et al., 2019; Graham & Hebert, 2010). Chapter 7 focuses on strategies for teaching students how to write brief responses, including text-based arguments and summaries. Teachers should also provide intensive writing instruction to build students' writing skills when demonstrating understanding (Biancarosa & Snow, 2006; Graham et al., 2016). In Chapter 8, we present effective approaches to strategy instruction for writing longer argumentative, informative/explanatory, and narrative compositions. Finally, students should have opportunities to further engage with content through inquiry activities that extend understanding (Graham & Perin, 2007). We conclude the after-reading chapters by examining the role of research and inquiry projects in content-area learning in Chapter 9. We offer a sample weekly and daily schedule for putting it all together in Chapter 10.

MOVING FORWARD

Preservice and inservice teachers often ask us why literacy is relevant to their content area. To be frank, neither of us entered the field of education expecting to write a book about content-area literacy instruction! We both became interested in literacy when we found that students in our high school ELA classes had difficulty comprehending and writing about the literature we assigned. John realized midway through his first year of teaching that reading entire works of literature aloud to each of his classes was not preparing his students for the independent reading they would be expected to do in college. Neither will relying solely on videos or PowerPoint lectures in order to avoid having students read textbooks in science and social studies. Using literacy in the content areas requires that all teachers know how to select appropriate texts for their students and then design effective instruction to support comprehension and learning before, during, and after reading, as well as through writing and inquiry. Our goal for this book is to help all teachers of adolescents feel confident that they can meet these requirements. The first step is to think about what makes the texts you assign difficult for your students. That's where we begin in the next chapter. Let's get started!

CHAPTER 2

Understanding Text Complexity

In the previous chapter, we discussed the unacceptable number of adolescents who are reading and writing below a proficient level according to national assessment data. One common way that teachers seek to address this issue is by assigning students in lower tracks to read below-grade-level texts (Hiebert, 2017; Northrop & Kelly, 2019). When speaking about the all-too-common practice of assigning these students to read high/low books (those with high interest and low readability) as a way to boost reading achievement, Dr. Alfred Tatum said that "low readability begets low readability" (UIC College of Education, 2013). In other words, limiting these students' reading selections to texts at low reading levels will only continue to perpetuate their low reading levels. More recently, Tatum (2017) tweeted the equally memorable expression "Leveled texts lead to leveled lives." We take the position that in order to prepare adolescents to be successful in their lives after high school, as well as to begin to move the needle on achievement, secondary teachers should not restrict students to reading texts below their grade level. Adolescents must read complex texts that will challenge them.

To illustrate the potential problems associated with assigning texts that are below grade level, consider the following example. When John was a first-year ELA teacher, his school had a policy of assigning ninth-grade students in honors sections to read *The Pearl* by John Steinbeck (1947) during the first 9 weeks of school. This novella, which tells the story of a Mexican pearl diver named Kino who grapples with issues of love for his family and man's inherent greed, is an appropriately complex piece of literature for incoming high school students. According to the Lexile Framework for Reading, *The Pearl* is written at a text complexity level appropriate for late middle school. In addition, it places considerable language and knowledge demands on adolescent readers and allows for interpretation of multiple themes (Karsten, 1965).

Students in lower-track classes were not assigned to read *The Pearl*. Instead, they read *Scorpions* by Walter Dean Myers (1988). This young-adult (YA) novel deals with a young male named Jamal who struggles to resist joining a gang called the Scorpions while trying to earn enough money to get his brother out of jail. This award-winning piece of YA fiction is particularly interesting to adolescent readers (Brooks, 2003). However, it is far less complex than *The Pearl* according to the Lexile Framework. Students who read *Scorpions* were exposed to less complex vocabulary and syntax, likely under the presumption that *The Pearl* would be too difficult. We believe that accessible YA texts certainly deserve a place in classrooms but not as a *replacement* for more complex texts, as you will see in our framework for using sets of connected texts in Chapter 3. This example reflects a national trend of teachers assigning less complex popular fiction in lower-track classes and more complex canonical novels in higher-track classes, a tendency that is even more problematic due to the underrepresentation of female protagonists and authors of color in the literary canon (Northrop & Kelly, 2019).

There are several reasons to consider assigning complex texts to all readers. First, complex texts have the potential to build reading skills, including fluency and vocabulary, as well as motivate readers when they are provided with appropriate instructional support (Lupo, Strong, & Conradi Smith, 2019; Shanahan, Fisher, & Frey, 2012). In addition, students' comprehension of more challenging texts is similar to their comprehension of easier texts when provided with knowledge supports (Lupo, Tortorelli, Invernizzi, Ryoo, & Strong, 2019). Thus, if readers are capable of comprehending complex texts when supported by their teacher, it makes little sense for that teacher to replace challenging text selections with easier ones.

There is another, more immediate, reason for teachers to assign complex texts. College and career readiness standards, including the CCSS, require students to read complex texts across content areas (NGA & CCSSO, 2010). Students must read texts of increasing complexity in each grade, initially with scaffolding and then independently, until they build the skills necessary to read at the college and career readiness level (see Figure 2.1). This approach, which Shanahan and colleagues (2012) suggest is akin to lifting heavier weights in order to build muscle, necessitates that teachers are able to determine when a text is at the right level of difficulty (or weight) for their grade. If it's too heavy, students won't be able to lift it. Too light and they won't build the muscle needed to lift something heavier. In this analogy, the teacher is the spotter who provides assistance when the lifter has difficulty lifting and provides the motivation to attempt a heavier weight than the lifter would be able to lift without support.

Providing appropriately complex texts with the right amount of instructional support is no simple undertaking. To do so teachers must be able to answer three questions: (1) What makes a text more complex in relation to other texts?; (2) How should teachers select complex texts for their students?; and (3) How can teachers provide appropriate instructional support? (Strong, Amendum, &

Grades 6–8	Grades 9–10	Grades 11–12
Grades 6–7: By the end of the year, read and comprehend texts in the grades 6–8 text complexity band proficiently, *with scaffolding as needed at the high end of the range.*	**Grade 9:** By the end of the year, read and comprehend texts in the grades 9–10 text complexity band proficiently, *with scaffolding as needed at the high end of the range.*	**Grade 11:** By the end of the year, read and comprehend texts in the grades 11–CCR text complexity band proficiently, *with scaffolding as needed at the high end of the range.*
Grade 8: By the end of the year, read and comprehend texts in the grades 6–8 text complexity band *independently and proficiently.*	**Grade 10:** By the end of the year, read and comprehend texts in the grades 9–10 text complexity band *independently and proficiently.*	**Grade 12:** By the end of the year, read and comprehend texts in the grades 11–CCR text complexity band *independently and proficiently.*

FIGURE 2.1. Level of text complexity standard in grades 6–12.

Conradi Smith, 2018). The goal of this chapter is to answer the first two questions. You will find the answer to the third question in the remaining chapters of this book.

We begin by describing each component of the three-part model of text complexity in the CCSS. According to the standards' authors, text complexity includes quantitative measures (those that can be counted), qualitative measures (those best judged by human readers), and considerations for matching texts with readers and tasks (NGA & CCSSO, 2010). Figure 2.2 displays our representation of this model as a pyramid. In the section that follows, we illustrate a process we have used to help teachers select appropriate texts for their students based on these three factors. In our process (and in our pyramid), quantitative measures serve as an initial check (and smallest part of the pyramid), qualitative measures are analyzed more in depth, and reader-task considerations (the largest part of the pyramid) receive the most attention (Strong et al., 2018). We conclude the chapter by providing examples of complex texts in ELA, social studies, and science recommended in the CCSS, as well as where these recommendations fall short.

QUANTITATIVE DIMENSIONS OF TEXT COMPLEXITY

Think about the most difficult book you read in high school. If you asked John's high school juniors, they might say F. Scott Fitzgerald's (1925) *The Great Gatsby.* Ask his high school freshmen, and they will say *To Kill a Mockingbird* by Harper Lee (1960). If you asked them about the most difficult nonfiction texts they read, they might say Henry David Thoreau's (1849) "Civil Disobedience" or Martin

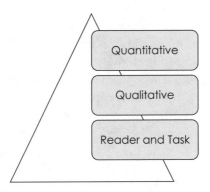

FIGURE 2.2. Three-part model of text complexity.

Luther King Jr.'s (1963) "I Have a Dream" speech, respectively. Few would argue that these selections are generally appropriate reading for students in ninth and eleventh grades. Teachers have long made decisions about which texts are appropriate to assign in each grade. But what makes some texts more difficult than others and, thus, more appropriate for some grades than others?

Some aspects of texts that contribute to their difficulty are best measured by computer algorithms. In Appendix A of the CCSS, these are referred to as quantitative dimensions of text complexity (NGA & CCSSO, 2010). Chances are that you have heard of the Lexile Framework for Reading (Stenner, Burdick, Sanford, & Burdick, 2007). Although there are many tools that measure quantitative dimensions of text complexity, Lexile is one of the most widely used (Cunningham & Mesmer, 2014). Put simply, Lexile is a measure of a text's complexity, typically ranging from 0L to 1800L, that takes into account two dimensions: semantic complexity (based on word frequency) and syntactic complexity (based on sentence length). The assumption underlying the Lexile Framework is that texts written using longer sentences and a higher proportion of less frequent words are more difficult to read (Stenner et al., 2007). While this might be true in many cases, Lexile measures should be interpreted cautiously. Whereas the difficulty of informational texts tends to be overestimated due to the repetition of rare words within them, the difficulty of narrative texts tends to be underestimated due to the short sentences typically used in dialogue (Hiebert, 2011). Consider the fiction and nonfiction texts John's freshmen and juniors read. Despite being appropriate text selections for ninth and eleventh grades, the two novels, *To Kill a Mockingbird* (870L) and *The Great Gatsby* (1010L), have lower Lexile measures than both "Civil Disobedience" (1340L) and "I Have a Dream" (1130L).

The potential benefits of Lexile are numerous but also require careful consideration on the part of the teacher. First, the Lexile Framework can be used to measure reader ability in addition to measuring text complexity. Assessments such as *Reading Inventory* can determine the Lexile measure associated with the texts a student has the ability to read with 75% comprehension (Stenner et al.,

2007). As a result, teachers can select texts for their students written at a Lexile level they will be able to comprehend. It is important to note, however, that teachers should also exercise caution in doing so. While students in lower-track classes are routinely given texts at a lower Lexile level (Northrop & Kelly, 2019), there is evidence to suggest that they can comprehend higher-level texts with instructional support (Lupo et al., 2019). As a result, we would never suggest restricting students' reading based solely on Lexile.

Another benefit of using the Lexile Framework is the ability to assign individual texts to a particular grade-level band. Lexile measures are available for most books using the "Find a Book" tool at *hub.lexile.com/find-a-book/search*. To determine a book's grade-level placement, the easiest place to look is in Appendix A of the CCSS, where you will find a table of text complexity grade bands (2–3, 4–5, 6–8, 9–10, 11–12) and corresponding Lexile ranges (NGA & CCSSO, 2010). In 2012, however, the Lexile ranges were updated to the current "stretch" ranges displayed in Figure 2.3 (CCSSO & NGA, 2012). You will notice that the "stretch" Lexile ranges are much wider than the CCSS Lexile ranges and much higher than the previous Lexile ranges. In John's ninth-grade ELA classroom, for example, students who were assigned *The Pearl,* which has a Lexile of 1010L, would have been reading a book at the high end of the grades 6–8 text complexity band under the previous Lexile ranges. Under the "stretch" Lexile ranges, this book is at the high end of the grades 4–5 band. Students who read *Scorpions,* which has a Lexile of 610L, were assigned a book in the grades 2–3 band.

If you have read either *The Pearl* or *Scorpions,* you should notice another limitation of Lexile when it comes to grade-level placement. In terms of content, neither belongs in an elementary school curriculum. So, why were they assigned to these grade bands? It helps to understand how the Lexile ranges were derived. Although Lexile measures typically range from 0 to 1800 (Stenner et al., 2007), the college and career readiness benchmark at the high end of the grades 11–12 text complexity band is 1385. The rationale underlying the grade bands is that students should be able to read college- and career-level texts by the end of high school. The Lexile ranges in each grade band represent the level of text complexity students would have to be able to read in order to ensure that they are able to read

Grade Band	Previous Lexile Ranges	CCSS Lexile Ranges	"Stretch" Lexile Ranges
2–3	450–725	450–790	420–820
4–5	645–845	770–980	740–1010
6–8	860–1010	955–1155	925–1185
9–10	960–1115	1080–1305	1050–1335
11–12	1070–1220	1215–1355	1185–1385

FIGURE 2.3. Lexile ranges in grades 2–12.

college and career texts (Williamson, Fitzgerald, & Stenner, 2013, 2014), which are typically within the grades 11–12 text complexity band (Stenner, Sanford-Moore, & Williamson, 2012; Wei, Cromwell, & McClarty, 2016). The problem, however, is that the Lexile Framework does not accurately place texts into appropriate grade bands except for those at the college level, often placing middle and high school texts into a lower grade band (Cunningham, Hiebert, & Mesmer, 2018). Many high school teachers would agree that *The Pearl* and *Scorpions* are likely placed in too low of a grade band.

So, if the Lexile Framework isn't always accurate at the secondary level, what should teachers use instead? There are alternative measures of the quantitative dimensions of text complexity, such as the Flesch–Kincaid Grade Level formula, but these too have limitations. Other measures are associated with commercial publishers, such as ATOS (Renaissance Learning), Degrees of Reading Power (DRP; Questar Assessment), the Reading Maturity Metric (RMM; Pearson), and TextEvaluator (Educational Testing Service). In Figure 2.4, we present grade-band ranges for each of these measures generated in two studies (Nelson, Perfetti, Liben, & Liben, 2012; Sheehan, 2015). However, similar questions remain as to whether these text complexity ranges are valid (Sheehan, 2017). Like Lexile, measures such as ATOS and DRP that rely on word frequency and sentence length work better for informational texts than narratives and for texts in lower grade bands (Graesser et al., 2014). In addition, Flesch–Kincaid tends to place texts at the middle and high school level into lower grade bands (Cunningham et al., 2018). If you use the Lexile Framework or one of these alternative measures at your school, we suggest using it as a starting point before considering additional quantitative measures for verification.

Additional tools for analyzing quantitative dimensions of text complexity are available to use but are limited in their functionality. One is Lexile Analyzer (*hub.lexile.com/analyzer*), which produces three scores for passages up to 1,000 words: Lexile measure, sentence length, and word frequency. Consider again the examples of texts read in John's ninth-grade ELA class. According to the Lexile Analyzer, a 1,000-word excerpt from *To Kill a Mockingbird* has an average

Grade Band	ATOS Analyzer	Degrees of Reading Power	Flesch–Kincaid	Reading Maturity Metric	TextEvaluator (SourceRater)
2–3	2.75–5.14	42–54	1.98–5.34	3.53–6.13	100–590
4–5	4.97–7.03	52–60	4.51–7.73	5.42–7.92	405–720
6–8	7.00–9.98	57–67	6.51–10.34	7.04–9.57	550–940
9–10	9.67–12.01	62–72	8.32–12.12	8.41–10.81	750–1125
11–12	11.20–14.10	67–74	10.34–14.2	9.57–12.00	890–1360

FIGURE 2.4. Text complexity bands for alternative measures.

sentence length of 12.82 and an average word frequency score of 3.56 (see Figure 2.5). An excerpt from Martin Luther King Jr.'s "I Have a Dream" has an average sentence length of 18.87 and an average word frequency score of 3.54. The higher Lexile measure for "I Have a Dream" reflects that this excerpt might be more difficult due to a greater number of words per sentence despite a similar number of infrequent words that students might not know. The Lexile range between 1100L and 1200L places it in the grades 9–10 text complexity band (see Figure 2.3), while the 800–900L range for the *To Kill a Mockingbird* excerpt places it in the 4–5 grade band.

One of the newer tools for measuring text complexity, Coh-Metrix, includes quantitative dimensions not measured by Lexile Analyzer. These include narrativity (i.e., similarity to oral conversation), syntactic simplicity (i.e., use of short and simple sentences), word concreteness (i.e., use of fewer abstract words), referential cohesion (i.e., words and ideas that overlap across sentences and the whole text), and deep cohesion (i.e., use of connectives that join ideas together; Graesser et al., 2014). The Coh-Metrix Common Core Text Ease and Readability Assessor (TERA) (*commoncoretera.com*) produces these five scores for passages up to 1,000 words. In addition, it produces the Flesch–Kincaid Grade Level. According to this tool, the excerpt from *To Kill a Mockingbird* is lower in referential cohesion (see Figure 2.5), which suggests that readers will be required to make inferences to connect ideas across sentences. The excerpt is also higher in its narrativity and syntactic simplicity, indicating that it is more story-like and has simple sentence structures. As such, the Flesch-Kincaid Grade Level estimate of 2.8 places the excerpt in the grades 2–3 band (see Figure 2.4), lower than the grade band recommended by the Lexile Analyzer. The excerpt from "I Have a Dream" is lower

Text Dimension	*To Kill a Mockingbird* Excerpt		"I Have a Dream" Excerpt	
	Lexile Analyzer	Coh-Metrix	Lexile Analyzer	Coh-Metrix
Sentence Length	12.82	—	18.87	—
Word Frequency	3.56	—	3.54	—
Narrativity	—	91%	—	50%
Syntactic Simplicity	—	82%	—	37%
Word Concreteness	—	45%	—	33%
Referential Cohesion	—	9%	—	51%
Deep Cohesion	—	43%	—	37%
Text Complexity	800L–900L	2.8	1100L–1200L	9.1
Grade Band	4–5	2–3	9–10	9–10

FIGURE 2.5. Comparison of text complexity analysis tools for sample text excerpts.

in narrativity and syntactic simplicity, indicating it is less story-like and has more complex sentences. The Flesch–Kincaid Grade Level estimate of 9.1 places it in the grades 9–10 text complexity band, consistent with the Lexile Analyzer. Thus, while both tools placed the "I Have a Dream" excerpt in the same grade band, the excerpt from *To Kill a Mockingbird* was placed in either grades 2–3 or 4–5 depending on which tool was used.

We hope that this example serves to illustrate the benefits and limitations of quantitative measures of text complexity. Their greatest benefit lies in the ability to compare one text against other texts in terms of dimensions that potentially, but don't always, make them more difficult to read. Their limitations are numerous and problematic for teachers who rely solely on quantitative measures to select texts for their students. Most notably, quantitative measures have the tendency to underestimate the readability of narratives and otherwise appropriate secondary-level texts.

QUALITATIVE DIMENSIONS OF TEXT COMPLEXITY

Common sense tells us that only looking at features that can be counted, such as sentence length and word frequency, does not entirely capture what makes texts complex. For example, Ernest Hemingway's writing style is characterized by short, simple sentences. However, Hemingway's (1926) novel *The Sun Also Rises* (610L) is totally inappropriate for second or third grade. The same can be said about Elie Wiesel's (1960) *Night* (590L), a book about the horrors of the Nazi Holocaust that no second- or third-grade teacher would assign to his or her students. These are just two examples of many texts that might be inappropriately assigned if teachers and school leaders relied on quantitative measures alone, a practice that is unfortunately all too common.

While quantitative measures may be necessary for making an initial determination about text complexity, they are not sufficient for helping teachers select texts and plan instruction for their students. In order to do so, teachers must move beyond quantitative measures and consider qualitative measures of text complexity, or those best judged by an attentive human reader. As indicated in our pyramid model of text complexity (see Figure 2.2), we suggest that teachers spend more time evaluating the qualitative measures when selecting texts than they do checking quantitative measures. Appendix A of the CCSS describes four qualitative dimensions of text complexity: levels of meaning or purpose, structure, language conventionality and clarity, and knowledge demands (NGA & CCSSO, 2010). Figure 2.6 shows whether literary and informational texts might be considered less or more complex based on these dimensions.

When selecting texts for students, teachers should consider the levels of meaning or purpose. For literary texts, such as novels or plays, those works with multiple levels of meaning are more complex than those with a single meaning.

Dimension	Literary Text		Informational Text	
	Less Complex	**More Complex**	**Less Complex**	**More Complex**
Meaning or Purpose	Single level of meaning	Multiple levels of meaning	Explicitly stated purpose	Implicit purpose or multiple purposes
Structure	Simple, conventional, explicit structure with events related in chronological order and no shifts in point of view	Complex, unconventional, implicit structure with events related out of chronological order and many shifts in point of view	Simple structure with explicit connections between ideas, traits that conform to a common genre or subgenre, or simple graphics that are unnecessary to understanding the text	Complex structure with implicit connections between ideas, traits specific to a particular discipline, or sophisticated graphics that are essential to understanding the text
Language	Literal language that is clear, contemporary, familiar, and conversational	Figurative or ironic language that is ambiguous or purposefully misleading, archaic or unfamiliar, and/or academic	Literal language that is clear, contemporary, familiar, and conversational	Abstract language that is ambiguous or purposefully misleading, archaic or unfamiliar, and/or domain specific
Knowledge Demands	Simple or single theme with common, everyday experiences or clearly fantastical situations told from a single perspective like one's own; require everyday knowledge and familiarity with genre conventions and have few references/allusions to other texts	Complex, sophisticated, or multiple themes with experiences distinctly different from one's own told from multiple perspectives; require extensive cultural and literary knowledge and have many references/allusions to other texts	Require everyday knowledge and familiarity with genre conventions and have few if any references to or citations of other texts	Require extensive or specialized discipline-specific content knowledge and have many references to or citations of other texts

FIGURE 2.6. Qualitative measures of text complexity.

Take, for example, Arthur Miller's (1953) *The Crucible.* On one level it is a play about the Salem witch trials in the late 1600s, but on a deeper level it is an allegory for McCarthyism in the United States at the time when the play was written. Understanding the implicit meaning within the play makes it more difficult than a short story that is solely about the Salem witch trials. Likewise, informational texts in which the author's purpose is explicitly stated are less complex than texts in which there are multiple purposes or in which the purpose is "deliberately withheld" (Fisher & Frey, 2014a, p. 240).

Structure is another important consideration when evaluating text complexity. Literary texts that follow a conventional plot structure (exposition, rising action, climax, falling action, and resolution) that is told in chronological order and from a single point of view are relatively less complex. A novel with many flashbacks in which events occur out of chronological order, such as Kurt Vonnegut's (1969) *Slaughterhouse-Five,* might be considered more complex in terms of structure. For informational texts, including science and social studies textbooks, those in which the text structure is explicitly signaled through text features are less complex than texts with an implicit structure or texts that combine multiple structures. A text that uses a simple structure such as sequence, cause–effect, or problem–solution might be less complex than one that uses a more difficult structure such as description or compare–contrast (Englert & Hiebert, 1984). In addition to organization, disciplinary texts that contain graphics such as charts and figures that supplement (rather than support) information in the written text are more complex.

The conventionality and clarity of language in a text also influence its complexity. Many readers find the archaic and unfamiliar language of Shakespeare's dramas and poetry, as well as their use of figurative language (e.g., similes, metaphors, personification), to be more difficult than literary works that employ more contemporary and familiar language. When considering informational texts about social studies, science, or technical subjects, those with unfamiliar academic or domain-specific vocabulary and those written using a formal register are more complex than texts written with familiar vocabulary and casual language (Fisher & Frey, 2014a).

Finally, the knowledge that authors assume readers will have when writing a text influences its complexity. Understanding complex literature often demands that readers possess sufficient literary and cultural knowledge to understand references or allusions to other works, such as the Bible or Greek mythology, as well as the background knowledge to interpret themes based on events that differ from one's own lived experiences. Complex informational texts often assume that readers have specialized or discipline-specific knowledge of key concepts in the text. For example, a primary-source document such as Patrick Henry's Speech to the Virginia Convention not only assumes that readers have prior knowledge of the historical context surrounding the American Revolution, but it also assumes that the reader has a working knowledge of the many mythological and biblical allusions that he uses for rhetorical effect.

Engaging in the thorough reading of a text to evaluate its complexity according to these qualitative dimensions is undoubtedly time consuming, but there are at least two clear benefits. Qualitative analyses of text complexity allow teachers to match readers with texts, and they allow teachers to identify the aspects of a text that will make it difficult for readers (Pearson & Hiebert, 2014). The first benefit is important, as teachers and school leaders might make a determination about in which grade to place a text based on qualitative dimensions. Think back to the example of *Night* by Elie Wiesel. Although its quantitative text complexity places it in the grades 2–3 text complexity band, the levels of meaning and knowledge demands make a high school placement more appropriate. The second benefit is, perhaps, more important. By taking notes about the meaning or purpose, structure, language, and knowledge demands of a text when reading it, teachers are well positioned to provide appropriate instructional supports for students. Although it may be unrealistic to expect teachers to read every text this closely, we recommend that grade-level or content-area teams share the responsibility of evaluating the qualitative dimensions of text complexity for each of the major texts assigned across a school year.

READER AND TASK CONSIDERATIONS

Whereas quantitative and qualitative measures are useful for determining how complex a text is in relation to other texts, reader and task considerations can help teachers determine how difficult a text will be for individual readers given specific tasks. Indicated by their placement at the bottom of our pyramid model of text complexity in Figure 2.2, we feel that reader and task considerations warrant the greatest attention. Despite the influence of reader and task variables on comprehension, the CCSS provide teachers with little guidance on matching texts with readers and tasks (Fisher & Frey, 2014a; Hiebert & Pearson, 2014). However, in a webinar following the release of the standards, the CCSSO (2012) provided more detail about the reader and task considerations described in Appendix A. Their guidance is summarized in Figure 2.7.

After teachers have checked quantitative measures of text complexity and analyzed qualitative measures, they should consider whether the text is a good match for the readers in their classroom. Factors such as readers' cognitive capabilities, reading skills, knowledge and experiences, and motivation can affect text comprehension (NGA & CCSSO, 2010; Snow, 2002). For example, working memory influences the reading skills required for comprehension, including inferencing and comprehension monitoring (Cain, Oakhill, & Bryant, 2004). In addition, readers with greater knowledge of vocabulary, prior knowledge about a topic, and motivation for reading informational texts comprehend them better

Reader Considerations		Task Considerations	
Cognitive Capabilities	Do readers at this grade level possess the necessary attention, memory, and critical analytic thinking skills to read and comprehend the text?	Reader's Purpose	What is the purpose (which might shift over the course of reading) for reading the text?
Reading Skills	Do readers at this grade level possess the necessary inferencing, visualization, and questioning skills to read and comprehend the text?	Type of Reading	What type of reading (e.g., skimming to get the gist, studying to retain content, close reading) is being done?
Knowledge/ Experience	Do readers at this grade level possess adequate prior knowledge and/or experience regarding the topic, vocabulary, genre, and language of the text to read and comprehend the text?	Intended Outcome	What is the intended outcome (e.g., increase in knowledge, solution to a real-world problem, and/or engagement with the text) of the task?
Motivation	Will readers at this grade level be interested in the content or develop an interest in the content of the text? Do the readers have the self-efficacy to believe they will be able to read and understand the text?	Task Complexity	Will the complexity of any tasks (or any questions asked or discussed) interfere with the reading experience?

FIGURE 2.7. Reader and task considerations.

(Best et al., 2008; Guthrie et al., 2007; Liebfreund & Conradi, 2016). In short, there is abundant evidence suggesting that teachers consider each of these factors when selecting texts for their students.

Equally important is considering the tasks in which students will engage while reading the text. Task considerations include the purpose for reading, the type of reading being done, the intended outcome, and the complexity of the task itself (NGA & CCSSO, 2010; Snow, 2002). Though less studied, there is also support for considering task factors. Simple tasks tend to make comprehending complex texts easier, but complex tasks can make comprehending even simple texts more difficult (Valencia, Wixson, & Pearson, 2014). For example, readers comprehend texts differently when asked to read for different purposes (e.g., reading for details versus reading for general impressions; Smith, 1967), when reading using different modes (e.g., oral versus silent reading; Holmes, 1985), when reading to complete an informal or formal outcome (e.g., classroom activities versus standardized testing; Mosenthal & Na, 1980), and when completing simple or complex tasks (Dreher & Guthrie, 1990). At the very least, beyond selecting what students should read, teachers should consider why and how students will read.

In our work with schools, we often see a disconnect between the complexity of the tasks expected in college and career readiness standards and the tasks that teachers assign to their students. Try as they might, teachers are unlikely to improve students' reading achievement by only increasing text complexity without also increasing the complexity of the tasks they ask them to complete (Fisher & Frey, 2015). Asking students to evaluate the impact of an author's choices on the meaning of a text or to integrate ideas across multiple texts, for example, are more complex tasks than asking students to recall literal-level details (Goldman & Lee, 2014; Valencia et al., 2014). Fortunately, unlike readers and texts, the tasks that teachers assign are more "malleable" (Amendum, Conradi, & Hiebert, 2018, p. 123). While teachers might assign easier tasks when introducing new instructional routines or when students read complex texts independently, they should assign rigorous, grade-level tasks and focus on making them easier through instructional support from the teacher or peers (Frey & Fisher, 2011; Strong et al., 2018). Complex tasks, when paired with appropriately complex texts and instructional support, are more likely to lead readers to deeper comprehension and content-area learning.

A PROCESS FOR TEXT SELECTION

Now that we have unpacked the quantitative, qualitative, and reader-task aspects of text complexity, we describe a process that we have used with teachers to select texts. We again want to stress that relying only on a single measure of text complexity will fail to result in selecting an appropriate text for students under many circumstances. Based on Hiebert's (2013) Text Complexity Multi-Index, we summarize a four-step process that weighs multiple measures when selecting texts and matching them with readers and tasks (Strong et al., 2018). We firmly believe that teachers should work together in their grade-level and content-area teams to evaluate the texts available to them in their school and select texts around which to plan their instruction. To aid in this process, we present a text complexity evaluation template in Figure 2.8.

First, check the complexity of a text you are considering, using a familiar source such as Lexile or an alternative quantitative measure. Once you have located the text complexity score, record it in the evaluation template. If you used Lexile, consult the Lexile Ranges in Figure 2.3 to see whether the text's complexity is appropriate for the grade-level band you teach. If you used an alternative measure, locate the associated grade-level band in Figure 2.4 and record it in the evaluation template. Remember that readability is only an indicator of a text's vocabulary and syntax. As such, it should serve as an initial check of whether the

Text Title:		
Quantitative Measures	Text Complexity Score(s):	Grade-Level Band(s):
Qualitative Measures	Meaning or Purpose:	
	Structure:	
	Language:	
	Knowledge Demands:	
Reader–Task Considerations	**Reader Considerations**	**Task Considerations**
	Cognitive Capabilities:	Reader's Purpose:
	Reading Skills:	Type of Reading:
	Knowledge/Experience:	Intended Outcome:
	Motivation:	Task Complexity:
Grade-Level Placement:		

FIGURE 2.8. Text complexity evaluation template.

text is grade appropriate. If the quantitative measure indicates that it is above or below grade level, that is not a disqualifier.

Second, consider using an additional text complexity analysis tool such as Coh-Metrix Common Core Text Ease and Readability Assessor. This step may only be necessary if the text's readability based on Lexile or another quantitative measure doesn't match your expectations. You might use Coh-Metrix to analyze a specific passage in the text in terms of its narrativity, syntactic simplicity, word concreteness, and cohesion (see Figure 2.5). It will also provide an associated grade level and an explanation of the analysis. Record this information in the evaluation template.

Third, spend some time reading the text and analyzing the qualitative dimensions of text complexity. As you read, record the levels of meaning or purpose, structure, language conventionality and clarity, and knowledge demands in the evaluation template. Consult Figure 2.6 for explanations of how literary and informational texts might be considered less or more complex according to each of these dimensions. An individual text might not fall neatly under one column or the other. It is likely that some dimensions will be more complex than others, and some dimensions might seem to fall somewhere in the middle. Although this may seem like a lot of work at first, remember that this step serves two purposes: determining whether the text is appropriate for the grade you teach and determining what aspects of the text will be challenging. The latter purpose is an important first step toward planning your instruction around that text.

Fourth, read the text one or two more times and ask yourself whether it is an appropriate match for readers and tasks at your grade level. As you read, record your answers to the questions posed for each of the reader and task considerations in Figure 2.7. Do readers in this grade level possess the cognitive capabilities, reading skills, knowledge and/or experience, and motivation necessary to comprehend the text (or will they be able to with support)? How will the task, including the reader's purpose, type of reading, intended outcome, and task complexity, influence comprehension? The answers to these questions based on a second reading of the text should help you make a final decision about a grade-level placement to record on the template.

FINAL THOUGHTS

When we first started working with middle and high school teachers to help them select texts, we found that the texts they wanted to use were not complex enough for the grade level they taught. On a recent school visit, John was pleased to hear about seventh- and eighth-grade ELA students analyzing issues of racial discrimination, bias, and manipulation in *Narrative of the Life of Frederick Douglass* (Douglass, 1845) and Shakespeare's *Othello*. For those teachers who feel they are a long way off from selecting complex texts and tasks for their readers, we urge you to read Appendix B of the CCSS (NGA & CCSSO, 2010). In this document, the standards' authors provide sample texts and tasks for each grade-level band in English language arts; history/social studies; and science, mathematics, and technical subjects. Select one of the text exemplars and sample performance tasks for your grade level and discipline, implement them, and reflect on students' performance in relation to the expected level of complexity and quality.

On a final note, there is one area where we feel the CCSS and other state standards are lacking in terms of guidance on text selection. The exemplar texts in Appendix B selected to represent the complexity, quality, and range of reading mostly represent canonical literature (including stories, drama, and poems) and literary nonfiction, primary and secondary source documents, and scientific and technical texts. Although these text types should probably make up a large percentage of what students read, they should also have opportunities to read YA literature that will motivate readers and that can be as complex as canonical texts (Flaherty & Chisholm, 2015; Glaus, 2014). In addition, although media texts are included in Appendix B, there is little guidance for analyzing visual text complexity (Cappello, 2017).

In the next chapter, we expand our notion of text to include these diverse text types and provide a framework for choosing and using multiple texts that build students' capacity for tackling complex, content-area texts. Instead of restricting students' reading to texts below their grade level, we urge you to select texts that will challenge them; then support their reading through the use of accessible texts that build background knowledge and through instructional scaffolds that can help them overcome the challenges you have identified. Evaluating text complexity takes time, but you are laying the groundwork for comprehension. You might be surprised what students are able to read with well-designed instruction.

CHAPTER 3

Designing Content-Area Text Sets

When Bill teaches comprehension theory to his preservice teachers every fall, he begins the discussion by having his students engage in the following reading task. He asks them to read silently and decide—without talking to a neighbor—what this passage is describing:

> The procedure is actually quite simple. First you arrange things into different groups. Of course, one pile may be sufficient depending on how much there is to do. If you have to go somewhere else due to lack of facilities that is the next step, otherwise you are pretty well set. It is important not to overdo things. That is, it is better to do too few things at once than too many. In the short run this may not seem important but complications can easily arise. A mistake can be expensive as well. At first the whole procedure will seem complicated. Soon, however, it will become just another facet of life. It is difficult to foresee any end to the necessity for this task in the immediate future, but then one never can tell. After the procedure is completed one arranges the materials into different groups again. Then they can be put into their appropriate places. Eventually they will be used once more and the whole cycle will then have to be repeated. However, that is part of life. (Bransford & Johnson, 1973, p. 400)

After they finish reading, Bill asks students to raise their hands if they are absolutely positive they know what the passage is about. Most semesters only 30–40% of students raise their hands to this initial question. Bill follows this query by providing them one word: laundromat. As recognition begins to move through the classroom (often accompanied by audible "ohs" and "ahs"), he again asks who knows what the passage is about. This time, usually, all hands go up. The answer to the question is, of course, washing clothes. Students may be able to recognize and know the meaning of every word of the passage; however, without the relevant background knowledge that includes the laundromat context, only half or less are able to *comprehend* what the passage is about. The students' background knowledge (or lack thereof) is directly related to their ability to successfully understand their reading. And it was one word from Bill that made the difference between comprehension and confusion.

Bill uses this example to illustrate an important point about learning in the disciplines—students need strategic, scaffolded support from their teachers if they are to comprehend demanding content-area texts and successfully achieve their teachers' instructional objectives and disciplinary goals. And as in the laundry example above, students need their teachers to support understanding *before* reading by providing the relevant, targeted background knowledge to fully engage these texts. In addition, teachers need to use *during*-reading strategies to support comprehension while students read and *after*-reading strategies to help students to synthesize and extend their understanding (Crafton, 1982). This is what many literacy teachers and researchers refer to as a Before–During–After (B-D-A) reading framework (e.g., Laverick, 2002).

In order to improve disciplinary learning and overall literacy outcomes, we also need to think hard about *how much* students are reading. This is what literacy experts call *reading volume,* which in mathematical terms can be defined as the total time spent reading multiplied by the number of words read (Anderson, Wilson, & Fielding, 1988; Cunningham & Stanovich, 1998). Reading volume is not only related to increased levels of comprehension, vocabulary knowledge, and general knowledge about the world (Cunningham & Stanovich, 1997; Sparks, Patton & Murdoch, 2014), it also provides students the practice and stamina they need to engage the increasingly complex texts they face in secondary school, college, and their careers. Unfortunately, both research into classroom reading practices and our own experiences working in secondary schools have shown us that the volume of students' reading within classrooms is often too low to support the levels of literacy development needed to learn important disciplinary concepts from increasingly difficult texts. Secondary teachers are either reading aloud to their students or having students listen to audio recordings of texts instead of reading independently or collaboratively (Swanson et al., 2016). It is not uncommon for teachers to avoid assigning reading altogether, instead choosing to present information in bulleted PowerPoints with worksheets for students to complete (Wexler, Mitchell, Clancy, & Silverman, 2017), or what we call *textless approaches* to instruction (Lewis et al., 2014; Lewis & Walpole, 2016).

Although these textless approaches are problematic, you may be thinking that adding more texts and tasks to an already full curriculum seems like an impossible assignment. However, in this chapter we provide you with a framework for designing integrated sets of related texts that not only provide your students increased reading volume but also give them the critical background knowledge needed to make complex texts accessible. Additionally, these sets create opportunities for students to make connections between texts, therefore extending their understanding of disciplinary concepts. We begin this chapter by providing an expanded definition of text and an explanation of why combining texts is important for disciplinary instruction. We then discuss comprehension theory and how integrated text sets, situated within a clear B-D-A reading framework, provide the critical background knowledge and strategic support needed to read and understand challenging disciplinary texts. We then provide a clear structure and content-specific examples for choosing these texts—multimedia, informational, young adult, websites, and visuals—that build both background knowledge and motivation, allow for differentiation, and expand student understanding of key disciplinary concepts.

EXPANDING OUR DEFINITION OF "TEXT"

Since this chapter focuses on how content-area teachers can leverage texts to achieve their disciplinary goals and improve their students' literacy outcomes, it is important to define just what we mean by "text." Content-area teachers usually think of their classroom textbooks when they hear that word (Berkeley, King-Sears, Hott, & Bradley-Black, 2014).

Although textbooks can be an integral part of classroom instruction, we argue for a broader definition of the word. For instance, one of author John Green's (2014) excellent "Crash Course" videos on race, class, and gender might be used to foster a deeper understanding of *To Kill a Mockingbird,* a novel that is ubiquitous in high school ELA classrooms (Mackey, Vermeer, Storie, & Deblois, 2012). Lyrics of Civil War songs from both the Union and the Confederacy on AmericanCivilWar.com (n.d.) can be important texts for social studies teachers who want students to analyze primary sources for how the North and South represented the conflict to themselves and the world. An online interactive simulation of a roller coaster from myPhysicsLab.com (Neumann, 2019) can be an important text for science teachers who want their students to experience the impact of friction, gravity, and mass on the motion of objects.

The point is that we have a great variety of texts with which we can build students' knowledge. Expanding our definition of text acknowledges this reality, but true knowledge building will only be accomplished by having students read multiple texts on a variety of topics.

THE LIMITATIONS OF A SINGLE TEXT

There are many reasons why teachers should include multiple texts in their content-area instruction. First, as we argued in our introduction, the volume of text reading that students do matters a great deal to their ability to independently comprehend text, develop their vocabularies, and add to their knowledge base (e.g., Sparks et al., 2014).

Another reason is that there are significant limitations to using a single classroom textbook to teach disciplinary concepts. Experts in social studies instruction have pointed out that their textbooks often provide only superficial coverage of historical events, or outright historical inaccuracies (Tschida & Buchanan, 2015). More importantly, using a single text prevents students from developing *historical thinking,* the ability to gather and evaluate multiple sources of information and to identify and reconcile competing perspectives of the past (Wineburg, 2001; Wineburg, Martin, & Monte-Sano, 2012). These important disciplinary skills require that teachers choose multiple texts (Bickford, 2013; Tschida & Buchanan, 2015) since multiple perspectives and competing historical accounts are rarely found in a single classroom textbook.

Science textbooks, too, have their weaknesses. Disciplinary experts in science point out that their textbooks often bounce from one idea to another, only superficially address important topics, and are unhelpful for building deep understanding of scientific concepts or scientific thinking (McGlynn & Kelly, 2019). Additionally, science texts are often *inconsiderate* (Daniels & Zemelman, 2003/2004), meaning that they can be poorly organized, overloaded with information, and difficult to read. McGlynn and Kelly (2019) have likened reading science textbooks to "looking at a well-organized 40-page menu at a restaurant and trying to decide what to order" (p. 36). It is no wonder, they argue, that students find them difficult to learn from.

ELA teachers also need to consider the drawbacks of single texts. Wells and Batchelor (2017) argue that although the individual stories, novels, plays, and poems that students read in ELA can be important reading experiences, they rob students of the opportunity to confront multiple perspectives. This limits students' ability to make more meaningful text-to-self, text-to-text, and text-to-world connections (Gritter, 2011), and prevents them from developing the ethical respect needed to empathize with those whose experiences are different from their own (Rabinowitz & Smith, 1998). Lewis and Flynn (2017) argued that without the critical background knowledge and context that multiple texts provide, students will not be able to apply what they learn from literary texts to contemporary issues of social justice and equity, an important National Council of Teachers of English (NCTE) standard (NCTE, 2012). For instance, although *To Kill a Mockingbird* directly addresses American racism, the novel is written by a white author, told from the perspective of a white narrator, and does not address contemporary racial problems facing our schools and communities (Lewis & Flynn, 2017). As in social studies and science, the single-text approach does not allow teachers to accomplish discipline-specific goals that require multiple perspectives embedded in multiple texts.

MULTIPLE TEXTS AND BACKGROUND KNOWLEDGE

There is a third important reason for using *sets* of texts instead of single texts. In Chapter 2, we spoke about the quantitative, qualitative, and reader-task considerations that can act as a barrier to students as they attempt to comprehend challenging texts. Although the Common Core State Standards—and other state standards that are aligned with them—require students to "read and comprehend complex literary and informational text independently and proficiently" (NGA & CCSSO, 2010, p. 35), many students need help to overcome the comprehension challenges that increasingly difficult texts pose (Best et al., 2008). Teachers must not only select instructional strategies that support comprehension before, during, and after reading, they must also think about how to strategically combine related texts in ways that build the relevant background knowledge needed to comprehend these demanding texts by reading other texts (Lupo, Strong, Lewis, Walpole, & McKenna, 2018).

Why should teachers focus on building background knowledge? First, as students get older, their accumulated background knowledge plays an increasingly important role in their ability to comprehend texts (Alexander, Kulikowich, & Jetton, 1994), and the more prior knowledge readers have, the better their comprehension is during reading (Arya, Hiebert, & Pearson, 2011; McNamara, Ozuru, & Floyd, 2011). Second, activating readers' prior knowledge before reading improves comprehension, regardless of whether students read easier or more challenging texts (Lupo et al., 2019). Because knowledge building is essential to designing instructional text sets, it is important first to understand how readers use their background knowledge to construct meaning from what they read. Understanding the comprehension process can help teachers think more strategically about the instructional strategies they employ and the texts they choose to support their students' understanding.

HOW READERS COMPREHEND TEXTS

Walter Kintsch (1988, 2013) provides us with a helpful representation of how readers use background knowledge to construct a comprehensive mental model of the text. He calls this the *construction–integration model*. In this conception, comprehension occurs in three distinct stages that are increasingly more complex (see Figure 3.1). At the first stage, *the surface code,* readers interpret individual words and phrases on a page or screen and construct the basic gist of a text, or what Kintsch (1988) calls the *text base*.

Although having a basic understanding is important, secondary teachers need their students to have a more comprehensive understanding of a text if they are to use reading to achieve challenging disciplinary goals. In this case, students must be able to integrate relevant background knowledge with this *text base* to

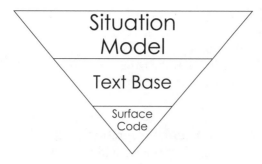

FIGURE 3.1. Levels of text representation.

form a *situation model,* a comprehensive representation of the text that refines and expands on their gist-level understanding. Unfortunately, research demonstrates that many adolescent readers are unable to develop this comprehensive situation model (Compton, Miller, Elleman, & Steacy, 2014). This is why teachers need to think hard about instruction that can provide students with the relevant background knowledge and experiences that can build this more robust textual representation.

To illustrate this process, let's look at a sample instructional segment that is focused on Shakespeare's *Romeo and Juliet,* a text that many of us are familiar with and that is another staple of the high school ELA curriculum (Mackey et al., 2012). In this segment the teacher is using the first act of the play to build her students' ability to analyze the development of Romeo and Juliet as characters, which is both an important disciplinary goal and meets a key standard for reading literature: "Analyze how complex characters (e.g., those with multiple or conflicting motivations) develop over the course of a text, interact with other characters, and advance the plot or develop the theme" (NGA & CCSSO, 2010, p. 38).

In the famous speech that follows their meeting at her family's masquerade ball, Juliet expresses both her love for Romeo and her despair over the fact that Romeo's family—the Montagues—are in a life and death feud with her own family, the Capulets. Juliet speaks:

> O Romeo, Romeo, wherefore art thou Romeo?
> Deny thy father and refuse thy name.
> Or if thou wilt not, be but sworn my love
> And I'll no longer be a Capulet.
> 'Tis but thy name that is my enemy:
> Thou art thyself, though not a Montague.
> What's Montague? It is nor hand nor foot
> Nor arm nor face nor any other part
> Belonging to a man. O be some other name.
> What's in a name? That which we call a rose

By any other name would smell as sweet;
So Romeo would, were he not Romeo call'd,
Retain that dear perfection which he owes
Without that title. Romeo, doff thy name,
And for that name, which is no part of thee,
Take all myself.

According to the construction–integration model, students begin the process by reading the surface code of the individual words and phrases on the page (see Figure 3.2). From this code (and possibly some translation support from the teacher) they are able to construct the gist, or text base, from this excerpt. In this case students will recognize that Juliet is a Capulet, Romeo a Montague and that, despite their family names and feud, Juliet has fallen deeply in love with him. However, in order to move past the text base to construct the situation model suitable for character analysis, discipline-specific background knowledge is needed.

Discourse analysts (Fahnestock & Secor, 1991; Wilder, 2002) and instructional specialists who focus on literature studies (Appleman, 2015; Beers & Probst, 2012) have pointed out that experienced readers of literature use specific types of interpretive background knowledge and critical frameworks to make sense of literary texts (Lewis & Ferretti, 2009). One well-known framework is the feminist critical lens in which readers interrogate a text for issues of gender, power, and language use (Appleman, 2015). For instance, if students are familiar with this gendered approach, they might focus on Juliet's relative lack of power in her family structure, a fact that is evidenced by her father's decision to marry her off against her will to a man she does not love and who is almost twice her age. It is no wonder, then, that Juliet wishes that Romeo could "deny [his] father

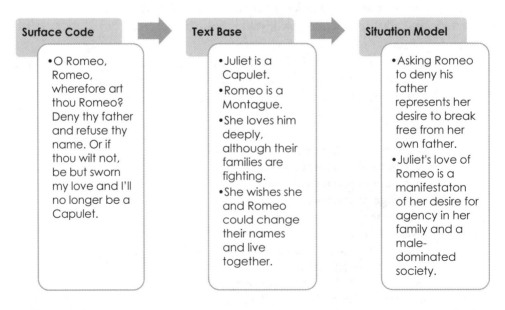

FIGURE 3.2. Illustration of the construction–integration process in *Romeo and Juliet.*

and refuse [his] name," something that she, too, wishes she had the power to do. Possessing this critical background knowledge, students can begin to move from a plot-level, text base understanding (Juliet loves Romeo but wishes he was from a different family) to a more comprehensive situation model of Juliet's "multiple or conflicting motivations" (NGA & CCSSO, 2010, p. 38). In this case students might construct the interpretation that Juliet's infatuation with Romeo is more than just the capricious whim of an adolescent girl who has fallen in love at first sight. It is, instead, a very real attempt to thwart her father's will and take back control of her life from the male-dominated society that treats women like possessions and perpetuates senseless feuds like the one that will eventually take her life.

It is clear that building this kind of interpretive situation model takes discipline-specific background knowledge that must be strategically taught. Otherwise, students will continue to operate at the plot or gist level and be unable to form a more comprehensive situation model where the work of the disciplines really happens. This leads to an important question. How do teachers actually go about building the background knowledge that is most critical to their students' understanding of disciplinary concepts and content-area material? Using before-reading instructional strategies is one way that they might begin this process, and in Chapter 4 we discuss several research-validated approaches to building background knowledge in this way. However, considering that reading volume and background knowledge are both crucial to students' learning, we also suggest building knowledge for reading challenging content-area texts by reading and viewing other related texts in an integrated collection of texts that we call the quad text set framework (Lewis et al., 2014; Lupo et al., 2018). In this way, we build background knowledge *for* reading *by* reading (Lewis & Walpole, 2016) and then expand our text set with other texts that will help students synthesize and extend their understanding.

DESIGNING A QUAD TEXT SET

In its most basic form, a quad text set is composed of four different kinds of texts, which are represented in Figure 3.3. The first is a challenging content-area text written at or above grade level that we call the *target text* (Lewis et al., 2014). The next three texts are selected to provide background knowledge that students need to construct meaning from the target text or to extend their understanding through text-to-text connections. These include an accessible and motivating *visual, video,* or *digital text* that serves to immediately engage students in the topic and activate the basic background knowledge needed to form a text base understanding of the target text (Lewis et al., 2014; Lupo et al., 2018). The next text type is an *informational text—or set of informational texts—*selected to build additional, discipline-specific background knowledge that students need in order to construct a situation model of the target text. The fourth text is an *accessible text*—young-adult fiction or nonfiction, magazine or newspaper articles, or texts

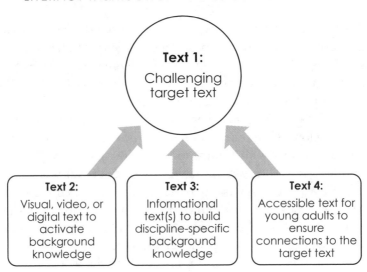

FIGURE 3.3. The quad text set framework.

drawn from popular culture—that helps students to make important text-to-text connections, extend their understanding of the target text, and find relevance in the disciplinary concepts that are the focus of instruction (Lewis et al., 2014; Lupo et al., 2018).

We would like you to think of the process of designing a quad text set as *planning backwards*. By this we mean that the first step in planning a quad text set is identifying the key learning objectives for the instructional unit or lesson from state learning standards. The second step is choosing a challenging target text that serves as an effective vehicle for achieving those learning objectives (Lewis et al., 2014). As we often say to our preservice teacher candidates, "We are not teaching *the text*; we are teaching skills *through the text*." Therefore, it is important that teachers choose a target text that is both complex enough to be challenging and rich enough to convey important disciplinary concepts. Teachers then work backwards from there to strategically choose other texts that build the relevant background knowledge and motivation needed to comprehend and make connections to the target text (Lupo et al., 2018). However, it is not enough to thoughtfully design a quad text set and then just assign the readings, hoping that students will be able to comprehend the target text without additional instructional support.

THE B-D-A FRAMEWORK AND THE QUAD TEXT SET

Without strategically planning instruction to support students when they read, it is still possible that they will not comprehend the texts that make up a quad text set, nor will they be able to achieve their teachers' instructional objectives. Before we provide examples of quad text sets designed for ELA, social studies, and science, we provide a brief preview of some research-based instructional strategies that we recommend using in concert with the sample quad text sets that follow. Remember that this is just a brief preview. We provide more specific explanations of these before-, during-, and after-reading strategies in subsequent chapters.

Before reading we recommend using strategies that provide students a preview of the texts they will read (e.g., Manzo & Casale, 1985), a graphic organizer that provides students a map of the text structure of their reading (e.g., Alvermann, 1981; Smith & Friend, 1986), or a visual representation of key vocabulary that students will encounter in the texts (e.g., Schwartz & Raphael, 1985). We focus on knowledge-building instructional strategies before reading because background knowledge—including vocabulary and text structure knowledge—is highly correlated to reading comprehension (Langer, 1984; Stahl, Jacobson, Davis, & Davis, 1989). A full menu of before-reading strategies to use with texts is presented in Chapter 4.

During reading we recommend providing comprehension support through carefully constructed reading guides that focus student attention and support the active construction of meaning from texts when reading independently (e.g., McKenna, Franks, Conradi, & Lovette, 2011; Wood, 2011) or through collaborative reading frameworks that support comprehension through strategic reading in pairs (e.g., Fuchs, Fuchs, & Kazdan, 1999) or small groups (Palincsar & Brown, 1984). A full explanation of several types of reading guides, the Peer-Assisted Learning Strategies (PALS) paired reading framework (Fuchs et al., 1999), and the Reciprocal Teaching small-group framework (Palincsar & Brown, 1984) are addressed in Chapter 5.

After reading we recommend supporting students in synthesizing textual information through text-based discussions (e.g., Sandora, Beck, & McKeown, 1999; Chinn, Anderson, & Waggoner, 2001), summary writing activities (e.g., Brown & Day, 1983; Buehl, 2014), or writing text-based arguments that encourage students to apply the information they gain from their reading (e.g., Lewis & Ferretti, 2011). A menu of these discussion and text-based writing activities can be found in Chapters 6 and 7, respectively. In addition, we recommend teaching students strategies for planning and revising argumentative, informative/explanatory, and narrative compositions (De La Paz & Graham, 2002), including the use of genre-specific text structures (Englert, Raphael, Anderson, Anthony, & Stevens, 1991). We discuss strategy instruction and the writing process for extended writing assignments in Chapter 8.

In the examples that follow, you will see that the instructional strategies we have selected for each text fit into the B-D-A reading framework that is embedded within the template we use to design quad text sets with teachers. Figure 3.4 presents that planning template. Beginning with this chapter, we demonstrate how we use this template to match texts and instructional strategies to meet content-area instructional objectives. We return to this template in subsequent chapters as we discuss the instructional strategies that we have used with teachers to support students' comprehension before, during, and after reading, as well as to improve students' writing.

	Instructional Objective(s):

	Visual Text:

Instructional Strategies	Before Reading:
	During Reading:
	After Reading:

	Informational Text(s):

Instructional Strategies	Before Reading:
	During Reading:
	After Reading:

	Target Text:

Instructional Strategies	Before Reading:
	During Reading:
	After Reading:

	Accessible Text:

Instructional Strategies	Before Reading:
	During Reading:
	After Reading:

	Extended Writing:

FIGURE 3.4. Quad text set planning template.

Quad Text Set Example for ELA

Let's take another look at our ELA teacher who is preparing her students to read *Romeo and Juliet*. Based on her school curriculum and state standards, she identifies character analysis as one of the key instructional objectives for her unit and decides to design a quad text set to achieve that goal. Specifically, she wants her students to learn to analyze how characters develop over the course of a play, interact with other characters, advance the play's plot, and develop the theme (NGA & CCSSO, 2010, p. 38). This instructional objective is displayed in the quad text set example for *Romeo and Juliet* in Figure 3.5. Keeping this objective in mind, she chooses Act I of *Romeo and Juliet* as an effective target text to teach this skill. Given its length, she decides that she will design a separate quad text set for each of the play's five acts. Planning backwards, she understands that the play presents several challenges to her students in achieving this objective, not the least of which is the Elizabethan language that can serve as a significant barrier to understanding the play at even the gist or text base level.

To help students overcome the language barriers—as well as to engage their interest—the teacher begins her quad text set by showing a brief video excerpt of Act I, Scene i, from Martinelli and Luhrmann's (1996) adaptation of the play set in modern California. This highly stylized and action-packed clip provides a gist-level understanding of the play's context and the feud between the Montagues and Capulets, as well as a helpful introduction to some of the play's main characters, including Romeo himself. Knowing that this is an important text for activating background knowledge, the teacher also provides instructional support before, during, and after viewing to make sure that students understand it and can apply what they learn when reading the target text. We describe the B-D-A supports for each text in this text set in subsequent chapters.

Because the teacher selected the target text to teach character analysis skills, discipline-specific background knowledge will also be needed to form a situation model of the play suitable for literary analysis and interpretation. First, the teacher understands that in order for her students to analyze what motivates Romeo and Juliet as characters, she must build their background knowledge of the Elizabethan era, the strict gender roles of the age that defined and controlled men's and women's behavior, and the general lack of rights that women had to control their own destinies. In order to provide that background knowledge, she chooses an online informational text on the lives of Elizabethan women (Elizabethi.org, 1998–2019) that provides students with an introduction to issues of gender and power, building the discipline-specific background knowledge needed to analyze the characters' deeper motivations in *Romeo and Juliet*.

Now that students understand the situational and social context of the play, they are ready to read the rest of Act I and analyze the "star-crossed lovers" as characters. Although the students have gained relevant background knowledge from the preliminary texts in the set, the teacher still needs to support

	Instructional Objective(s): Analyze how characters develop over the course of a text, interact with other characters, advance the plot, and develop the theme.		
	Visual Text: Video of Act I from contemporary film version of *Romeo and Juliet*		
Instructional Strategies	**Before Reading:**		
	During Reading:		
	After Reading:		
	Informational Text(s): Article on gender roles and power in Elizabethan England		
Instructional Strategies	**Before Reading:**		
	During Reading:		
	After Reading:		
	Target Text: Act I of Shakespeare's *Romeo and Juliet*		
Instructional Strategies	**Before Reading:**		
	During Reading:		
	After Reading:		
	Accessible Text: Selected chapters from *Eleanor and Park* by Rainbow Rowell		
Instructional Strategies	**Before Reading:**		
	During Reading:		
	After Reading:		
	Extended Writing:		

FIGURE 3.5. ELA quad text set on *Romeo and Juliet.*

comprehension through B-D-A instructional choices. In this case she knows that she will have to provide students with help in understanding both the plot and vocabulary of the first act. More importantly, she will need to plan the strategic supports that will encourage students to focus on Romeo and Juliet as characters and to make inferences about how and why they fall in love so quickly based on their knowledge of Elizabethan gender roles.

To reinforce how the gendered expectations of society can impact the characters, the teacher chooses her fourth text, a selection of chapters from a contemporary YA novel, *Eleanor and Park* (Rowell, 2012). This story traces the relationship of two very different high school students: Eleanor, an introverted and awkward newcomer whose family lives in poverty and in constant fear of her violent and controlling stepdad, and Park, a comic-book-loving teen from a loving and supportive mixed-race family who, nonetheless, has to deal with his father's narrow definition of manhood. Although this young adult love story takes place in the mid-1980s (instead of the late 1500s), both characters, like Romeo and Juliet, have to negotiate the societal expectations of what it means to be a man and a woman. Connecting key chapters to the play encourages students to extend their understanding of the representations of gender and power in *Romeo and Juliet.*

At the conclusion of this quad text set, the teacher wants her students to demonstrate their understanding by writing an expository essay that explores gender and power and its impact on character. Recognizing that her students may have difficulty without instructional support for planning before writing, she provides a graphic organizer to help her students select evidence from the texts and organize ideas using a compare–contrast structure (Englert et al., 1988). The teacher plans to adjust the amount of support she provides based on students' needs, allowing most students to draft their essays independently before editing and revising them with peer assistance. We address these kinds of extended written assessments in Chapter 8.

The Order of Texts

It is important to note here that our experiences using the quad text set approach with teachers have indicated that the order in which texts are presented to students is important (Lupo et al., 2018). Interspersing knowledge-building texts with chunked or repeated reading of the target text can improve students' understanding and motivation to read the challenging target text (Lupo et al., 2018). For instance, in the *Romeo and Juliet* quad text set, the teacher may have students reread Act I, Scene iv (where Lady Capulet encourages Juliet to reconcile herself to the arranged marriage) after students read the chapters from *Eleanor and Park.* The targeted reread of this scene allows students to directly apply their knowledge of gender and power in this accessible text to their analysis of Juliet's situation and provides insight into her character's motivation. The point is that teachers can strategically and flexibly order the texts within a quad text set to provide students with both increased reading volume and the opportunity to acquire important disciplinary knowledge and skills.

Quad Text Set Example for Social Studies

In order to illustrate the flexible use of the framework, we discuss an example of a quad text set that includes an inquiry extension, one that might be used in a high school social studies classroom. This quad text set is based on one designed by one of Bill's teacher candidates. It is a particularly strong example of how quad text sets can be used to build both critical background knowledge and disciplinary literacy skills. Based on the curriculum and state social studies standards, this teacher decided to focus her quad text set on cultivating students' ability to trace the development of the idea of segregation over time and explain patterns of continuity and change in contemporary United States history (Delaware Department of Education, 2018, p. 1). She also would like to attend to the disciplinary literacy skill of determining the central idea of a primary source and summarizing its key details (NGA & CCSSO, 2010, p. 61). These two instructional objectives, focused on both content and literacy skills, are reflected in the social studies quad text set example in Figure 3.6. You can also see that this teacher has chosen the *Brown v. Board of Education* decision as a challenging target text that serves as an appropriate vehicle for meeting her instructional objectives.

Working backwards from the target text, the teacher understands that she needs to activate students' background knowledge about segregation and therefore chooses a video text called "Kids Talk about Segregation" (WNYC, 2016). This is a short but engaging interview with Bronx fifth graders who are studying the topic in a predominately minority school. In the video the children define what segregation is in simple terms and provide moving examples of segregation that still manifest themselves in their current school communities.

To build more discipline-specific background knowledge, the teacher chose an informational text that detailed the history of racially segregated schools and communities in the United States (Nodjimbadem, 2017). This text, titled "The Racial Segregation of American Cities Was Anything But Accidental," introduces two important historical terms that are critical to their understanding of this concept: *de jure segregation,* which is segregation that happens through laws (like Jim Crow laws), and *de facto segregation,* which is segregation that is not legally prescribed but occurs despite the fact that there are no segregation laws in place (like the racial divide between inner-city and suburban schools in the North). This text is important because it provides a chronology of both kinds of segregation in the United States and raises questions about whether the de facto segregation of the northern states was, in fact, segregation by law.

Now that students have background knowledge of both historic and contemporary examples of segregation, they are ready to read the target text, the *Brown v. Board of Education* decision (Warren, E., & Supreme Court of the United States,

	Instructional Objective(s): Analyze historical materials to trace the development of an idea over time and explain patterns of continuity and change; determine the central idea of a primary source and accurately summarize the central idea and key details.
	Visual Text: "Kids Talk about Segregation" video
Instructional Strategies	**Before Reading:**
	During Reading:
	After Reading:
	Informational Text(s): Article on the history of racial segregation in the United States
Instructional Strategies	**Before Reading:**
	During Reading:
	After Reading:
	Target Text: *Brown v. Board of Education* decision
Instructional Strategies	**Before Reading:**
	During Reading:
	After Reading:
	Accessible Text: Article on racial disparities in modern U.S. public schools
Instructional Strategies	**Before Reading:**
	During Reading:
	After Reading:
	Extended Writing:

FIGURE 3.6. Social studies quad text set on segregation.

1953). This landmark Supreme Court decision ruled that state-sanctioned segregation of public schools was unconstitutional. It is a text that is both a rigorous primary-source document and an important vehicle for achieving the teacher's disciplinary goals.

Because the teacher wants her students to analyze segregation for patterns of continuity and change over time, she chooses a fourth text to connect to the *Brown v. Board of Education* decision, a magazine article published by the American Psychological Association (Weir, 2016). The article, "Inequality at School," details the impact of racial bias on contemporary school systems and how this bias not only leads to inequities but also to de facto segregation in many modern schools. She chose this text because she wanted her students to see that although state-sanctioned segregation was deemed unconstitutional in the past, segregation is still found in many schools and leads to continuing inequities. This text is an important tool that encourages students to analyze whether the *Brown v. Board of Education* decision actually worked given what they now know about segregation in today's schools.

Leveraging the knowledge that students now have about de jure and de facto segregation, the teacher encourages students to extend their understanding through a structured inquiry project. For this quad text set, she designed a project that both encourages students to apply what they learned about segregation and also gives them practice using the authentic tools of inquiry that social scientists actually use (Lewis et al., 2014). We discuss research and inquiry activities in greater detail in Chapter 9.

Quad Text Set Example for Science

Science teachers, too, can leverage quad text sets to improve learning and literacy outcomes and meet the rigorous Next Generation Science Standards (NGSS Lead States, 2013). Let's examine the case of a middle school science teacher who is designing a unit on climate change. This is a challenging subject for a number of reasons. First, climate change is highly politicized, and debates about the issue have both obscured the science and led to widespread confusion among his students about the topic. Additionally, this teacher's aging textbook does not adequately cover climate change, nor does it contain up-to-date data on global changes or visual representations of that data. These limitations make it very difficult to meet the science standards that he intends to focus on with this quad text set: the impacts of humans on Earth's systems, as well as using graphs, charts, and images to identify patterns in data (NGSS Lead States, 2013, p. 72). He also intends on addressing the disciplinary literacy skill of integrating technical information expressed in words in a text with a visual representation of the information (NGA & CCSSO, 2010, p. 62). You will see these two instructional objectives displayed in the science quad text set example in Figure 3.7.

Starting from the instructional objectives, he chooses his target text. In order to overcome the limitations of his textbooks, he locates a set of five connected web pages that explain how individuals, businesses, communities, nations and the world can act to mitigate climate change (National Geographic Partners, 2015–2019). Not only does this text align with the NGSS around human impacts on Earth's systems, it also provides his students with a blueprint for taking action against this threat.

To mitigate the uneven background knowledge of his students, the teacher begins to plan backwards. He plans to build the relevant background knowledge needed to understand the target text by choosing a short video called "Climate Change 101" with Bill Nye (National Geographic, 2015). This video text provides a working definition of climate change and presents several clear arguments for why climate change represents a very real threat to life on Earth. Not only is this text an entertaining—though serious—introduction to the topic, it serves an important role in helping this teacher overcome students' misconceptions about climate change.

To build more specific background knowledge, the teacher chooses the digital informational text "Climate Change: How Do We Know?" from the National Aeronautics and Space Administration (NASA, 2019) Global Climate Change website. This text not only provides discipline-specific background information about the issue, it also includes interactive graphs and visualizations to help students to track global temperatures, sea-level rise, land ice mass, and ocean acidification over time. The ability to interpret visual representations of data is an important element of the science and disciplinary literacy standards that the teacher hopes to achieve with this unit. To make efficient use of time, the teacher uses the jigsaw method (Poindexter, 1994) to support students' comprehension. First, students get into "expert groups" where each group is assigned one section of the text to read. Next, students meet with a new group—the "jigsaw group"—containing one member from each of the expert groups. Here they share the information that they found in each of their sections. Although some teachers bristle at the fact that students only read one section of this text, this strategic decision provides his students more time to read and comprehend the target text.

To extend student understanding of the impacts of climate change, he assigns the first chapter of the award-winning YA novel *Ship Breaker* by Paolo Bacigalupi (2010). This novel takes place in a post-oil dystopia ravaged by climate change and the rising sea levels and superstorms that are generated by a warmer, wetter Earth. This chapter, which introduces a group of child laborers who break up ships for scrap to eke out an existence, allows students to apply what they learned about the natural and economic impacts of climate change to a fictional world where characters are controlled by a degraded and unstable environment.

Now that students have a fuller understanding of the scope of the problem, they are ready to read the target text on mitigating climate change. The teacher supports comprehension before, during, and after reading, and then encourages them to share their understanding of the target text in an extended writing assignment.

Instructional Objective(s): Construct an argument supported by evidence (e.g., patterns in graphs, charts, and images) for how humans impact Earth's systems; integrate technical information expressed in words in a text with a visual representation of that information.		

Visual Text: "Climate Change 101" video with Bill Nye

Instructional Strategies	**Before Reading:**
	During Reading:
	After Reading:

Informational Text(s): "Climate Change: How Do We Know?" website

Instructional Strategies	**Before Reading:**
	During Reading:
	After Reading:

Accessible Text: Chapter 1 of *Ship Breaker* by Paolo Bacigalupi

Instructional Strategies	**Before Reading:**
	During Reading:
	After Reading:

Target Text: "5 Ways to Curb Climate Change" articles

Instructional Strategies	**Before Reading:**
	During Reading:
	After Reading:

Extended Writing:

FIGURE 3.7. Science quad text set on climate change.

FINAL THOUGHTS

The quad text sets we described in this chapter accomplish three important goals. First, they provide students with the critical background knowledge needed to read and understand challenging content-area texts by reading and viewing more accessible texts. Second, the use of multiple texts increases the volume of literary and informational text reading that students need to develop reading stamina, improve their vocabulary knowledge, and gain knowledge about the world. Third, sets of connected texts allow students to make important connections that extend their understanding of concepts across texts. It is clear that quad text sets offer students many more learning opportunities than a single classroom textbook or teacher lecture can provide.

That being said, finding texts and designing quad text sets can be difficult for teachers who already have a lot on their plates. It is crucial, then, that teachers work together with their school and department colleagues to determine instructional objectives, identify target texts that are effective vehicles for those objectives, and then find and vet texts that build the appropriate background knowledge and extend student understanding. Although it can be frustrating and time consuming to design text sets independently, by working together with colleagues, teachers can share the burden and improve the quality of their text sets through creative collaboration.

At first glance, it may also seem like a lot of work to fill in the quad text set planning template with before-, during-, and after-reading supports for each text. However, we argue that doing so may actually require less planning time, not more. Remember that we provided only a preview of a handful of instructional strategies in this chapter. After reading about them in more detail in subsequent chapters, you will have a toolkit of strategies for supporting comprehension at your disposal. Once learned, you will be able to select from each of these tools based on your instructional objectives and the demands of the texts in your quad text set.

It is equally important that once teachers build their quad text sets, they need to organize digital or physical sites to store them and the supporting materials. Bill often tells the story of how, because of retirements, changing schools, or other reasons, nearly 40% of teachers left the high school where he was teaching during one particular school year. And nearly all of the materials that those teachers found, created, and used over the course of their careers walked out the door with them. This disadvantaged not only the teachers who had to take their places but, more importantly, the students who no longer had access to the plans and materials of experienced teachers. Therefore, when you design your quad text sets, we suggest that you work together, thoroughly vet texts and materials, and get them stored!

CHAPTER 4

Building Background Knowledge before Reading

When delivering professional development in schools, Bill often recalls the time he taught Jack Schaefer's (1953) novel *The Canyon* in his sophomore ELA class. This text relates the exciting adventures of Little Bear, a young Sioux warrior living in the time before European colonization of North America, and his struggle to understand himself and his place within his society. Bill chose this text because it was both appropriately complex for this grade level and because it was a perfect vehicle for achieving his instructional goals related to character development. Given his adolescent audience, who themselves were trying to find their way in adult society, Bill felt that this story, especially the conflicts Little Bear faces and the understanding that he gains, was something to which they could easily relate.

After a week of reading and discussion, tracing the development of Little Bear as a character and linking that character development to broader thematic issues in the text, Bill paused during a classroom discussion when one of his students raised her hand. Thinking that she was going to add to the discussion with an insightful comment about character development, theme, or a poignant text-to-self connection, Bill listened intently. However, he was shocked when she instead asked, "Mr. Lewis, you mean that Little Bear was a guy, not a bear?"

As Bill tells it, he went through most of the stages of grief after hearing that question—denial, anger, bargaining, depression. The last stage, acceptance, finally came when he realized that his student's honest question did not stem from a lack of motivation in ELA or because she was not engaged in the reading or classroom discussions. It came because the student did not have adequate background knowledge of Native American culture. Further, Bill failed to provide that background knowledge before they read, assuming that this contextual knowledge was already firmly in place. While Bill believed that his students were all thinking deeply about Little Bear as a character and how his struggles were illustrative of the tension we all feel between society and ourselves as individuals, some of his students were only thinking about how a talking bear could accomplish all of the human actions that were described in this narrative.

This, of course, is an extreme example! However, what it demonstrates is how critical background knowledge is to all kinds of learning. Whether it be general reading comprehension (Stahl, Hare, Sinatra, & Gregory, 1991), mathematical problem solving (Hart, 1996), the comprehension of history texts (Tarchi, 2010), or literary interpretation (Lewis & Ferretti, 2009, 2011), nearly all learning processes are more effectively facilitated when students' background knowledge is stronger. Therefore, when it comes to supporting students' comprehension of challenging disciplinary texts, it is important to think critically about the challenges that texts pose to readers and the before-reading strategies that can help them overcome those challenges.

It is important to note that we don't want teachers to take a deficit view of students. *All* students have a great deal of general background knowledge that is generated from their personal life experiences. The problem is that as they get older and the topics that they read about become less familiar and more culturally removed from their life experiences, students need topic-specific background knowledge that is only generated in academic contexts (Hattan, 2019).

For instance, after Bill's interaction with the student who did not comprehend *The Canyon,* he understood that she lacked academic background knowledge on Native American culture and traditions that would help her to make sense of this text. He also recognized that, like his own children who watched the animated television series *Little Bear,* this student may have been accessing *personal* experiences because more relevant *academic* experiences were missing.

As you can see, comprehension is complicated by the fact that it is a personal cognitive construction that is grounded in an interaction between the background knowledge readers have about the topic of their reading, the texts they read, and their purposes for reading (Snow, 2002). Like the young woman in Bill's classroom, adolescent students will bring different types and amounts of background knowledge to the literacy tasks their teachers plan. This will significantly impact how much students will benefit from those tasks if they benefit from them at all.

This important point should not be lost. The more students know in advance, the easier it is for them to read to learn new information. Further, students who read more often generate more background knowledge through reading, which makes *new* reading easier. For students who do not have the academic background knowledge needed for a particular text, the converse will be true, experiencing what has been called the Matthew effect in reading (Stanovich, 1986). This effect occurs because readers with greater initial knowledge will read more easily and build more complex understandings than those with more limited initial knowledge who will acquire more basic information. In other words, those with greater knowledge will build richer, more coherent *situation models,* while those with lesser knowledge will remain at a poorer, less coherent *text base* or gist level of understanding (Kintsch, 1988, 2013). We have argued that targeted building of background knowledge by teachers will allow students to spend more time reading more complex texts (Lupo et al., 2018). This will help students to achieve instructional objectives and will also build useful and relevant knowledge for their future reading.

Given the critical role that background knowledge plays in reading comprehension, the purpose of this chapter is to help teachers make efficient use of instructional time so that students with different amounts of academic background knowledge can engage in the productive reading of challenging texts that build both literacy skills and content knowledge. First, we describe different sources of background knowledge and provide insights into researchers' explorations of the role of background knowledge in comprehension. Next, we focus on strategies that build two types of knowledge before students read: knowledge of the discipline-specific words in the text and prior knowledge of how the concepts in the text are structured. Research suggests that both teaching difficult vocabulary and previewing texts before reading improve comprehension (Stahl et al., 1989). Although accomplishing both of these goals with a relatively limited amount of instructional time might seem like a challenge, the research-validated strategies we have selected can be used to build knowledge quickly and in a variety of contexts. The five strategies in this chapter will help teachers determine what their students know and what they need to know in order to learn new information during reading. At the end of this chapter, we demonstrate how to use these before-reading strategies to build knowledge for reading the disciplinary texts in the quad text sets we introduced in the previous chapter.

WHAT IS BACKGROUND KNOWLEDGE, AND HOW DO WE BUILD IT?

When we use the term *background knowledge,* we are referring to everything that students already know before reading a text. Students acquire background knowledge in all of the ways that they learn. It comes from having interactions with people, traveling to new places, and attending events or experiences. It also comes from Internet searches, what students learn formally in schools and, yes, their prior reading experiences (Fisher, Frey, & Lapp, 2012; Lewis et al., 2014). Background knowledge, therefore, is a blanket term for all of the different types of knowledge that students bring to their learning experiences. As we illustrate in Figure 4.1, that blanket covers four sources of background knowledge.

The first source is *vocabulary knowledge,* which can be defined as the understanding of word meanings. Returning to our example of *Romeo and Juliet* from Chapter 3, readers must know or be able to infer the meanings of nearly all the

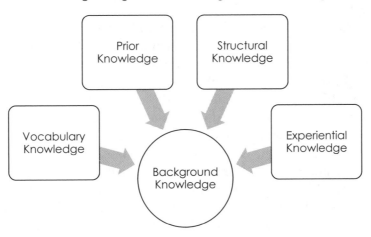

FIGURE 4.1. Sources of background knowledge. Adapted with permission from Lewis, Walpole, and McKenna (2014). Copyright © 2014 The Guilford Press.

words that Shakespeare uses, from *star-crossed* to *ancient* to *portentous*. The second source, a reader's *prior knowledge,* will also be brought to bear to make sense of the text, including knowledge of Shakespeare's tragedies, the Elizabethan era, and the gendered expectations of the time. Additionally, as we explained in Chapter 3, this prior knowledge can be bolstered by the teacher's choice of digital and informational texts that are strategically grouped together in a text set.

The third source, *structural knowledge,* will help readers to leverage their grammatical knowledge to interpret the language of Shakespeare's plays. At a higher level, their genre knowledge about how dialogue is formatted in a play, Shakespeare's use of blank verse in his soliloquies, and how the action of the play is partitioned into five distinct acts and individual scenes will all influence comprehension. Finally, readers possess *experiential knowledge* based on their lived experiences. Although students cannot have experiential knowledge of living in Elizabethan England, they will likely bring to bear the experiential knowledge of an adolescent crush or falling in love for the first time. Students' experiential knowledge of conflicts between themselves and parents (or of parents having different sets of expectations for male siblings and female siblings) could also be helpful for understanding the conflicts in the play.

Proficient readers strategically coordinate these varied and complex sources of background knowledge to make sense of the texts they read. If readers have insufficient knowledge in one or more sources, it can jeopardize comprehension. Take, for example, Recht and Leslie's (1988) study of the effects of background knowledge on comprehension, known colloquially as the baseball study. When asked to read a story about baseball, middle school students who had greater knowledge of baseball but who were otherwise considered poor readers comprehended the text better than so-called good readers who had limited knowledge of baseball. In short, the poor readers' knowledge of the vocabulary and structure associated with a baseball game (which was likely acquired through experiences playing or attending baseball games or watching them on television) was enough to compensate for their poor reading abilities. The important message here is that these individual sources of knowledge are related and that readers with more relevant and sufficient background knowledge are able to comprehend and learn more easily because they have multiple ways to store information.

Building the specific academic vocabulary knowledge that is part of each specific content area, then, is a component of building relevant background knowledge. As students get older, their accumulated background knowledge in different subjects has a more significant role in their ability to comprehend texts (Alexander et al., 1994). Secondary students must read and comprehend challenging primary source documents and commentaries in history; novels, poems, and dramas in ELA; and a variety of challenging informational texts in the sciences. Each of these types of text has its own specialized language that is particular to each domain, and students' comprehension relies on their knowledge of that specialized language.

Taking a thoughtful and strategic approach to vocabulary instruction is important for another reason. Research demonstrates that students from low-income families, those who have reading difficulties, and English learners often come to school with vocabularies that are half the size of their more skilled or affluent peers (Rupley & Slough, 2010). Because these students do not have the same amount of discipline-specific vocabulary knowledge, their ability to make sense of challenging texts in different content areas suffers disproportionately. Therefore, providing students with strategically integrated vocabulary instruction in *every* content area is more than a comprehension issue—it is also an equity issue. Every student deserves to have the background knowledge that is needed to make sense of the complex texts from which they will be expected to learn. Unfortunately, what often passes for vocabulary in schools—decontextualized lists of unrelated words that students define and then write sentences about (and then often forget!)—is not only ineffective for building students' lexicons, it does not have any measurable impact on reading comprehension (Nagy, 1988), which should be the ultimate goal of the vocabulary instruction we deliver in schools (Wright & Cervetti, 2017). We ignore effective vocabulary instruction at our—and our students'—peril!

TEACHING ACADEMIC VOCABULARY: WHICH WORDS?

Now that you understand the important role that vocabulary knowledge plays in text comprehension, let's think about how to strategically choose the words that we teach students. As you read the complex disciplinary texts that you assign, you might be overwhelmed by the number of words you could choose to teach. For example, a quick Internet search of vocabulary for Act I of *Romeo and Juliet* gave us a suggested list of 40 words! However, in the case of teaching academic vocabulary, more is definitely not better. That is because research demonstrates that students learn only around 15% of new words they encounter in contextual reading, and they need an estimated 12 encounters with those words to learn the new concepts (McKeown, Beck, Omanson, & Pople, 1985; Swanborn & de Glopper, 1999). Given these numbers, you can see that it is practically impossible to provide rich, contextualized exposure to anywhere near the 40 vocabulary words that were suggested for just the first act of *Romeo and Juliet*. Teachers need to be strategic in choosing a smaller number of words for instruction, spending time only on the words that are critical to students' understanding.

However, knowing that students need multiple encounters with words still leaves the practical question of how to choose vocabulary words for content-area instruction. Vocabulary researchers and former teachers Kevin Flanigan and Scott Greenwood (2007) have expressed the frustration that many secondary teachers feel—that although they understood the general recommendations for effective vocabulary instruction, including active engagement in word learning and providing students multiple exposures to words in multiple contexts, they were not well prepared for the nuts-and-bolts task of actually choosing the words that would be best to accomplish their instructional goals. Nor were they prepared to determine the amount of instructional time they should spend on each word. As former high school teachers ourselves, this, too, has been our experience. Therefore, we have found that Flanigan and Greenwood's (2007) "four-level framework" for content-area vocabulary is an excellent guide for strategically choosing the academic words students need to learn to comprehend the texts they read, as well as to develop increasingly robust conceptual knowledge about disciplinary content.

Their method is based on the tiered vocabulary frameworks of Beck, McKeown, and Kucan (2013) and Graves and colleagues (2014) with which you might already be familiar. Beck and colleagues' (2013) framework, for example, describes three different "tiers" of words and their relative importance in instruction. It is represented in Figure 4.2.

Although the three-tiered vocabulary framework is useful, we believe that the four-level framework of Flanigan and Greenwood (2007) provides a more helpful heuristic for actually choosing words, determining when to teach the words in a B-D-A reading framework, and deciding on how much time to spend on the vocabulary words that are selected. A visual representation of the four-level framework for vocabulary is shown in Figure 4.3.

Critical "before" words, or Level 1 words, are those that are absolutely critical to understanding a passage. They represent key concepts that students need to construct meaning from the passage. Therefore, these words should be few in number and taught *before* the students read (Flanigan & Greenwood, 2007). Similarly, Graves and colleagues (2014) describe these words as "essential words" (p. 336), because they tend to be repeated frequently in order to convey key concepts in informational texts or story elements in narratives. They suggest teaching around two to three of these essential words at a time. For example, in our social studies quad text set, *de jure segregation* and *de facto segregation* would be examples of Level 1 words because they are critical for understanding the changing nature

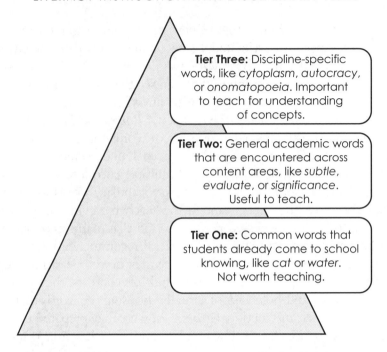

FIGURE 4.2. Three-tiered vocabulary framework.

of segregation over time. *Gendered criticism* would be an example taken from one of the texts in our *Romeo and Juliet* quad text set since students must interrogate this text for issues of gender and power, which is the key concept embedded in this term. Given their importance, Flanigan and Greenwood (2007) recommend devoting between 15 and 20 minutes to teach these critically important words before students read.

Level 2 words, or "foot-in-the-door" words, are also necessary for understanding a passage; they should be few in number and should be addressed before students read (Flanigan & Greenwood, 2007). However, students need only a

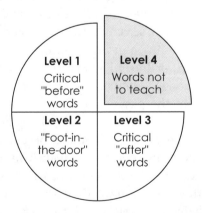

FIGURE 4.3. Four-level framework.

basic understanding of Level 2 words to get the gist of the passage. As a result, these words can be taught relatively quickly. For instance, in our science quad text set on climate change, a teacher might select *greenhouse gas* as a word to teach because it is important to understanding how human beings impact the environment. However, providing students a brief definition and some context for understanding this concept would be enough to get their foot in the door, so to speak. For example, before reading an informational text on the effects of climate change, the teacher could concisely explain that greenhouse gases are human-made gases that trap heat in the atmosphere and warm the planet, much as the greenhouses we often see for plants trap heat within their glass panels.

Critical "after" words, or Level 3 words, are those that teachers believe students should know but that are not crucial to comprehending the text (Flanigan & Greenwood, 2007). Graves and colleagues (2014) refer to these words as "valuable words" that teachers should select based on their students' existing vocabulary knowledge (p. 336). This category also includes words that are clearly defined in the text, high-utility words that are seen in many contexts including other academic content areas (e.g., *mutiny* and *discreet* from our *Romeo and Juliet* vocabulary list), and words that can be used to teach craft and structure issues, as when an author might use the term *bolted* instead of *ran fast* to describe a person's movement. These words can be dealt with on the fly while students are reading, or they can be addressed after reading is finished (Flanigan & Greenwood, 2007). In other words, teachers do not need to spend very much time on them.

We believe that the Level 4 words are among the most important for teachers to recognize. These are the words "not to teach at all." Flanigan and Greenwood (2007) describe Level 4 words as those that students either already know, much like Beck and colleagues' (2013) Tier One words, or words that are inconsequential for achieving a lesson's instructional goals. For example, our 40-word vocabulary list for the first act of *Romeo and Juliet* includes words such as *rapier* (a type of sword) and *trencher* (a type of long serving dish). Although students are unlikely to know these words, they are not crucial to understanding the text, they are generally easy to understand in context (or can be quickly explained), and they will very rarely (if ever) show up in any other readings. It would be foolish, then, to spend any time teaching these words when they have little utility either inside or outside the context of the play.

STRATEGIES FOR TEACHING VOCABULARY

Now that you have a framework for choosing words, it is time to turn to some research-validated strategies for teaching vocabulary that support students' comprehension and understanding of disciplinary concepts. In the section that follows we provide two strategies: one that will help you to build background knowledge on a central concept before reading and one that will allow you to teach a group of related words before, during, or after reading. We know that two strategies might not seem like a lot after we have stressed how important vocabulary instruction is to student understanding! However, the reason that we are focusing on these two strategies is to reinforce the point that if a word is not critical to understanding a text or if it cannot be easily grouped with other related terms, it probably is not worth teaching in advance.

Concept of Definition

Concept of definition (CD; Schwartz, 1988; Schwartz & Raphael, 1985) is an excellent strategy choice if the text you have selected is about one central concept that must be understood in advance. In Flanigan and Greenwood's (2007) terms, this strategy would be appropriate for Level 1 words that are critical to understanding a passage and should be taught before reading. This strategy encourages students to make multiple connections to a word, including its category, characteristics, examples, and non-examples. The CD strategy has the additional benefit of offering a visual representation for how the target concept is connected to related words and concepts. Figure 4.4 shows a blank CD map that indicates what words the teacher and students should generate for each box.

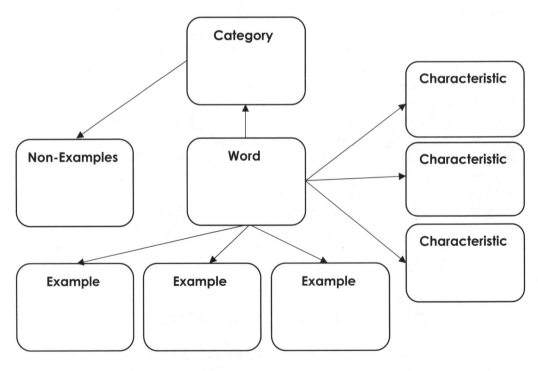

FIGURE 4.4. CD map.

In order for students to benefit from this instructional strategy, teachers must describe a CD map in a specific way. It's not enough to present students with a completed diagram to copy or a blank diagram to complete on their own. Teachers must explain the conceptual information to students as they construct the CD map in order to explicitly demonstrate the connections between the key concept and its definitional elements. In Figure 4.5 we have constructed a sample CD map for the key concept of *climate change* based on our science quad text set.

Here is an example of a teacher's explanation while constructing this CD map:

"Climate change is a meteorological phenomenon stemming from human activity on Earth's systems. It is characterized by rising global temperatures, rising sea levels, and violent and unpredictable weather such as droughts, floods, and hurricanes. The 2019–2020 Australian bushfires that ruined homes and killed people and animals are an example of the effects of climate change. The 2018 California wildfires are also an example because they were caused by a long drought that is related to climate change. The warming temperatures that have caused the polar ice caps to melt, leading to rising sea levels, increased coastal flooding, and severe hurricanes are also an example. Local weather patterns are not considered climate change because they are centered in very small areas. Climate change refers to global patterns."

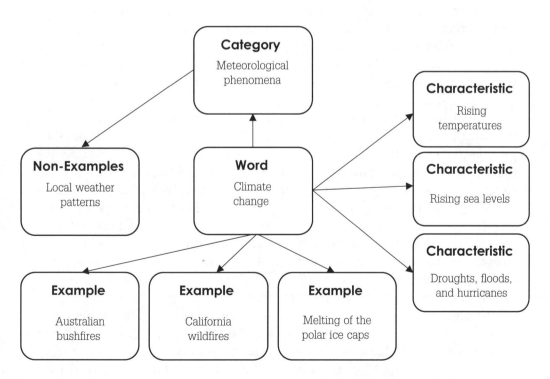

FIGURE 4.5. CD map for climate change.

As you can see, the structure of a CD map mirrors the relationships among ideas in the text. In the center is the central concept that belongs to the superordinate category above. To the right of the central concept are the concept's defining characteristics, and, underneath, there are specific examples of the concept. Connected to the superordinate category on the left is a non-example that belongs to the same category but differs from the central concept in its terms of its characteristics and examples. When teaching Level 1 words before reading, concept of definition is both quick and easy to use, making it well worth the instructional time.

Semantic Feature Analysis

Because content-area materials are usually structured around groups of related words, it is important to choose strategies that not only help students to understand the meaning of these words but also make the relationships between the words clear. For instance, an earth science reading might compare and contrast cirrus, stratus, cumulus, and nimbus clouds. An introductory government class might read a piece about the executive, judicial, and legislative branches of our representative democracy. An English literature class could compare the Italian, Shakespearean, Spenserian, and Miltonic types of sonnets. The point here is that providing students with the opportunity to connect key disciplinary concepts is the best way to both learn these new concepts and build their understanding of the structure of the discipline. Therefore, when choosing texts to use for content-area instruction, teachers need to look closely at the readings they assign and search for the related words that express these important disciplinary concepts. Using the Flanigan and Greenwood (2007) framework, we see that these words will generally fall into Level 2 and Level 3, important words that should be addressed either before, during, or after reading.

A semantic feature analysis (SFA; Anders & Bos, 1986) is a graphic organizer that allows teachers to introduce related concepts in a text selection and then provide students with multiple opportunities to compare, contrast, and discuss these related concepts through a set of features or attributes that the concepts either do or do not possess. To complete an SFA chart, the teacher and students use an agreed-upon symbol system to note the relationship between key terms and features. For example, you might choose to note whether a term is (Y), is not (N), or is somewhat (S) associated with each feature. Or you might choose to note whether a key term has a positive (+), negative (−), or no relationship (0) with each feature. If students are unsure of whether a term is associated with or related to a feature, they might use a question mark (?).

Because it is difficult to describe an SFA chart without seeing one, let's look at Figure 4.6 for a sample chart that our social studies teacher constructed for an informational text in her quad text set that describes two different types of racial segregation. This SFA chart features two important vocabulary words that are

Important Features

Important Vocabulary	School segregation in the 1950s South	School segregation in 1990s Boston	Separate bathrooms for different racial groups	The bus system that Rosa Parks boycotted	Fewer African American students in AP classes	Fewer White students suspended from school	Urban housing policies and zoning ordinances
De jure segregation	Y	N	Y	Y	N	N	?
De facto segregation	N	Y	N	N	Y	Y	?

FIGURE 4.6. SFA chart for types of racial segregation.

arranged on the vertical axis: *de jure segregation* and *de facto segregation*. On the horizontal axis the teacher has arranged the important features that will help her students to compare and contrast the two key terms. In this case the features are specific examples of segregation that the students must decide are either de jure (segregation by law) or de facto (segregation as a matter of fact or circumstance). This exercise provides students the background knowledge needed to understand the reading and to accomplish instructional goals by analyzing the legality of America's currently segregated school systems.

Once you have constructed an SFA chart, it can be used flexibly to achieve your instructional objectives. For instance, if you believe that the words you have selected are either critical to understanding the text (Level 1 words) or "foot-in-the-door" words for which students must have a basic understanding before reading (Level 2 words), you can display a filled-in SFA chart on an interactive whiteboard and review the terms with students before they read. If the words are not critical to comprehending the passage but still important terms that you want students to know, students can fill in the chart during or after reading. In the example in Figure 4.6, the teacher might choose to display and guide students through the filled-in chart but then leave question marks in the column for urban housing policies and zoning ordinances. Finding out whether these policies are examples of de jure or de facto segregation now becomes the purpose she provides her students for reading this text.

Teachers will often need to create a chart with more than just two related concepts. Bill designed the SFA chart in Figure 4.7 for a reading selection he assigned to his ELA students on the periods of American literature, a text that was well suited as an introduction to the chronological approach he took to the course. Because students needed only a basic understanding of the terms before they read—but needed to differentiate between these important academic terms after reading (Level 2 and Level 3 words)—he previewed them, thinking aloud about each term and its attributes to provide students a "foot-in-the-door" understanding. After reading, Bill returned to this SFA chart to allow students to discuss whether his initial ratings were accurate based on their reading and to possibly amend the chart after their discussion.

For our quad text set on global climate change, the teacher decided to construct an SFA for academic vocabulary related to specific solutions to the climate crisis (see Figure 4.8). On the vertical axis the teacher placed the names of the potential solutions, and on the horizontal axis he listed features associated with what entities are primarily responsible for each of the solutions. This SFA is an efficient and effective way for students to understand the connections between each of the solutions and to actively discuss why and how each entity is responsible for mitigating the impacts of climate change. However, because the features are also directly related to the informational text structure in the reading, this SFA chart also provides a structural preview of what students will be reading along with the conceptual knowledge about these terms.

Important Features

Important Vocabulary	Concerns the objective presentation of reality	Concerns the power of the individual	Concerns the workings of individuals in society	Primarily influenced by Darwinian theory	Concerns the troubled depths of the human mind	Concerns scientific truth and reason	Directly influenced by the horrors of war
Puritanism	N	N	N	N	N	N	N
Neoclassicism	Y	Y	Y	N	N	Y	N
Romanticism	N	Y	N	N	Y	N	N
Regionalism	S	S	Y	N	N	N	N
Realism	Y	N	Y	N	S	S	Y
Naturalism	Y	N	Y	Y	S	Y	Y
Modernism	Y	N	Y	S	S	S	Y

FIGURE 4.7. SFA chart for periods of American literature.

Important Features

Important Vocabulary	You	Businesses	Cities	Nations	World
Green buildings	N	Y	Y	N	N
Stratospheric aerosols	N	N	N	N	Y
Offshore energy	N	N	N	Y	N
Repowering	N	Y	Y	Y	N
Water management	N	N	Y	N	N
Green bonds	N	N	N	Y	N
Carbon capture/removal	N	N	N	Y	Y
Smart streets	N	N	Y	N	N
Space sunshade	N	N	N	N	Y
Big data	N	Y	N	N	N
Efficient vehicles	Y	Y	Y	Y	N

FIGURE 4.8. SFA chart for solutions to climate change.

Figure 4.9 provides a blank SFA chart (based on Anders & Bos, 1986) that you might find useful when designing your own. We encourage you to look closely at a content-area text that you will assign in the next few weeks or as part of a quad text set and see if you can determine which groups of related words, and their associated features, you would choose as you construct an SFA that would build the conceptual background knowledge that students need to comprehend that text.

Teaching academic vocabulary before reading is a good way to spend your instructional time. Research shows that explicitly teaching the meanings of words that students will encounter in reading passages significantly improves their comprehension of those passages (Wright & Cervetti, 2017). This comprehension benefit comes from both relatively brief and more time-intensive instruction of words that will appear in a reading passage (Apthorp, 2006; Beck, Perfetti, & McKeown, 1982; Hawkins, Musti-Rao, Hale, McGuire, & Hailley, 2010; Stahl, 1983). Although there are many strategies for teaching vocabulary in context, graphic organizers such as the CD map and the SFA chart are two go-to strategies that will significantly improve both your students' word knowledge and their understanding of challenging disciplinary texts.

Important Features

Important Vocabulary

FIGURE 4.9. SFA template.

STRATEGIES FOR PREVIEWING A TEXT

Although vocabulary knowledge is necessary to students' understanding of a text, more is needed if students are going to be able to comprehend challenging content-area material. As we have asserted in this chapter, having well-structured prior knowledge about a topic makes it easier for students to read and learn from texts written about that topic. Therefore, providing students with an explicit preview of the content and structure of a text can be one of the simplest and most straightforward ways to build the requisite knowledge needed to comprehend the text, turning a text that was inaccessible to one from which students can learn. In the section that follows, we present three instructional approaches to previewing a text focused on either building or activating prior and structural knowledge before reading. The first strategy is teacher directed and more appropriate for complex texts about topics for which students have little background knowledge on which to draw. The last two strategies are more student directed and collaborative, making them useful for when students have some general knowledge about the topic of the text.

Listen–Read–Discuss

When a colleague first introduced Listen–Read–Discuss (LRD) to us, we thought that she was joking. The reason we had this reaction was that it seemed way too simple and straightforward to be an effective strategy for adolescent literacy instruction. However, after using LRD both in our own classrooms and in the classrooms of the teachers with whom we have worked in professional development, we found that its simplicity does not undermine its effectiveness for building the content and structural knowledge that students need to comprehend challenging disciplinary texts. In fact, the power of the LRD is in its simple elegance and the ease by which teachers can incorporate it into their instructional routines. It is easy to see why Manzo and Casale (1985) describe LRD as an applicable before-reading strategy for both new teachers and veteran teachers who might be skeptical about content-area literacy instruction.

   As we said, the LRD strategy is very simple. It is represented in Figure 4.10. To implement LRD, you start by delivering a fast-paced lecture before reading a specific text. You can introduce your lecture by reviewing what the class has been learning and telling students that you want them to be successful in engaging with a text that you have chosen to meet your instructional objectives about those learning goals. You then provide a brief preview of the text. Here, students *listen* as you offer an outline of what they will read and explanations of the difficult concepts in the order in which they are found in the text. After the preview stage, you could end by posing a focus question or by setting a specific purpose for their reading.

   Next, students *read* the text that you have selected. Comprehending the text will be made easier for students because you have already provided definitions of

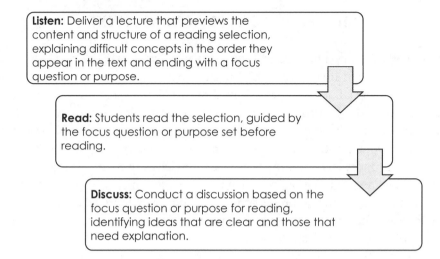

FIGURE 4.10. Steps for implementing LRD.

difficult words and concepts and have previewed the text's structure during the listen phase of the strategy. After students have listened to your lecture and read the text, they *discuss* the text with the focus question or purpose in mind, identifying ideas that students understood clearly, those that need to be clarified, and those about which students still have questions. The power of this strategy is that students have three opportunities to learn the information: once through your preview, a second time through their reading of a complex text, and a third time through a whole-class discussion.

The *listen* portion of the strategy should not be a full-blown lecture. This preview is specifically designed to be brief. Bill recalls his graduate student who had designed LRD professional development for her school and then tracked the implementation of the strategy in classrooms. She was disappointed to find that although many teachers were using the LRD strategy correctly and some students were benefiting from it, some teachers' *listen* previews were 40 to 50 minutes in length! The beauty of LRD is that it should encourage teachers to talk less and students to read more. We recommend no more than 5–10 minutes of structured teacher previewing before students begin the reading portion of the LRD strategy.

Let's consider what this strategy looks like with one of the texts that we have chosen for our quad text set on segregation in social studies, the *Brown v. Board of Education* decision (Warren, E., & Supreme Court of the United States, 1953). Since college and career readiness standards require that students read primary-source documents that are often written in a way that can be confusing to students, they represent perfect texts for which LRD can be used. Before reading our sample LRD preview, we suggest that you read the text for yourself on the Library of Congress website (*www.loc.gov/item/usrep347483*). Afterward, we encourage you to read our LRD preview, followed by a second reading of the text, to see how we represented its structure.

"I have chosen an important document for you to read today that has shaped the way that school systems and society have treated people from different races and backgrounds. As you know, we have been studying segregation. The *Brown v. Board of Education* decision directly impacted society because it changed the laws that segregated people of different races in schools. The period in history is the early 1950s, a time when African American children and White children in many states had to attend entirely different schools— segregated schools. This was not their choice; it was the law. This is what is called *de jure segregation,* or segregation 'by the law.' This case came to the Supreme Court in 1952 after Kansas students who were prevented from attending school with White children brought a case against their school system. The school system said that segregation was legal because even though students of different races were separate, the schools they attended were equal. The phrase 'separate but equal' was the legal rationale that people gave for maintaining segregated schools. The plaintiffs, the people who brought the case, argued that separate school facilities are inherently unequal and, therefore, should be abolished. After the arguments were made on both sides, the Chief Justice of the Supreme Court wrote an opinion about how the majority of the Court ruled on this case. An *opinion* is an argument for the way they viewed the case. The majority opinion is then enforced and becomes the law.

"Before you start to read, I want to give you a preview of the opinion. First, Chief Justice Earl Warren lays out the case of the children who believed that African American students should be able to attend schools with their White peers. He uses the term *Negro children,* which is an old, racist term for African Americans that is not acceptable to use today. He begins by reviewing the cases in which children were deprived of attending school and how they were not provided their constitutional rights under the 14th Amendment, which says that all American citizens should have equal protection under the law. They were arguing that being forced to attend segregated schools did not provide them 'equal protection.'

"In the next section, Justice Warren describes the many court cases that found that separating races in public places was legal because the facilities were determined to be separate but equal and, therefore, did not violate the Equal Protection Clause. He specifically mentions the *Plessy v. Ferguson* case that the Supreme Court decided in 1896. In this case the court found that having separate train cars for Black and White passengers was legal because they were, and here comes that phrase again, 'separate but equal.'

"Now here is the important part. The Chief Justice writes that the people who support segregation do so because they argue that the buildings, teachers, teacher pay, and other factors are equal in schools for White and Black children (separate but equal). However, he goes on to say that this case is not just about equal facilities and resources, it is about something more important. He also says that we have to think hard about these more 'intangible,' or less concrete, factors, because education is critical to developing good citizens and a stable and democratic society. Because of these intangible factors, the Court decided in favor of the children and provided their argument for their decision. So when you get to the final part of the opinion, I want you to identify the reasons that Chief Justice Warren says that 'separate but equal' can no longer be a reason to separate people of different races, and that it does violate the Equal Protection Clause of the 14th Amendment.

"Now I am going to give you 15 minutes to read the Court's decision and to determine why Chief Justice Warren believes that 'separate but equal' is no longer a rationale for separating children from different races in school. When you are done, we will discuss the parts of the argument that are clear to you and what parts you still want to discuss. However, think hard about why 'separate but equal' is inherently unfair and unconstitutional."

When planning an LRD preview, we encourage you to write a script that previews the content and structure of the main ideas in the text. If it is a text with which you are very familiar, you may be able to use an outline or notes instead. Whatever method you choose, we suggest that you make these preparations so that the *listen* portion of the LRD strategy does not expand into a full-class lecture. Remember that we want students to construct meaning of this text while they read, not give the ideas to them in a lecture. A few minutes spent planning a preview, and an explicit focus or purpose for student reading, can be a powerful tool for helping students to comprehend the text and extend their understanding through a productive whole-class discussion.

Prereading Plan

Another straightforward strategy for previewing the content and structure of a text before reading is the Prereading Plan (PreP), which was developed by Judith Langer (1981, 1984). The PreP strategy allows students to activate their prior knowledge on a topic and reorganize that knowledge in their memory through a prereading discussion. When planning to use the PreP strategy, the teacher chooses a set of key words that represent the main concepts in the text students will read that day. Like the ideas in an LRD preview, the teacher presents the words in the order in which they appear in the text. However, they are presented one at a time to allow for students to fully engage their background knowledge for each word.

The PreP strategy involves three phases of teacher questioning, which are represented in Figure 4.11. First, the teacher asks students to provide their initial

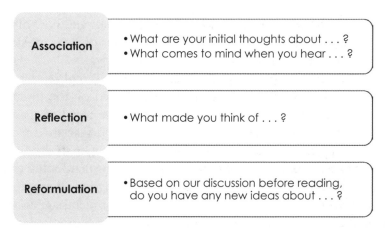

FIGURE 4.11. Steps for implementing a PreP.

associations between the concepts and their prior knowledge. Second, the teacher asks students to share their *reflections* on their own and their classmates' initial associations. In the third phase, students are asked to explain the *reformulation* that occurs as they integrate new ideas from the discussion with their prior knowledge before the discussion.

Let's consider the visual text that is part of our science quad text set on climate change, "Climate Change 101" (National Geographic, 2015). This fast-paced and entertaining video by Bill Nye introduces important concepts about climate change that will be crucial to students' understanding of challenging texts that come later in the quad text set. Leading students in a discussion using the PreP strategy can be an efficient way to provide a preview of the content and structure of the text and help students to activate and reorganize their understanding of climate change before viewing the video. For this text, the teacher can center a previewing discussion on the following words that Nye highlights in his presentation in chronological order: orbital variation, industrial revolution, greenhouse gases, ocean acidification, and glacial melt.

In the association phase, most students will be able to contribute initial associations with these words based on their previous learning. Some might immediately recognize that these concepts are all related to issues of climate change or that they associate ocean acidification with the coral bleaching that the Great Barrier Reef in Australia is suffering. Others might offer that they have seen videos of large chunks of glaciers "calving" into the ocean.

During the reflection phase, the teacher probes students to think more deeply about their initial associations and why these came to mind. For instance, the student who talked about coral bleaching might relate an experience she had at an aquarium where she became fascinated by the fish and other marine animals at a coral reef display. The student who saw videos about the calving of glaciers might relate the experience his uncle had backpacking in Alaska and how his uncle not only saw calving glaciers up close but also took pictures of areas in Alaska where glaciers had been retreating because of climate change.

In the reformulation phase, students are asked to verbalize any new ideas, elaborations, or associations that they have made based on the discussion. For example, a student who listened to the story about the receding glaciers might make the connection that increased glacial calving and glacial retreat are both caused by warming temperatures due to climate change. The student who offered her aquarium experience might elaborate on that idea by mentioning that the loss of habitat due to coral bleaching could cause a severe food shortage for people who rely on the ocean for their meals. The idea is that students are encouraged to elaborate on their own knowledge using the collective background knowledge of the group. By the end of the discussion, students are now ready to encounter the challenging concepts in the video.

The benefits of the PreP strategy were found only for average and above-average readers in a study of sixth-grade students, suggesting that students with reading difficulties might require more extensive knowledge-building support (Langer, 1984). However, because the strategy encourages students to activate and verbalize their prior knowledge, attentive teachers can quickly assess the background knowledge of the group and provide more support where needed. In addition, a recent study of ninth-grade students suggests that the next strategy we describe, the K-W-L strategy, might provide the level of instructional support necessary for students with reading difficulties, including English learners, to comprehend challenging content-area texts (Lupo et al., 2019).

K-W-L Strategy

To be honest, we were a bit wary of adding the K-W-L strategy to a book on adolescent literacy. Although K-W-L and its variations have been used for a long time as a prereading strategy for activating prior knowledge (Blachowicz & Ogle, 2008; Carr & Ogle, 1987; Ogle, 1986, 1992), the increasingly specialized and discipline-specific texts that students read in high school can pose significant problems for teachers who want to use K-W-L to prepare their students to read challenging content-area material about which they have little to no relevant prior knowledge.

For instance, if Bill asked students in his undergraduate YA literature class to discuss everything they knew about deconstructionist criticism at the beginning of a lesson, it would be a very short lesson! However, when students have enough relevant prior knowledge about a topic, the K-W-L strategy can be helpful for activating and organizing that knowledge in a way that leads to setting clear purposes for reading and improved comprehension of disciplinary texts.

As you probably know, K-W-L stands for *"Know," "Want to Know,"* and *"Learned."* In its most basic form teachers engage students in a conversation about what they know about a topic (K) before reading a text, a straightforward brainstorming session that allows students to activate and share their prior knowledge. Students are then guided to identify what they "want to know" (W) about the topic, which provides a purpose for their reading. After these prereading steps are complete, students read the text. After reading, students identify what they learned from their reading (L). A chart for the K-W-L strategy is shown in Figure 4.12.

Let's say that a social studies teacher has chosen an informational text as an introduction to the American Civil War. Although her students may not have extensive prior knowledge about this seminal event in the history of the United States, she knows that students have learned about some aspects of the Civil War in previous grades. She decides that she can leverage the K-W-L strategy to activate that prior knowledge and provide a purpose for reading the text selection. A sample of the completed K-W-L chart for this text is represented in Figure 4.13.

She begins using the K-W-L strategy by encouraging her students to list what they know (or think they know) about the topic. Teachers should remind students that some of the things that they think they know about a topic might be unreliable and, therefore, must be confirmed by reading reliable sources (Buehl, 2014). During this initial step, the students might contribute the following ideas: The Civil War was fought to free slaves, the Union was fighting against the Confederacy, the North wanted to keep the Union together, Gettysburg was an important battle, the North won, slavery was abolished, Lincoln delivered the Gettysburg Address, General Lee was the leader of the southern troops, General Grant was the leader of the Union forces, and the war ended at Appomattox.

During the next step, the teacher encourages her students to generate questions about what they want to know about the topic and record those questions in the middle column of the K-W-L chart. Students might ask the following: "How did the war start?" "Why is the Battle of Gettysburg important?" "Did slaves fight for the Union?" "Were they forced to fight for the Confederacy?" "What happened at Appomattox Courthouse?" "What happened to General Lee after he lost?" "Were there any other reasons for the war?" "Why is the Gettysburg Address important?"

Following this step, students are directed to read the passage, where they look for answers to their questions and check if their prior knowledge was confirmed by the reading. The answers to these questions are then listed in the "What We Learned" section of the K-W-L chart. As you can see from the sample chart, many of the students' questions are answered in their reading, while others—like what happened to General Lee after he lost—were not.

You may have noticed that we did not yet address the very bottom of the K-W-L chart. This section is part of Ogle's (1986) K-W-L strategy that we rarely see teachers use. After students brainstorm their prior knowledge on a topic (but before they fill out their questions in the "Want to Know" section), Ogle (1986) suggests that teachers help students group their prior knowledge into related

Topic:		
What We **K**now	What We **W**ant to Know	What We **L**earned

Categories of information we expect to see:

FIGURE 4.12. K-W-L strategy chart. Adapted with permission from Blachowicz and Ogle (2008). Copyright © The Guilford Press.

categories that they expect to see in the reading selection. If you are using the K-W-L strategy to read an informational text, we believe that this section is worth adding to your K-W-L chart because it can serve as an effective preview of the structure of the text.

In the example in Figure 4.13, the teacher guides students in listing the categories of information they expect to see based on their prior knowledge. For example, in the "What We Know" section students listed both Slavery and Fort Sumter, which fit under the category of "how and why the Civil War began." In addition, students listed Generals Grant and Lee, who both fit under the category of "the leaders of each side." They also listed the categories of "how the Civil War ended" and "the impact of the Civil War" based on what they expected to learn.

Topic: The Civil War		
What We Know	**What We Want to Know**	**What We Learned**
• Fought to free slaves • Union (North) fought the Confederacy (South) • North wanted to keep the United States together • Gettysburg was an important battle • The North won • Fort Sumter • Slavery was abolished • Gettysburg Address • General Lee led the South • General Grant led the North • Appomattox	• How did the war start? • Why is the Battle of Gettysburg important? • Did slaves fight for the Union? • Were slaves forced to fight for the Confederacy? • What happened at Appomattox Courthouse? • What happened to General Lee after he lost? • Were there any other reasons for the war? • Why is the Gettysburg Address important?	• The war started when the Confederates attacked Fort Sumter in Charleston. • The Battle of Gettysburg is important because the Confederacy lost many men, and they had to retreat back into Virginia. • Nearly 180,000 free Black men and escaped slaves fought for the Union. • There were more reasons for the war than slavery. States' rights played a role as well as the southern economy that relied on cotton and slave labor to harvest it. The South also did not support Lincoln. • The Gettysburg Address is important because it focused on equality, which has been the hallmark of America ever since.
Categories of information we expect to see: • How and why the Civil War began • The leaders of each side • How the Civil War ended • The impact of the Civil War		

FIGURE 4.13. Completed K-W-L strategy chart for passage on the Civil War.

By having students see how their ideas are related, they can then make predictions about how that information will be structured in the text they will read. This provides a framework for organizing the material in a meaningful way (Ogle, 1992). The power of the K-W-L strategy, then, is that it allows students to activate and organize their prior knowledge, predict a text structure, actively engage texts through questioning, and set clear purposes for their reading.

BEFORE-READING STRATEGIES IN DISCIPLINARY TEXT SETS

Now that we have a concise menu of before-reading strategies, we want to show you how they can be integrated into the ELA, social studies, and science quad text sets introduced in Chapter 3. As you have seen, we have already explained how some of these texts can be scaffolded through before-reading strategies that build the vocabulary, content, and structural knowledge that allows students to fully engage with these texts. We will briefly revisit those while explaining our teachers' strategic choices for the rest of the texts in their quad text sets.

English Language Arts

The first text in our ELA quad text set on *Romeo and Juliet* is a contemporary film version of Act I of the play (see Figure 4.14). Even though students have some general background knowledge about *Romeo and Juliet* and the romance that is its focus, few students understand the context of the play, the family dynamics that drive the action, or how or why Romeo and Juliet meet and fall in love. Therefore, to provide the critical background knowledge that students need to achieve her instructional goals, the teacher chooses to deliver an LRD preview to build both the content and structural knowledge of Act I of the play.

To begin, our teacher provides an engaging oral introduction to Shakespeare's tragedy and explains why the tragedy is important for exploring issues of gender and power. She then provides a brief chronological preview that focuses on the major conflicts of Act I as well as Romeo and Juliet's developing relationship. She highlights the initial fight between the Montagues and Capulets in Scene i, Juliet being promised in marriage to the much older Paris in Scene ii, and the dangerous "love at first sight" meeting of Romeo and Juliet at a Capulet masquerade party in Scene v. However, most importantly, the teacher provides a very clear purpose for viewing this act. In this case she wants students to focus on the differences between how men and women act in the play and what society seems to expect from each of these groups. After the students view the act, the teacher guides them in a discussion of this important focus question in order to prepare them for the more intensive gendered interpretive work to come. We illustrate this after-reading discussion when we revisit this quad text set in Chapter 6.

	Instructional Objective(s): Analyze how characters develop over the course of a text, interact with other characters, advance the plot, and develop the theme.		
	Visual Text: Video of Act I from contemporary film version of *Romeo and Juliet*		
Instructional Strategies	**Before Reading:** Listen–Read–Discuss		
	During Reading:		
	After Reading:		
	Informational Text(s): Article on gender roles and power in Elizabethan England		
Instructional Strategies	**Before Reading:** Concept of Definition		
	During Reading:		
	After Reading:		
	Target Text: Act I of Shakespeare's *Romeo and Juliet*		
Instructional Strategies	**Before Reading:** K-W-L strategy		
	During Reading:		
	After Reading:		
	Accessible Text: Selected chapters from *Eleanor and Park* by Rainbow Rowell		
Instructional Strategies	**Before Reading:** Prereading Plan		
	During Reading:		
	After Reading:		
	Extended Writing:		

FIGURE 4.14. ELA quad text set with before-reading strategies.

The second text in the quad text set is an informational text reading on the gendered expectations of men and women in Elizabethan England. Because the goal for this reading assignment is to understand the male-dominated nature of Elizabethan society, the teacher decides to focus on the term *patriarchal* as a word that is critical to understanding the text and contributes to her students' ability to understand the choices that Romeo and Juliet make as characters. Introducing the term before reading, the teacher constructs a concept of definition map (see Figure 4.4) with the term *patriarchy* in the center, *power* as the superordinate category, and *matriarchy* as the non-example. Moving to characteristics, she lists "men as breadwinners," "male leaders," and "women need to be cared for," and then she provides three specific examples from the reading of the patriarchy's influence: "women could not own property," "women could not act on a public stage," and "women could not vote." This activity now prepares students to understand the multiple manifestations of a patriarchal society in their text reading.

The third text in the quad text set is Shakespeare's original text of Act I of *Romeo and Juliet*. Because students have already viewed a modern video interpretation of the act and are familiar with the conflicts and the gendered expectations of the time period, the teacher decides to use the K-W-L strategy to activate that prior knowledge and to set purposes for their reading based on her learning objectives. After students fill in their prior knowledge from their initial viewing of Act I in the "What We Want to Know" column (see Figure 4.12), she encourages students to develop reading goals based on issues of gender and power. For instance, students might write, "I want to know why Juliet has to marry Paris," "I want to know why the Montague and Capulet men have to fight," or "Are gendered expectations part of the reason that Romeo and Juliet fall in love so quickly?" These "Want to Know" questions set a purpose for their reading, which culminates in students discussing their questions and purposes after they read.

The accessible text is a selected chapter from *Eleanor and Park* by Rainbow Rowell. Like Romeo and Juliet, Eleanor and Park are also "star-crossed lovers," both characters coming from different racial and socioeconomic groups and struggling with the gendered expectations of their society. Because this novel is set in modern times, is written in contemporary language, and is focused on awkward romantic relationships with which secondary students are familiar, the teacher chooses to use the PreP strategy (see Figure 4.11) to activate, reflect on, and reformulate their background knowledge in order to help them make connections between this text and *Romeo and Juliet*. She begins by choosing five key terms that appear chronologically in the selected chapter (*sexist, vulnerable, infatuation, leer, masculinity*) and then guides her students through the three-step process of making associations with the concept, reflecting on those associations, and then reformulating their understanding by offering new ideas after the guided discussion. They are then prepared to read the text and make substantive connections about the impact of gendered expectations on both Eleanor and Park and Romeo and Juliet.

Social Studies

For the quad text set on segregation, our teacher introduced the topic through the video "Kids Talk about Segregation," a first-hand account of the impact of racially segregated schools on children in modern New York City (see Figure 4.15). Since students already have some generalized knowledge about segregation in the United States, the teacher decided on the PreP strategy to help them to activate, reflect on, and reformulate that knowledge to prepare for viewing the video (see Figure 4.11). The teacher begins this process by choosing five key concepts from the video in the chronological order in which they are presented in the video (*awkward*, *comfort*, *separate classes*, *opportunity*, and *diversity*). She guides her students in making associations with each of these key terms, followed by reflections about what made her students think about those ideas, and then by inviting them to reformulate their background knowledge about segregation in order to prepare for the video by adding new ideas or making new connections between what they generated about the key terms in the video.

For the second text in this quad text set, the teacher decides on a semantic feature analysis chart (which we illustrated previously in this chapter in Figure 4.6). She chose this text to highlight the key vocabulary that is critical to students' comprehension of the article on the history of segregation in the United States and to make sure that they understand the difference between de jure and de facto segregation. For the challenging target text, the *Brown v. Board of Education* decision, the teacher chose the LRD strategy as an explicit structural preview of this challenging Supreme Court decision (which we also addressed earlier in this chapter).

Because the accessible text is focused on continuing racial disparity in American schools, the teacher chooses a concept of definition map (see Figure 4.4) to provide students the opportunity to make multiple connections to that key term both before and during reading. Beginning with the term *racial disparity* in the middle of the CD map, she connects it to the superordinate category *injustice* above and then writes three key characteristics of racial disparity in the right-hand boxes: "unequal treatment in housing," "unequal treatment in the justice system," and "unequal treatment in the education system." Now that students have a general idea of what the word means, they can begin reading, filling in more specific examples of racial disparities during reading, and then discussing their examples after reading.

Science

Our science teacher began his quad text set on climate change (see Figure 4.16) with Bill Nye's "Climate Change 101" video and decided to activate prior knowledge using the PreP strategy, which we illustrated earlier in this chapter. The teacher begins by introducing five key terms in the order in which they appear in

	Instructional Objective(s): Analyze historical materials to trace the development of an idea over time and explain patterns of continuity and change; determine the central idea of a primary source and accurately summarize the central idea and key details.	
	Visual Text: "Kids Talk about Segregation" video	
Instructional Strategies	**Before Reading:** Prereading Plan	
	During Reading:	
	After Reading:	
	Informational Text(s): Article on the history of racial segregation in the United States	
Instructional Strategies	**Before Reading:** Semantic Feature Analysis	
	During Reading:	
	After Reading:	
	Target Text: *Brown v. Board of Education* decision	
Instructional Strategies	**Before Reading:** Listen–Read–Discuss	
	During Reading:	
	After Reading:	
	Accessible Text: Article on racial disparities in modern U.S. public schools	
Instructional Strategies	**Before Reading:** Concept of Definition	
	During Reading:	
	After Reading:	
	Extended Writing:	

FIGURE 4.15. Social studies quad text set with before-reading strategies.

	Instructional Objective(s): Construct an argument supported by evidence (e.g., patterns in graphs, charts, and images) for how humans impact Earth's systems; integrate technical information expressed in words in a text with a visual representation of that information.

Visual Text: "Climate Change 101" video with Bill Nye

Instructional Strategies	**Before Reading:** Prereading Plan
	During Reading:
	After Reading:

Informational Text(s): "Climate Change: How Do We Know?" website

Instructional Strategies	**Before Reading:** Listen–Read–Discuss
	During Reading:
	After Reading:

Accessible Text: Chapter 1 of *Ship Breaker* by Paolo Bacigalupi

Instructional Strategies	**Before Reading:** K-W-L strategy
	During Reading:
	After Reading:

Target Text: "5 Ways to Curb Climate Change" articles

Instructional Strategies	**Before Reading:** Semantic feature analysis
	During Reading:
	After Reading:

Extended Writing:

FIGURE 4.16. Science quad text set with before-reading strategies.

the video and then guides students through the processes of making associations, reflecting on those associations, and reformulating and extending their ideas. Since students have a great deal of generalized background knowledge on climate change because of the scientific and political attention it has been given in the press, the PreP strategy is an excellent choice for activating and extending that knowledge before they view the video.

The next text in the quad text set is an informational text that highlights nine specific measurable impacts of climate change, for which the teacher chose to build background knowledge using the LRD strategy (see Figure 4.10). The online text's clear headings and relatively high number of academic vocabulary words lend themselves to the more explicit structural and background knowledge building that are a key feature of well-organized LRD scripts.

The accessible text is a chapter from Paolo Bacigalupi's novel *Ship Breaker*. This novel is set in a dystopian post-oil world where children eke out a meager existence by venturing into the bowels of beached ships to scavenge copper and other treasures. The book is particularly interesting to our teacher because it is set in a future New Orleans, flooded by rising sea levels and wracked by powerful and unpredictable hurricanes, a horrifying example of what humanity might face if we continue on our current climate-change trajectory. His students have a great deal of background knowledge on climate change because of their reading and viewing of the first two texts. Therefore, he decides to use the K-W-L strategy (see Figure 4.12) to activate students' background knowledge about dystopian literature so that he can help encourage them to leverage both their genre and content knowledge that they have already learned to comprehend this text.

Beginning with the "What We Know" phase of the strategy, the teacher encourages his students to tell him what they already know about dystopian literature. For instance, in the "What We Know" section, students might list "violence," "a central evil government," "group survival," and "destroyed environment" as some of the qualities they know about dystopias. In the next step the teacher asks students what they "Want to Know." However, to make this phase more productive, he provides a bit more background knowledge about the text, explaining that the novel takes place in a world where climate change has completely altered the land, weather patterns, and society. "Knowing this," he says, "what do you want to know about *Ship Breaker* before we read this first chapter?" Using their knowledge of both dystopias and climate change, the students are now much more likely to generate specific questions that can guide their reading of the chapter and help them connect what they read to their previous learning about the dangers of climate change. For example, students might ask if sea-level rise will cause problems for the characters in this book or if specific environmental issues, like powerful storms, might impact its plot and conflicts. Other students might begin to see that *Ship Breaker* will probably have some important lessons for our society and, therefore, ask more thematic questions like "How is this society like or unlike our own?" or "What kind of lesson is the author trying to teach us with this book?" After students finish the reading, the teacher leads them to write and discuss what they have learned, particularly focusing on the author's purpose for writing this dystopian novel and how it relates to our contemporary climate reality.

The quad text set ends with a more hopeful informational text that explains specific ways to combat climate change and who is primarily responsible for making these changes: individuals, businesses, cities, countries, or the whole world. Because these potential solutions are clearly a group of key terms related to the organizing concept of mitigating climate change, the teacher develops an SFA chart, which we illustrated earlier in this chapter (see Figure 4.8).

FINAL THOUGHTS

We realize that there are many more ways to build students' background knowledge than what we have presented in this chapter. However, these five instructional strategies have some important similarities that are worth revisiting. First, they are all research-validated approaches that build vocabulary, content, and/or structural knowledge. Second, these strategies are all relatively easy to implement because they are straightforward and take little instructional time. This is important because it leaves more time for students to read, discuss, and write about complex texts, which we address in the next three chapters. One of the most important similarities, however, is what these strategies do for teachers. They will force you to carefully read the texts you choose for instruction, specify your teaching and learning goals in advance, and choose strategies that provide students with the critical background knowledge they need to accomplish those goals. As the content-area expert and teacher, you know the goals you have for instruction, the demands of the texts you choose to meet those goals, and the background knowledge of your students. By thinking about these elements, you can leverage the strategies in this chapter so that all students can read, comprehend, and successfully achieve those goals.

CHAPTER 5

Supporting Comprehension during Reading

Over the last 5 years, we have spent a great deal of time working with teachers, instructional coaches, and administrators in middle and high schools. In doing this work, we have been consistently impressed with their dedication and desire to improve students' disciplinary knowledge and literacy outcomes. However, as we discussed in Chapter 3, we have also been troubled by both the relatively low volume of text reading and the flawed methods by which reading is accomplished in many of these classrooms. Too often we observe teachers reading aloud large chunks of text to students—or playing audio recordings of those texts—instead of having students work in pairs or small groups to collaboratively construct meaning from challenging disciplinary texts. We observe students engaged in deadening round-robin or "popcorn" reading (where students read aloud a small chunk of a text while other students listen) instead of focused silent reading followed by robust classroom discussion. As former high school teachers, both of us have been guilty early in our careers of translating challenging informational texts into focused PowerPoint lectures (where students copy notes instead of reading and discussing the texts from which the information is drawn). This instructional choice is all too common in secondary classrooms (Wexler et al., 2017).

The question that we pose to both the educators with whom we work and the preservice teachers we teach is why teachers are choosing these "textless approaches to instruction" (Lewis & Walpole, 2016, p. 34) when these methods provide neither reading volume and stamina nor opportunities for critical engagement that students need to comprehend, analyze, and interpret challenging disciplinary texts. This is especially true of round-robin reading, which can actually damage students' social and emotional growth (Ash, Kuhn, & Walpole, 2009; Ivey, 1999).

As you can imagine, the answers to this question are varied. Some teachers might say that students can't or won't read what is assigned, and so they must find alternative ways to expose them to content. Others might believe that their students enjoy being read to and that dramatic reading of whole texts builds an intrinsic love of reading and literature, history, or science. Still others think that lectures and accompanying PowerPoint presentations are the only way to cover a jam-packed curriculum in the small amount of time allotted to them during the course of a school year. Although these rationales for textless approaches might seem reasonable on the surface, as we discussed in Chapter 1, the fact remains that approximately two-thirds of students continue to struggle with reading comprehension (NCES, 2019). We have argued that students will only get better at reading if they are provided with the opportunity to engage in substantive reading experiences with a high volume of challenging texts (Lupo et al., 2018). Although perfection is difficult to achieve, the old adage "practice makes perfect" applies to reading as much as it applies to any other human endeavor, from learning a foreign language, to playing a sport, to learning an instrument. We only get better by consistently practicing that particular endeavor.

Besides these reasons, our own experience as secondary teachers and our work in secondary classrooms across the country show us that many teachers are choosing textless approaches simply because they are do not know of any research-based alternatives for engaging and supporting students in their classroom reading (Meyer, 2013). For instance, when Bill teaches his preservice teachers about during-reading strategies, he freely admits to using round-robin and popcorn reading approaches when he began his career teaching high school in the mid-1980s, despite how disengaged, frustrated, and sometimes painfully embarrassed his students were when they were asked to read aloud this way in class. Like many teachers, he chose these methods not because he did not care about his students' literacy development but rather because he had been consistently subjected to these reading methods in his own schooling experiences and was not prepared to support his students' in-class reading in any other way. Keeping these contextual factors in mind, we can understand why some teachers still practice round-robin reading (and its variations) even when they fully understand the potentially damaging effects of this approach (Ash et al., 2009; Kuhn, 2014). If teachers do not have an alternative, they go to what they have been exposed to in their own classroom experiences as students, most often teacher read-alouds, round-robin reading, and lectures with note taking.

The purpose of this chapter is to provide you with a menu of research-based alternatives for supporting students' reading that will build both the stamina and skill needed to make meaning from challenging disciplinary texts. The strategies we present might require you to substantively rethink how you use classroom time to allow for sustained reading. Many teachers believe that lecturing is the most efficient way to cover content, or that round-robin or teacher read-alouds are the most efficient way to ensure students have "read" a text. Instead, we encourage you to replace these less effective activities by following up on the targeted background-knowledge building strategies discussed in Chapter 4 with strategies for supporting real reading of challenging texts that will prepare students for classroom discussions and text-based writing. (We cover these strategies in the next two chapters.) Only then will students have the practice and experience they need to fully engage with challenging texts and acquire the content knowledge and skills they need to be successful in college and the workplace.

DURING-READING FRAMEWORKS

As you already know from reading the first four chapters of this book, this is a strategy-oriented text. We believe that having a toolbox of research-based strategies can help teachers to improve their students' comprehension and learning from texts. That being said, we want to make it clear that we see teaching comprehension strategies as a means to an end instead of the end goal itself. What we mean by this statement is that we do not see your role as teaching comprehension strategies for their own sake. Instead, we suggest that you quickly teach and model the strategies we present here as a way to facilitate student engagement in real reading and collaboration around disciplinary texts. Instead of viewing strategies as the goal of instruction, we want you to see them as useful frames for students to use when reading together. We believe that student reading is a more efficient and effective way of building content knowledge than either lecturing about content-area concepts or teaching decontextualized comprehension strategies.

The question remains, however, about how to accomplish the in-class reading part of this formula. We begin this chapter by describing a large-scale effort to improve adolescents' comprehension by leveraging cooperative grouping options for classroom reading. We then describe three during-reading frameworks that utilize the same design features to build more knowledgeable and skilled readers of disciplinary texts: Reciprocal Teaching, Peer-Assisted Learning Strategies, and reading guides. We have specifically chosen one strategy to support reading in small groups, one for collaborative pairs, and one for independent reading in order to encourage flexibility in how you assign in-class reading. We demonstrate how each of these research-based approaches can be easily worked into your instructional routines and improve students' content acquisition and comprehension of disciplinary texts.

COLLABORATIVE STRATEGIC READING

To illustrate how a collaborative reading framework can be used to support in-class engagement with texts, it is helpful to first look at a large-scale research effort dedicated to improving comprehension for adolescents, including students with disabilities and those who struggle with reading. This intervention is called Collaborative Strategic Reading (CSR). Although it was first developed and tested in an upper-elementary setting (Klingner, Vaughn, & Schumm, 1998), CSR has also been rigorously tested in middle school ELA classrooms (Vaughn et al., 2011) as well as in secondary social studies and science classrooms (Boardman, Klingner, Buckley, Annamma, & Lasser, 2015). In all studies, CSR has been shown to have a beneficial impact on reading comprehension when compared to "business-as-usual" instruction.

The CSR instructional model uses a clear B-D-A reading framework to support students as they engage with challenging disciplinary texts. The four strategies in this B-D-A framework are represented in Figure 5.1. CSR instruction begins with teachers explicitly teaching the four strategies to the whole group, followed by modeling and teacher think-alouds about each of these strategic steps (Boardman et al., 2016). Teachers then gradually release responsibility for use of the strategies to students.

After learning the four strategies and practicing them with a sample text, students work in small groups of four to six to read a challenging text that the teacher has strategically segmented in advance of the lesson, using a CSR learning log that scaffolds their collaborative interactions with the text (see Figure 5.2). *Before reading,* the teacher and students begin by previewing the text, making connections to background knowledge, setting purposes for reading, and pre-teaching

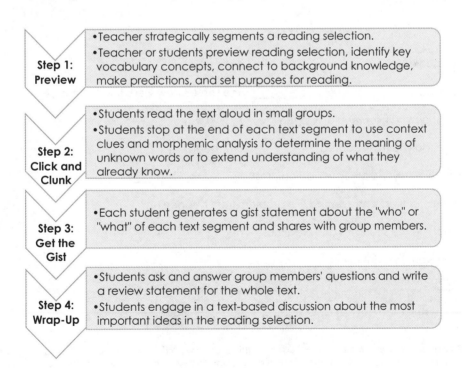

Step 1: Preview
- Teacher strategically segments a reading selection.
- Teacher or students preview reading selection, identify key vocabulary concepts, connect to background knowledge, make predictions, and set purposes for reading.

Step 2: Click and Clunk
- Students read the text aloud in small groups.
- Students stop at the end of each text segment to use context clues and morphemic analysis to determine the meaning of unknown words or to extend understanding of what they already know.

Step 3: Get the Gist
- Each student generates a gist statement about the "who" or "what" of each text segment and shares with group members.

Step 4: Wrap-Up
- Students ask and answer group members' questions and write a review statement for the whole text.
- Students engage in a text-based discussion about the most important ideas in the reading selection.

FIGURE 5.1. CSR framework.

Before Reading	Brainstorm:	Predict:
		Purpose for Reading:
	Key Vocabulary:	
During Reading	Gist Statement 1:	
	Gist Statement 2:	
	Gist Statement 3:	
	Gist Statement 4:	
After Reading	Questions: How were _____ and _____ the same? How were they different? What do you think would happen if _____? What do you think caused _____ to happen? How would you compare and contrast _____ and _____? What might have prevented the problem from happening? What are the strengths and weaknesses of _____? How would you interpret _____?	

FIGURE 5.2. A CSR learning log.

key vocabulary concepts. *During reading,* students monitor their comprehension through the "click-and-clunk" strategy, recognizing when textual information "clicks" with their background knowledge or purpose for reading and "clunking" when their comprehension breaks down. When this happens, students are taught to apply fix-up strategies to help them determine word meanings or concepts that they do not understand. At the end of each text segment, students identify the important "who" and "what" of that segment and write a gist statement to share with their group members. *After reading* the entire passage, students engage in the "wrap-up" phase in which they ask and answer their own questions and then review and summarize the key ideas in the full text (Boardman et al., 2016). To manage the CSR group discussions, individual students are assigned the roles of leader, clunk expert, gist expert, and question expert. Since questioning a text is such an important skill for comprehending it, we recommend that this part of the wrap-up be scaffolded through use of sentence stems that you can see in Figure 5.2 (Vaughn, Klingner, & Bryant, 2001).

Alternatively, you might teach a strategy that prepares students to ask and answer different types of questions (explicit, inferential, and critical), such as Question–Answer Relationships (QAR; Raphael, 1986). The QAR strategy teaches students to answer two types of questions using information from the text: "right there" questions, which require locating the answer that is explicitly stated in a single sentence, and "think and search" questions, which require drawing inferences from multiple places in the text. In addition, students are taught to answer two types of questions using their background knowledge: "author and me" questions, which require making inferences by piecing together background knowledge and information in the text, and "on my own" questions that require students to use their knowledge and experiences to answer questions that may include critical evaluations of the text (Raphael & Au, 2005).

We believe that CSR has tremendous potential in secondary content-area classrooms, and we encourage you visit their comprehensive website (*http://toolkit. csrcolorado.org*) that describes the project and provides professional development modules, as well as access to materials, videos, and instructional scripts that can be used with your students. However, we also choose to highlight CSR because it incorporates several important high-utility strategies that successful adolescent readers use to make sense of texts that are strategically chosen and chunked by the teacher (see Figure 5.3). You will see that these strategies are important features of the other during-reading frameworks we have chosen for this chapter as well.

The first key feature is that students read strategically segmented or "chunked" texts. Chunking texts allows students to focus on smaller segments of the reading assignment, ensuring that they are not overwhelmed with too much textual information at one time. It also helps students to see how text segments are related to one another. Research demonstrates that chunking informational texts and highlighting text structure promote reading comprehension (Brozo, Schmelzer, & Spires, 1983; Duffy et al., 1989). Therefore, we encourage you

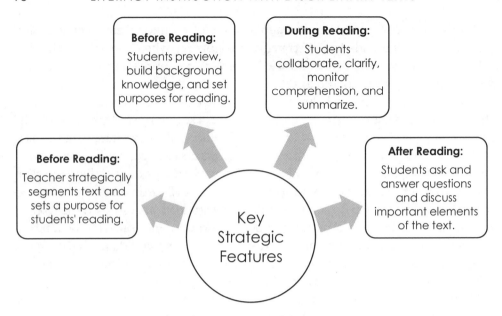

FIGURE 5.3. Key features of during-reading support frameworks.

to determine where students should pause their reading of challenging texts to reflect, question, and summarize what they have learned in that text segment before they continue reading.

Another key feature of these strategies is that students are provided with an opportunity to preview the text before they read, building and activating background knowledge about textual concepts—including key vocabulary—and determining a purpose for their reading. Since successful readers make sense of texts by drawing on background knowledge relevant to their purposes (e.g., Hattan, 2019; Langer, 1984), providing students this opportunity is critical.

The most important feature of the CSR strategy is that students read texts collaboratively with other students, applying fix-up strategies and clarifying when comprehension breaks down, and periodically summarizing what they have read. This is very different from the widely used practices of teacher read-alouds and listening to audio recordings of texts in secondary classrooms (Swanson et al., 2016). The final key feature, asking and answering questions about a text to discuss what students have learned after reading, is covered in greater detail in Chapter 6.

We have chosen to highlight these features because the difference between those who are good comprehenders and those who struggle is that poor comprehenders do not engage in active construction of meaning, which is the hallmark of successful comprehension of challenging content-area texts. Because these cognitive activities occur inside the "black box" of their more successful peers' cognitive processes, poor comprehenders can mistakenly come to believe that good comprehenders automatically understand challenging text because they cannot see the questioning, rereading, predicting, and summarizing that go on in a successful reader's mind. Therefore, teachers need to choose instructional frameworks and strategies that make the comprehension process visible (Hart & Stebick, 2016) and give students the practice and opportunity to automatize these thinking processes in their own reading.

RECIPROCAL TEACHING

We have chosen to discuss Reciprocal Teaching (RT) next not only because this during-reading framework leverages the high-utility strategies that we see in CSR, but also because we have used RT extensively in our own teaching in secondary schools and in our work with content-area teachers in supporting their professional learning. Although this strategy was first designed as an elementary intervention (Palincsar & Brown, 1984), it has since been used in nearly all grade levels and content areas. It has been studied extensively, including with older students in high school (Alfassi, 1998) and community colleges (Hart & Speece, 1998). RT has become a flexible and successful "go-to" in-class reading strategy for engaging students in reading a broad range of text types in a variety of content-area classrooms.

Like CSR, RT utilizes small heterogeneous groups of four to six students. Although we have observed classrooms in which students work in informally arranged groups, we believe that teachers should be more strategic when grouping students. We recommend doing so by using students' Lexile scores or other reading achievement data from standardized assessments used in your school. As an example, let's say that we have 28 students in our class and have rank-ordered them from our highest (1) to lowest performing student (28). Using these data, we can create five separate groups (represented in Figure 5.4) and then go down the list, assigning each student to a different group in order.

Group 1		Group 2		Group 3		Group 4		Group 5	
Student	Lexile	Student	Lexile	Student	Lexile	Student	Lexile	Student	Lexile
1	1200	2	1180	3	1100	4	1040	5	1040
6	1000	7	1000	8	990	9	990	10	980
11	960	12	960	13	960	14	960	15	950
16	950	17	940	18	940	19	900	20	890
21	860	22	820	23	800	24	800	25	700
26	700	27	700	28	650	–	–	–	–

FIGURE 5.4. Heterogeneous grouping for RT based on Lexile scores.

We assign the five highest performing students to each of the five groups. The process begins again by placing student 6 in group 1 and then continuing in the same fashion until all students are assigned to a group. Once students are grouped, the teacher can provide a brief preview of the text they will read, building and activating prior knowledge as well as providing a clear purpose for reading. Students then engage in silent reading of a passage that either is clearly segmented by text features (e.g., headings), or strategically chunked by the teacher beforehand. While reading, they engage in a structured discussion that uses four of the high-utility strategies that we saw in CSR: predicting, questioning, clarifying, and summarizing. Before the process begins, teachers or students choose a discussion leader who will guide his or her group through the first text segment. The leader guides the group in *previewing* the chunk of text, encouraging the group to make predictions based on any available information (e.g., titles, subheadings, illustrations, previous readings, or reading purposes provided by the teacher). The leader then directs the group to silently *read* that chunk of text. After they read, the discussion leader guides the group in *asking questions* about the passage and encouraging the group to *clarify* any textual information that they previously had questions about during reading, much like the "clunk" strategy that is embedded in CSR. The leader then guides the group in *summarizing* the text chunk before passing the responsibility of discussion leader to another student, who begins the cycle again. This cycle of reading and discussion activities is repeated until the group finishes the assigned text. The role of the teacher during an RT discussion is to coach the groups as they read and discuss the text, making sure that the discussion remains on track and that the groups are moving forward through the text at a reasonable pace. The cycle, based on Palincsar and Brown (1984), is depicted in Figure 5.5.

We would like to note that although the discussion leaders are primarily responsible for moving the group through each stage of the RT cycle, all students should be encouraged to predict, read, question, clarify, and summarize. When working in schools, we have been in classrooms where teachers have assigned static roles for each reading assignment: one student assigned as discussion leader, one as predictor, questioner, clarifier, and summarizer. However, since comprehending a text requires that students strategically and flexibly coordinate the use of multiple strategies (Lysynchuk, Pressley, & Vye, 1990), RT is more effective—and more engaging—if students participate in each strategy in the RT cycle together.

Introducing RT

Although Palincsar and Brown (1984) recommended teaching each of the RT strategies over 5 consecutive days of instruction, secondary content-area teachers cannot spend this amount of time introducing RT into their classrooms. Therefore, when starting RT in middle and high school classrooms, we believe that a

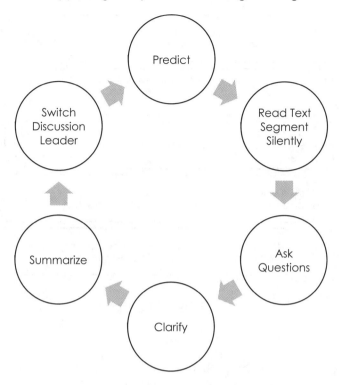

FIGURE 5.5. RT cycle.

more recent study of RT (Hacker & Tenent, 2002) provides a helpful procedure for introducing the framework in a short one-class-period introduction. This procedure is outlined in Figure 5.6.

When first introducing the strategy, the teacher can form the collaborative groups and lead students in a teacher-directed version of RT, briefly explaining the individual strategies within the RT cycle, and then using the strategies to read and discuss a content-area text that is aligned with the teacher's instructional goals for the day. After the teacher initiates the process in this way, he or she can quickly cede responsibility to the students to use the framework independently, with the teacher circulating among the groups and providing assistance when needed. Since more engaged student reading is our goal, and not comprehension instruction per se, we recommend moving quickly into student engagement in reading content-area texts.

Implementing RT

As an illustration of how RT can be implemented with a variety of text types, let's look at how Bill used RT to scaffold the challenging seventeenth-century poem "Verses upon the Burning of Our House" by Anne Bradstreet in his high school American literature class. Before learning about RT, Bill took a relatively

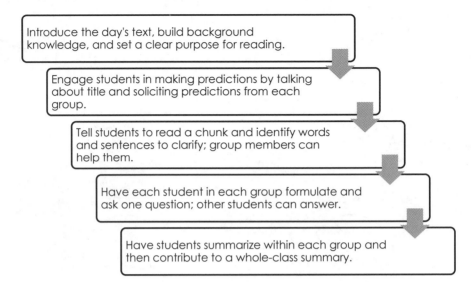

FIGURE 5.6. Strategy for introducing RT.

"textless" approach to teaching this poem, first reading aloud to his students Bradstreet's poetic description of the speaker losing her house to fire, then rereading each stanza of the poem followed by rapid-fire questioning. Sound boring? Bill will freely admit that it was. However, when he used the RT framework to scaffold real student reading of the poem, things changed for him and his students.

To begin the RT lesson, Bill first needed to determine the purpose of his students' reading. In the case of this poem, Bill wanted his students to develop a robust understanding of the Puritan worldview and how that worldview is both represented and resisted in Anne Bradstreet's poem. The second step was to strategically chunk the text to better achieve those instructional objectives. As you may know from your own reading of the poem in high school, the narrator progresses through several distinct emotional stages as she comes to terms with this tragedy. The first is Bradstreet's shock and despair at the loss of her house, followed by the narrator parroting the common beliefs of Puritan society at the time: that the house was God's, not hers, and that she should not complain about losing something that she did not possess in the first place. The next section, however, contains a very honest discussion of the possessions that she had lost in the fire, the speaker mourning the memories that will no longer be made there. The next stage represents an emotional change in the poem when she shakes herself out of her sadness and refocuses on the spiritual, not physical, aspects of life. The poem ends with a complex extended metaphor of a "heavenly house" that will eventually take the place of all her earthly dwellings. To illustrate, consider the first section of Bradstreet's poem:

In silent night when rest I took,
For sorrow near I did not look,
I wakened was with thund'ring noise
And piteous shrieks of dreadful voice.
That fearful sound of "fire" and "fire,"
Let no man know is my Desire.
I, starting up, the light did spy,
And to my God my heart did cry
To straighten me in my Distress
And not to leave me succourless.
Then, coming out, behold a space
The flame consume my dwelling place.

Bill began the RT lesson by arranging his students into small heterogeneous groups of four to six. He also provided students with a graphic organizer with spaces to record their predictions, questions, clarifications, and summaries (Palincsar & Brown, 1986; see Figure 5.7). Before reading, he provided them a quick summary of the context of the poem and previewed some archaic vocabulary terms that might interfere with comprehension (e.g., *succourless*). During this short text preview, Bill reminded his students that their purpose for reading was to analyze the poem for its adherence or resistance to the Puritan beliefs that they had already learned about.

Bill began the during-reading portion of the lesson by identifying the initial discussion leaders and encouraging those leaders to guide their groups in previewing the first chunk of text, predicting the events and emotions that would be discussed there (e.g., "I think she is going to talk about how sad she is about her house burning down"). The group members then read the first chunk silently to check their prediction. Once finished, they began their discussion of the chunk by forming questions about what they had just read (e.g., "I wonder what she means by 'Let no man know is my Desire.' Is she feeling guilty? Did she burn down her own house?"), clarifying where possible (e.g., "Maybe it means that the event is so terrible she doesn't want anyone else to have to experience it?"), and then summarizing (e.g., "The narrator wakes up, sees that her house is on fire, and cries to God to help her. Running out of the house, she sees the house destroyed by fire"). The group ended the cycle by switching discussion leaders and then moving to the next chunk. After reading the full poem, students engaged in a whole-class discussion of how the speaker both represents and resists Puritan philosophy throughout her spiritual journey.

When Bill taught this poem by reading it aloud to students and followed up with questions about each stanza, he found that the instruction took a full 50-minute class period. After adopting the RT framework, however, he was surprised to find that the more literacy-rich instruction took no more instructional time than the original textless approach did. Instead of Bill reading and interpreting the poem for his students, however, the responsibility for reading and making

Predict	Question
What do you predict will happen next?	What questions do you have about the text?

Clarify	Summarize
What is unclear and needs to be clarified?	What are the most important details?

FIGURE 5.7. RT graphic organizer.

meaning now fell squarely on their shoulders. Replacing teacher reading with collaborative student reading was an effective and efficient way to provide students with more opportunities to read, and the lesson was more engaging, motivating and—yes—fun for the students!

PEER-ASSISTED LEARNING STRATEGIES

Peer-Assisted Learning Strategies (PALS) is a procedure for in-class reading that leverages student collaboration and discussion within a framework of specific text-based activities. It is also a procedure that we have used successfully in our work in middle and high schools in a variety of content-area classrooms. Originating from the work of Doug and Lynn Fuchs at Vanderbilt University, PALS was originally developed to improve the reading of elementary students in grades 2 through 6 (Fuchs, Fuchs, Mathes, & Simmons, 1997). However, research on PALS has been expanded to include kindergarten, first grade, and high school students (Fuchs et al., 2001), including secondary students with significant reading problems (Fuchs et al., 1999). We encourage you to check out the website of the Fuchs Research Group at Vanderbilt University (*https://frg.vkcsites.org/what-is-pals*), which provides a thorough description of the PALS framework, as well as access to PALS products and training.

One way that PALS is different from RT is that it relies on collaborative pairs of students working together with a shared text instead of heterogeneously grouping students. Like RT, however, it is important that teachers strategically assign student pairs so that they can reap the full benefits of the framework. Pairing students begins with teachers rank ordering them from highest achieving to lowest achieving using reading assessment data and then splitting the list in half. This means that the highest performing students are paired with those in the middle, and those in the middle are paired with the lowest-performing students. Figure 5.8 shows how the Lexile data we used to assign our RT groups can be split to assign PALS pairs. In this example, our highest-achieving student (student 1) is paired with a middle-achieving student (student 15). Although we used Lexile data in this example, you can use any data that you have available.

When used with elementary students, PALS pairs are often kept together for several weeks at a time as they learn, practice, and use the strategy. However, research on the use of PALS with secondary students suggests that switching PALS partners can be more motivating for older students and can help to overcome the difficulties associated with the increased absenteeism of students in secondary school (Fuchs et al., 2001). Switching partners means, of course, that your PALS pairs might not always be perfectly aligned with their performance data. This is acceptable as long as the pairs contain a stronger and weaker reader and as long as the pairs are arranged so that your strongest students are not paired with your weakest.

Student	Lexile	Student	Lexile
1	1200	15	950
2	1180	16	950
3	1100	17	940
4	1040	18	940
5	1040	19	900
6	1000	20	890
7	1000	21	860
8	990	22	820
9	990	23	800
10	980	24	800
11	960	25	700
12	960	26	700
13	960	27	700
14	960	28	650

FIGURE 5.8. Pairing students for PALS based on Lexile scores.

We saw the importance of strategically pairing students when we were observing a lesson in a secondary ELA classroom that was utilizing PALS to read an informational text. Instead of strategically pairing students, the teacher allowed her students to pick their own PALS partners. Students quickly paired with their friends, leaving one last pair that was composed of a student with limited English proficiency and one with a reading disability. Although both English learners and those with reading disabilities can certainly benefit from the PALS framework, pairing two students who significantly struggle with reading grade-level text is going to lead to a frustrating and unsuccessful reading experience for both students.

Once you have formed your PALS pairs, students are ready to read the text using the four distinct timed PALS activities: Partner Reading, Retelling, Paragraph Shrinking, and Prediction Relay. Figure 5.9 shows the progression of activities and timing for each activity.

In the *Partner Reading* phase, Partner A (the stronger reader) begins reading the text aloud for 5 minutes while Partner B (the weaker reader) tracks the text, watching for mistakes and miscues, and prompting Partner A to correct his or her mistakes. After 5 minutes, Partner B begins reading where Partner A left off while Partner A tracks the text, looks for mistakes, and prompts corrections during the next 5 minutes for a total of 10 minutes of engaged reading. We have

Reader	Activity	Time
Partner A	Partner Reading	5 minutes
Partner B	Partner Reading	5 minutes
Both	Retelling	2 minutes
Partner A	Paragraph Shrinking	5 minutes
Partner B	Paragraph Shrinking	5 minutes
Partner A	Prediction Relay	5 minutes
Partner B	Prediction Relay	5 minutes
Total time required:		32 minutes

FIGURE 5.9. Timing for activities in PALS.

found that when students are first learning to use PALS, providing them with a partner reading script (or projecting a script on an interactive whiteboard), like the one displayed in Figure 5.10, can help facilitate engagement during the partner reading phase of the PALS protocol (Fuchs et al., 2001). After the 10 minutes of Partner Reading have elapsed, students take turns *Retelling* what they just read, recapping the main points of their reading over the next two minutes.

In the *Paragraph Shrinking* phase, pairs continue reading the text aloud from where they left off for 10 minutes, 5 minutes of reading per partner. However, this time they take turns reading the text in sections, pausing after each chunk to summarize what they just read. For instance, if partners are reading a narrative text, the reader reads a half to a full page before pausing to paragraph shrink. If it is an informational text, the reader reads one to two full paragraphs or a focused

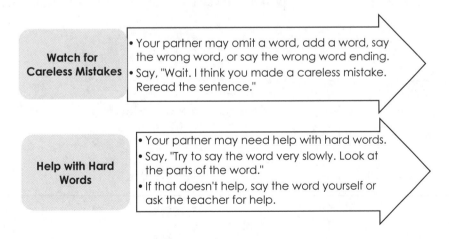

FIGURE 5.10. Partner Reading script.

chunk of text that is clearly marked by a heading or subheading. The key here is that the chunks of text are large enough to effectively summarize but also short enough so that the readers are not overwhelmed by having to summarize too much information. As each partner reads, the listening partner uses a series of prompts to help the reader summarize each of the chunks (Fuchs et al., 2001). These prompts are represented in Figure 5.11.

In research on PALS, the listener actually counts the words in the reader's summary of the main idea, directing the reader to "shrink it" if using more than 10 words (Fuchs et al., 2001). That being said, it is not harmful if paragraph summaries come in a word or two over 10. The key is that the reader is able to read the passage, quickly summarize its main idea, and then get back to reading. During this phase, the same reader continues reading and summarizing for the full 5 minutes. Then the partners switch roles, continuing for another 5 minutes.

The *Prediction Relay* stage adds one more task to what students do while Paragraph Shrinking. The listener asks the reader to make a prediction about what is going to happen in the next half page or paragraph. After the reader predicts and reads the chunk, the listener asks the reader to evaluate his or her prediction and then guides the reader to summarize the chunk using the Paragraph Shrinking script in Figure 5.11. These four steps are displayed in Figure 5.12.

The role of the teacher during a PALS session is to keep time and walk among the pairs, asking and answering students' questions and praising students for staying on task and implementing the scripts. It is important to note that teachers must also be able to tolerate some constructive noise when implementing PALS sessions because classrooms can be noisy places given the oral reading, retelling, summarizing, and predicting activities. That being said, ambient noise can be controlled by having student pairs share the same copy of the text. By sharing a single text, pairs of students will naturally be forced closer together, thus eliminating the need to speak loudly across a greater distance. Additionally,

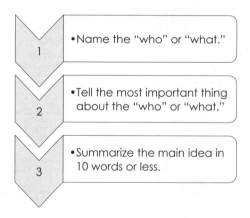

FIGURE 5.11. Paragraph Shrinking script.

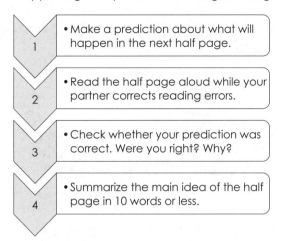

1 • Make a prediction about what will happen in the next half page.

2 • Read the half page aloud while your partner corrects reading errors.

3 • Check whether your prediction was correct. Were you right? Why?

4 • Summarize the main idea of the half page in 10 words or less.

FIGURE 5.12. Prediction Relay steps.

teachers should be prepared to help students make accommodations for the noisier reading environment. For instance, students can easily get off track when they are separated by only a beat or two from a pair that is reading nearby, leading to an annoying echo effect. Simply having one of the pairs stop reading for several seconds to allow for the other pair to read ahead can eliminate this common problem. We believe that the benefits of PALS to students' literacy development and content acquisition is well worth the minor inconveniences you might experience when first implementing this strategy.

Using PALS Flexibly

Once students are familiar with the PALS framework, you might find ways to use pieces of PALS when you want students to read portions of text in a time frame that is greater than or less than the 32 minutes that PALS instruction generally takes. For example, you might have students read just two or three pages of a chunked informational text, using the Paragraph Shrinking strategy after each chunk. Alternatively, you might have students use only Prediction Relay to read a short chapter of a narrative text. John had his ninth-grade students use the full PALS framework when reading each chapter of *To Kill a Mockingbird*. After student pairs completed the PALS procedures for a given chapter, each student finished reading the chapter independently before engaging in a Retelling of the main points with their partner. After a classroom discussion demonstrated that Bill's Advanced Placement students did not comprehend a complex section of Joseph Conrad's (1902) "Heart of Darkness," he engaged them in a 15-minute collaborative rereading of the section using Paragraph Shrinking. This relatively short amount of instructional time was all that was needed to improve students' understanding of that section of text and prepare them for an engaged discussion of the segment.

READING GUIDES

Reading guides differ from CSR, RT, and PALS in that reading guides are generally completed as students read independently, not in strategically chosen pairs or groups. Even though students are reading by themselves, however, it does not mean that they are not being supported in their reading or that their reading is not "collaborative."

First, before we describe what reading guides are, we want to clarify what reading guides are not. They are *not* comprehension questions at the end of a chapter, story, or poem. Those are assessments, not reading guides! Instead, reading guides are written directions from the teacher to his or her students that focus their efforts during reading, assist them in processing content, and provide a model for active and strategic reading (McKenna et al., 2011). Although they are reading alone, a well-constructed reading guide allows you to be personally at your students' sides even if you are not physically reading with them.

Because reading guides can take many forms and can be customized and personalized for individual students or classes, we are wary about dictating the form that your guide should take. That said, we suggest a general process for creating reading guides, as follows.

1. Read the entire text that you want students to read, identifying specific places where you anticipate they will have difficulty or where there is a natural break in the text where students could pause in order to predict, question, clarify, or summarize.
2. Return to each of the places you identified and create a support for each comprehension roadblock or an activity to help students synthesize or extend their understanding of textual information. Here are some possibilities:
   a. Write a brief explanation to clarify the problem area.
   b. Help students make a specific connection to a text they have previously read, viewed, or discussed in class.
   c. Write a guiding question that can focus their attention on key information.
   d. Include a visual image (or encourage students to draw one) for students to annotate that will help them to visualize what they have read.
   e. Create a graphic organizer to help students organize textual information and show how ideas are related.
3. Compile your supports and include very specific directions for how your students will move from your guide to the text and back.

Reading Guides for Disciplinary Texts

Now that you have a general procedure for creating a reading guide, it may be helpful to look at a few guides that we have created for our own secondary students or have used in our professional development work with teachers. One form of a guide that we have found particularly helpful is called a Reading Road Map (RRM; Wood, 2011). Looking very much like the step-by-step directions that we might get from Google Maps when starting out on a journey, RRMs segment a student's "journey" through a text, providing clear directions for each step, as well as indicating how fast students should read, their purpose for reading each text segment, and helpful notes as they travel through the text.

For instance, let's take a look at a guide that John created for an informational article from ReadWorks (2013) on lightning-related wildfires in the Florida panhandle. John chose this article because of its alignment with key science standards that are related to Earth's systems and the impact of humans on those systems (NGSS Lead States, 2013). The article describes why Florida receives more lightning strikes than any other state, the dangers and benefits of lightning-related fire on Florida's ecosystem, and how fire crews work to protect people from the dangers. Following the process described above, John read the full article and noted areas of the text that might confuse students or areas to which he wanted to draw their attention. Once finished, he returned to those areas and created supports in an RRM that you can see in Figure 5.13.

Knowing that the location and geographical features of Florida are key to understanding why the state receives so many lightning strikes, John started his RRM with two maps to help students visualize what they were reading. He also recognized that the article's authors used the word *adapted* in the second paragraph. Since adaptation is a key disciplinary science concept, his RRM directs students to "STOP" their reading and provides a short contextual explanation of this vocabulary word to be sure that his students understand its meaning. In the third paragraph, John drew students' attention to the main ideas in that text section with an inferential question on the benefits of fire on certain species of wildlife. He did this because he understands that a key concept in the article is that wildfires are both natural and beneficial, and answering that question would help students to understand that. A key feature of this RRM is that John has his students skim the paragraph that provides information on the prescribed fire crews. Although this section may interest some students, it is not critical for achieving his instructional objectives, leaving more time for focusing on the work of those crews in paragraphs 5 and 6 and the evidence-based class discussion on the relative helpfulness or harmfulness of Florida's wildfires.

Reading guides can take other forms as well, depending on your instructional goals and the unique features of the texts you choose to meet those goals. For instance, take this reading guide that we created to help social studies teachers guide students through Patrick Henry's speech to the Virginia Convention.

Destination	Speed	Mission
End of first paragraph SLOW	Slow.	Visualize a map of the United States while you read. Label the map below using the details in this paragraph. How does this help you understand why Florida receives the most lightning strikes in North America?
Second paragraph, line 2 STOP	A quick minute,	Stop for a minute after reading this sentence: "Many plants and animals in Florida depend on fire, and they have adapted to the constant presence of fire." **Adapted** means that plants and animals changed in order to live with fire.
End of third paragraph	Moderate.	This section provides examples of plants and animals in Florida that depend on fire. Think about the relationship between fire, wiregrass, and gopher tortoises. Why are regular fires important to gopher tortoises?
Fourth paragraph	Fast!	The author is introducing readers to something called a prescribed fire crew that lights fires on purpose. Skim this paragraph.
Fifth and sixth paragraphs SLOW	Slow down.	Pay attention to the two reasons that prescribed fire crews light fires. How and why do they fight fire *with* fire?
STOP		Get ready for our discussion. Based on the passage, do you think fires in Florida are more helpful or harmful? Look for evidence in the text that supports your argument.

FIGURE 5.13. RRM for "Lightning and Fire" (ReadWorks, 2013).

As you look at Figure 5.14, you will notice that the guide is *not* a set of comprehension questions. Instead it is a self-paced reading support that is created for a specific group of students with a specific reading purpose in mind. In this case, the purpose is to engage students in a discussion of the impact of Henry's rhetorical choices on the reader or listener. You can find a copy of the speech as well as an audio recording online (*https://etc.usf.edu/lit2go/133/historic-american-documents/4956*).

You can see that this reading guide scaffolds students' comprehension of the text by guiding them through an initial reading that provides a gist-level understanding and then through a targeted second reading that encourages students to analyze the impact of Henry's rhetorical choices on the meaning and impact of the speech.

Although reading guides are usually designed to support individual students reading by themselves, we would also encourage you to consider using reading guides with pairs of students. Just as a journey is often more enjoyable with a traveling companion, a paired "journey" through a text can be equally enjoyable and allow students to take advantage of the benefits of collaboration if they get lost in that journey and comprehension breaks down.

Reading Guides for Multiple Texts

Although both of these examples focus on a single text, reading guides can also be used to help students navigate back and forth through multiple texts. For instance, Wood (2011) describes using RRMs to guide students from specific portions of a print article or book chapter to websites chosen in advance by the teacher (or student-chosen websites) and then back into the print text. As an example of how this can be accomplished, we modified the RRM that Bill originally created (Lewis et al., 2014) for his American literature students for Edgar Allan Poe's (1845) short story "The Pit and the Pendulum." Before we show you the guide, we would like to give you some context about why he created it.

When Bill first taught Poe's story, he assigned it to his students to read independently and without support. However, after students in a particular class did poorly on a postreading quiz, a student approached Bill and admitted that the first two paragraphs were so difficult that he just gave up. This comment forced Bill to reconsider the challenges that this text posed to students, and it also provided some important insight into his students' thinking and the strategic cost–benefit analysis they made when faced with challenging content area material. If students laboriously read and reread a section of text and yet still do not understand it, they are going to be less likely to spend additional time and cognitive energy reading more of that text if they feel that the outcome will end with the same frustrating lack of comprehension. Bill now understood that creating a reading guide for that text would provide both the strategic scaffolding to comprehend the text and the motivation needed to push through the difficult parts.

Directions: Please number your paragraphs before you begin; that will make it easier for you to use this guide while you read. If I have a tip for you, it is numbered by paragraph. Read my tip first. I want you to actually read the speech twice—once quickly for the main idea, and then again more slowly to help you understand Henry's rhetorical choices.

First Reading:

1. Henry is addressing an audience that may disagree with him about breaking away from England. Think about why he used this type of introduction.

3–4. Henry says that hoping the British government will change is natural, but that he is guided by the "lamp of experience." What do you think he means by "lamp of experience"?

5. Henry lists a clear reason Britain changing is unrealistic. What is that reason?

6–9. Henry is discussing what the colonies have done to keep from breaking away from England. What did the colonies do, and what was the reaction?

10. Do you agree that fighting against England was the only thing that the colonies could do? Why or why not?

11–13. Henry is trying to address critics who think that the colonies are too weak to fight England. Identify two reasons that Henry thinks this is not a good argument.

14. This paragraph addresses the battles between the colonies and England taking place in the north. Why does he mention this?

14. This paragraph ends with the line "Give me liberty or give me death!" Why do you think he chose to end it with this direct statement?

Second Reading: Now let's look at Henry's rhetorical choices. Read the selection again, focusing on the following sections. Number a blank sheet of paper with each of the paragraphs listed below and explain how each choice lends persuasiveness to Henry's argument.

Paragraph 3: Metaphor	"We are apt to shut our eyes against a painful truth, and listen to the song of that siren, till she transforms us into beasts. Is this the part of wise men, engaged in a great and arduous struggle for liberty?"
Paragraph 5: Biblical allusion	"Is it that insidious smile with which our petition has been lately received? Trust it not, sir; it will prove a snare to your feet. Suffer not yourselves to be betrayed with a kiss."
Paragraph 10: Repetition	"If we wish to be free—if we mean to preserve inviolate those inestimable privileges for which we have been so long contending—if we mean not basely to abandon the noble struggle in which we have been so long engaged, and which we have pledged ourselves never to abandon until the glorious object of our contest shall be obtained, we must fight! I repeat it, sir, we must fight!"
Paragraph 11: Rhetorical questions	"They tell us, sir, that we are weak—unable to cope with so formidable an adversary. But when shall we be stronger? Will it be the next week, or the next year? Will it be when we are totally disarmed, and when a British guard shall be stationed in every house? Shall we gather strength by irresolution and inaction? Shall we acquire the means of effectual resistance, by lying supinely on our backs, and hugging the delusive phantom of hope, until our enemies shall have bound us hand and foot?"
Paragraph 14: Appeals to emotion (pathos)	"Why stand we here idle? What is it that gentlemen wish? What would they have? Is life so dear, or peace so sweet, as to be purchased at the price of chains and slavery? Forbid it, Almighty God! I know not what course others may take; but as for me, give me liberty, or give me death!"

FIGURE 5.14. RRM guide for Patrick Henry's "Speech to the Virginia Convention."

Revisiting the short story with this lens, Bill noticed that the first four paragraphs were extraordinarily complex, with multiple embedded clauses, archaic vocabulary, and a setting that is unfamiliar to most students: Inquisition-era Spain. Additionally, this text section is told from the standpoint of a terrified and confused narrator who moves in and out of consciousness as he attempts to reconstruct his trial and judgment for the readers. No wonder students had difficulty comprehending this challenging text section! What Bill also noticed is that after this first section of the story, it becomes much clearer and more interesting, with significantly less interior monologue and more action. Therefore, instead of creating a guide for the whole story, he created an RRM for just the first four paragraphs. Using Wood's (2011) framework for including digital texts in reading guides, we modified the original RRM that Bill constructed to include helpful web-based supports from digital texts. See the RRM in Figure 5.15.

As you can see, this guide provides helpful background knowledge about the setting and context of the story, and it also encourages students to skip sections that are not crucial to their understanding. This leaves instructional time for reading more important parts of the text, or discussion and summarizing activities. Additionally, this guide provides students the opportunity to personally connect to the text by having them make explicit text-to-self connections with the narrator's plight, independently search the web for visual representations of the setting, and use text-based evidence to summarize what they have read, followed by predictions about the rest of the story. Like CSR, RT, and PALS, Reading Road Maps encourage students to use the active cognitive reading strategies that successful readers leverage to make sense of text.

Collaborative Listening–Viewing Guides

Since the text sets that we have been building together over the course of the last chapters often use visual or video texts to build relevant background knowledge, it is worthwhile to end this section with a strategy that also comes from the work of Karen Wood (1990, 2011; Wood & Mraz, 2005) and is specifically designed to guide students to engage with information that is not in traditional print or digital print form. Calling it the Collaborative Listening–Viewing Guide (CLVG), Wood designed a simple process for listening or viewing that is represented in Figure 5.16.

As an example of how to use this strategy, let's say that we decide to use a short video text titled "Why Florida Has Become the Lightning Capital of the Country" (CBS Evening News, 2017) as a way to build background knowledge before students read the informational text "Lightning and Fire" discussed earlier in the chapter. The teacher provides students with a graphic organizer (see Figure 5.17) and guides them in completing the *preview–review* section, in this case brainstorming information they know about Florida, lightning, and thunderstorms. Setting a clear purpose for viewing, the teacher instructs students to

Destination	Speed	Mission
How the Spanish Inquisition worked: *https://history.howstuffworks.com/ historical-figures/spanish-inquisition. htm*	Start your engines!	This story takes place during the Spanish Inquisition when they were arresting, trying, and executing people who were accused of going against the Catholic Church. Many of them burned alive at the stake! Quickly read the description of this era.
First paragraph, line 10: The courtroom	Proceed with caution.	Get a sense of the narrator's mental state after he is sentenced to death by the Inquisition. What are the things that he hears and sees? Why would his senses be so affected by this death sentence?
First paragraph, line 20: The courtroom SLOW	Slow.	The narrator begins to focus on the candle flames in the courtroom. How might candle flames be symbolic of the narrator?
Torture and punishment during the Spanish Inquisition: *https://history.howstuffworks.com/ historical-figures/spanish-inquisition3. htm* STOP	A quick minute.	This is a brief description of the torture methods that were used during the Spanish Inquisition. Skip this part if you are feeling squeamish!
End of first paragraph STOP	A quick minute.	Think about how you might react knowing that you were about to face imprisonment, torture, and death. How might your reaction be similar to the narrator's?
End of second paragraph	Fast!	The narrator describes going in and out of consciousness. Skim this passage.
End of third paragraph	Fast!	The narrator is being carried down to a dungeon and regains consciousness. Skim this passage.

(continued)

FIGURE 5.15. RRM for "The Pit and the Pendulum." Adapted with permission from Lewis, Walpole, and McKenna (2014). Copyright © 2014 The Guilford Press.

Destination	Speed	Mission
End of fourth paragraph: The dungeon SLOW	Slow down.	The narrator is in the dungeon in the pitch darkness. Choose a sentence that you think best describes the most terrible part of being imprisoned and summarize it here.
Google Images	A quick minute	Quickly search Google images with the word *dungeon*. Find a picture of a dungeon that best represents the picture that you have in your head.
STOP		Based on what you have read so far, what do you think is going to happen to the narrator in the next few pages given his mental state right now?

FIGURE 5.15. *(continued)*

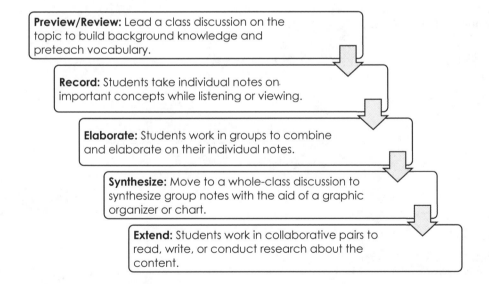

FIGURE 5.16. Procedure for the CLVG.

Video Title:

Student Name:

Group Members:

Preview–Review:

Record (Individually):	Elaborate (Group):

Synthesize (Whole Class):

Extension:

FIGURE 5.17. CLVG. Adapted with permission from Wood and Mraz (2005). Copyright © 2005 The Guilford Press.

individually take notes on the important concepts while viewing the video in the *record* section. Moving into collaborative groups, students compare their notes, *elaborate* on what they wrote, and reorganize information in meaningful ways. Following this stage, students then *synthesize* their group notes as a full class, highlighting the most significant elements of what they listened to or viewed. The strategy ends with the *extension* phase during which the teacher encourages them to read the informational text to extend their understanding of the effects of Florida's lightning. Although John had originally designed an RRM for individual reading of the "Lightning and Fire" article (see Figure 5.13), he could just as easily have students work in PALS pairs or in RT groups after completing the CLVG. The key is that, like the scaffolding we provide for print texts, students' interactions with visual or audio texts also need strategic scaffolding.

DURING-READING STRATEGIES IN DISCIPLINARY TEXT SETS

Based on our goals for instruction and the unique features of each text, we have chosen specific during-reading (or viewing) strategies to support student comprehension in our ELA, social studies and science quad text sets. In the following sections, we provide a brief summary and rationale for our during-reading instructional choices.

English Language Arts

Figure 5.18 represents the during-reading strategies chosen for each of our four texts in the ELA quad text set. The visual text is a contemporary video version of Act I of *Romeo and Juliet* designed to build background knowledge about the characters and conflicts in the play. The teacher has chosen to support student comprehension through a CLVG, which is helpful for constructing meaning from nonprint texts. The next text, an informational text on gender roles in Elizabethan England, has clear text features like headings and subheadings. Therefore, she decided to use RT, with students stopping at the end of each chunk to predict, question, clarify, and summarize. A reading guide is her choice for the first act of *Romeo and Juliet,* the target text. Since this is a complex text, the reading guide allows her to provide targeted scaffolding to help students comprehend Shakespeare's language and to distinguish among the individual character traits of the Montague and Capulet family members. She used the selections from the contemporary young-adult novel *Eleanor and Park* to encourage students to compare and contrast the gendered expectations they see in *Romeo and Juliet* with those in a contemporary setting. Thus, the questioning phase of CSR is perfect for encouraging students to ask critical questions about the similarities and differences between the main characters of the play and the novel, and how all are influenced by gendered expectations.

	Instructional Objective(s): Analyze how characters develop over the course of a text, interact with other characters, advance the plot, and develop the theme.
	Visual Text: Video of Act I from contemporary film version of *Romeo and Juliet*

Instructional Strategies	Before Reading: Listen–Read–Discuss
	During Reading: Collaborative Listening–Viewing Guide
	After Reading:

Informational Text(s): Article on gender roles and power in Elizabethan England

Instructional Strategies	Before Reading: Concept of Definition
	During Reading: Reciprocal Teaching
	After Reading:

Target Text: Act I of Shakespeare's *Romeo and Juliet*

Instructional Strategies	Before Reading: K-W-L strategy
	During Reading: Reading Guide
	After Reading:

Accessible Text: Selected chapters from *Eleanor and Park* by Rainbow Rowell

Instructional Strategies	Before Reading: Prereading Plan
	During Reading: Collaborative Strategic Reading
	After Reading:

Extended Writing:

FIGURE 5.18. ELA quad text set with during-reading strategies.

Social Studies

Figure 5.19 includes the during-reading supports developed for the social studies quad text set on segregation in the United States. As in the ELA text set, a CLVG is best suited for constructing meaning from this video text, followed by RT for the informational text because of the clear headings and subheadings that conveniently chunk the reading for students. The goal for this reading assignment is building background knowledge about the chronology of racial segregation in the United States and to differentiate between *de jure segregation* and *de facto segregation*. Therefore, the teacher would have students produce a timeline of both types of segregation in their RT groups based on their reading. The *Brown v. Board of Education* decision is the challenging text in this quad text set, and so the teacher decided that the Paragraph Shrinking phase of PALS—with its paired oral readings—would best support her students in their comprehension of this text. This would be followed by a contemporary article on the continued racial disparities experienced in American school systems. The goal for this reading is to have students reflect on whether the *Brown v. Board of Education* decision was effective in eliminating racial segregation in American public schools. An RRM can focus students on that question and scaffold their ability to contrast contemporary examples of continued segregation in schools with the intentions of the Supreme Court's decision.

Science

The science quad text set on climate change in Figure 5.20 begins with a video from the famous scientist and TV personality Bill Nye to build background knowledge. The teacher feels that, like the other quad text sets, the CLVG strategy will work well with this video because it not only allows him to focus students on the reality of climate change before viewing but also encourages students to elaborate and synthesize their individual notes about important concepts in the video related to the reality of climate change. The second text is an interactive digital text that is chunked into several sections, each addressing a different element of climate change. The teacher assigns heterogeneously grouped students into "expert" groups, with each group assigned a different text section. Since each text section requires students to digitally manipulate graphs and charts throughout the reading, he designs a reading guide for each group with directions on how to read, interact, and take notes on what they find in their text segment. When students finish their section, the teacher will organize the students into new "jigsaw groups," each group composed of one member of the different expert groups. Here students will share what they found with the other group members and summarize their findings. The third text is a contemporary young adult novel set in a dystopian future in which the United States is ravaged by the impacts of climate change. The Paragraph Shrinking phase of PALS can work well here,

Instructional Objective(s): Analyze historical materials to trace the development of an idea over time and explain patterns of continuity and change; determine the central idea of a primary source and accurately summarize the central idea and key details.		
Visual Text: "Kids Talk about Segregation" video		
Instructional Strategies	**Before Reading:** Prereading Plan	
	During Reading: Collaborative Listening–Viewing Guide	
	After Reading:	
Informational Text(s): Article on the history of racial segregation in the United States		
Instructional Strategies	**Before Reading:** Semantic Feature Analysis	
	During Reading: Reciprocal Teaching	
	After Reading:	
Target Text: *Brown v. Board of Education* decision		
Instructional Strategies	**Before Reading:** Listen–Read–Discuss	
	During Reading: PALS (Paragraph Shrinking)	
	After Reading:	
Accessible Text: Article on racial disparities in modern U.S. public schools		
Instructional Strategies	**Before Reading:** Concept of Definition	
	During Reading: Reading Guide	
	After Reading:	
Extended Writing:		

FIGURE 5.19. Social studies quad text set with during-reading strategies.

Instructional Objective(s): Construct an argument supported by evidence (e.g., patterns in graphs, charts, and images) for how humans impact Earth's systems; integrate technical information expressed in words in a text with a visual representation of that information.

Visual Text: "Climate Change 101" video with Bill Nye

Instructional Strategies	**Before Reading:** Prereading Plan
	During Reading: Collaborative Listening–Viewing Guide
	After Reading:

Informational Text(s): "Climate Change: How Do We Know?" website

Instructional Strategies	**Before Reading:** Listen–Read–Discuss
	During Reading: Jigsaw Groups with Reading Guide
	After Reading:

Accessible Text: Chapter 1 of *Ship Breaker* by Paolo Bacigalupi

Instructional Strategies	**Before Reading:** K-W-L strategy
	During Reading: PALS (Paragraph Shrinking)
	After Reading:

Target Text: "5 Ways to Curb Climate Change" articles

Instructional Strategies	**Before Reading:** Semantic Feature Analysis
	During Reading: Reciprocal Teaching
	After Reading:

Extended Writing:

FIGURE 5.20. Science quad text set with during-reading strategies.

with students pausing at the end of each page of the opening chapter of the book to summarize what they have read, making sure that each partner understands how the impacts of climate change are manifested in the setting described in the chapter. The quad text set ends with an informational text on how to mitigate climate change which, because of the clearly defined headings, makes it a natural choice to use with Reciprocal Teaching.

FINAL THOUGHTS

We know that we have given you a lot to think about in this chapter. We have asked you to rethink the use of your classroom time. And we have asked you to think about stepping away from the podium and replacing teacher reading, audio recordings, and PowerPoint lectures with more active and engaged student reading using research-validated collaborative and independent reading frameworks. Although these frameworks might represent significant shifts in your classroom instruction, we believe that using them will not only help you build your students' content knowledge but also build more mature literacy skills that will help them to be successful independent readers and thinkers in college, the workplace, and society at large.

CHAPTER 6

Conducting Discussions
after Reading

In the previous chapter, we told you about some of the most common methods of reading we have seen in our visits to middle and high school classrooms. Too often, we find that teachers aren't having their students read enough during class time. When they do, they tend to return to the same routines that they likely experienced as students: teacher read-alouds, round-robin reading, and even PowerPoint lectures in place of student reading. Unfortunately, the same pattern is present in classroom discussions. For example, Applebee, Langer, Nystrand, and Gamoran (2003) found that secondary students participated in fewer than 2 minutes of discussion during a 60-minute class period. Swanson and colleagues (2016) observed discussions in less than 20% of secondary ELA and social studies classes. To make matters worse, only a handful of teachers were responsible for all of those observations, with some teachers never engaging students in discussion. Our own observations in middle school have also revealed classroom discussions to be few and far between (Walpole, Strong, & Riches, 2018). When we do see them, they usually follow the same structure that many of us experienced as students.

Think back to the classroom discussions you had as a middle and high school student. They were probably, most often, whole-class discussions, with the teacher posing a set of literal-level questions meant to check for understanding before moving on to the next question. As former high school teachers and current teacher educators, we too have been guilty of leading this type of discussion in our own classrooms. Consider the following example from John's ninth-grade ELA class. After his students read Richard Connell's (1957) "The Most Dangerous Game," a short story about a big-game hunter who is tasked with surviving a fellow hunter's sadistic game of hunting humans, he led a discussion that began something like this:

> JOHN: Let's review the story "The Most Dangerous Game." Who can tell me the name of the main character? (*Malik raises his hand, and John calls on him to answer.*)
>
> MALIK: Rainsford?
>
> JOHN: Correct! What about the setting? Who can tell me where the story takes place? (*Malik raises his hand again. Lauren is looking in the text for the answer*). Lauren?
>
> LAUREN: I'm not sure.
>
> JOHN: Let's see if we can figure it out. Remember that Rainsford and his friend Whitney were on a ship in the beginning of the story, right? And then what happened?
>
> MALIK: Rainsford heard a sound and fell overboard.
>
> JOHN: That's right, Malik. But please remember to raise your hand next time. Okay, so Rainsford fell overboard and then what? Where did he wake up? It was an island, right? Lauren, can you tell me the name of the island? (*Lauren looks in the text.*)
>
> LAUREN: Is it Ship-Trap Island?
>
> JOHN: Yes! Good job, Lauren. The setting of the story is Ship-Trap Island.

Chances are that you have been either on the giving or the receiving end of this type of discussion. We all have! John, asking his students to recall the names of the main character and the island setting, attempted to check whether his students had understood the story. It was clear that Malik had read it and was excited to volunteer to answer every question. When Lauren found the name of the island in the text, John was pleased that she understood where the story was set. However, John's questions probed only a surface-level understanding of the text, not the higher levels of comprehension represented by the text base or situation model we described in Chapter 3. This example, the default method of many teachers, is a far cry from the discussions we would hope to see—students engaging in meaningful discourse with each other and using evidence in response to higher-level questions about texts (Swanson et al., 2016).

In this chapter, we describe several options to help teachers move beyond this default method of questioning to conducting more robust discussions that probe higher levels of comprehension. Some of the strategies in this chapter will be easier to implement for teachers who prefer to retain control over classroom discussions. Others will require transferring control to students as they lead and participate in small-group discussions. We begin by diving deeper into the limitations of traditional classroom discussions and the characteristics of effective discussions. Next, we take a look at the expectations for discussion in college and career readiness (CCR) standards for speaking and listening. In the rest of the chapter, we present and illustrate instructional strategies for facilitating different types of text-based discussions. We conclude, as in previous chapters, by returning to our quad text set examples in ELA, social studies, and science. We demonstrate how to select discussion formats that will both promote comprehension after reading and prepare students to write about what they have read.

EFFECTIVE CLASSROOM DISCUSSIONS

The example at the beginning of the chapter certainly was not an effective classroom discussion. The method of teacher-led discussion that was employed is often referred to as an initiation–response–evaluation (IRE) pattern (Cazden, 1988; Mehan, 1979). In an IRE pattern, the teacher *initiates* by asking a question, solicits a student *response* to the question, and then provides an *evaluation* of the student's response. The problem with this method of "discussion" is that it is really not much of a discussion at all. It is better characterized as a *recitation* in which "students' responses to questions are assessed, and issues are seldom explored" (Alvermann, O'Brien, & Dillon, 1990, p. 306). Despite the fact that the IRE pattern provides limited opportunities for students to engage in elaborated discussion, it persists as the dominant method in content-area classrooms (Alozie, Moje, & Krajcik, 2009; Reisman, 2015; Tytler & Aranda, 2014).

What can teachers do to lead more effective discussions? We cannot understate the importance of planning in advance. According to Reisman (2017), "Good discussions have little to do with magic and everything to do with careful planning and pedagogical savviness" (p. 34). In our work with teachers regarding planning lessons, we argue that it is simply not enough to plan on having a discussion. The discussion itself, including the questions you ask and the moves you make, must be carefully planned in order to avoid falling into the trap of IRE recitations.

In their review of discussion-based approaches to reading instruction, Lawrence and Snow (2011) identify five characteristics of effective discussions that are helpful to consider:

1. Effective discussions begin with open-ended questions worthy of discussion.
2. Interpretive authority and control of turns are shared between the teacher and students.
3. There is substantial time for peer interaction and dialogue.
4. A specific topic, activity, or goal for the discussion is clearly stated.
5. All participants know the rules for contributing to the discussion.

These characteristics indicate why the discussion at the beginning of the chapter was not effective. First, there were no open-ended questions worthy of authentic discussion. They were merely assessment questions that elicited either a correct or an incorrect response. Second, there was no shared authority or control of turns between the teacher and students, with John serving as arbiter in the matters of interpreting the text and leading the discussion. Third, there was no interaction between Malik and Lauren nor any of the other students who presumably listened as the "discussion" unfolded. Fourth, although there was a stated purpose of reviewing the short story, there was no clear goal or outcome for engaging in this discussion. Finally, there was evidence that at least one student (Malik) didn't understand the rules of contributing to the discussion when he didn't raise his hand to respond. Now that we have established what a discussion should and should not look like, we turn our attention to meeting the CCR standards for discussion.

STANDARDS FOR DISCUSSION

In Chapter 1 we introduced the CCR anchor standards to which we have been attending throughout this book. In addition to reading and writing, we believe that it is important for all content-area teachers to be familiar with the CCR standards for speaking and listening, which outline requirements for developing students' oral communication and collaboration skills. One standard in particular, Anchor Standard 1, is especially relevant when considering the role of discussion in improving comprehension of content-area texts (Fisher & Frey, 2014b).

Anchor Standard 1 requires students to "prepare for and participate effectively in a range of conversations and collaborations with diverse partners, building on others' ideas and expressing their own clearly and persuasively" (NGA & CCSSO, 2010, p. 22). There is a lot to unpack there. We find it especially helpful to look at the specific requirements delineated in a particular grade-level standard. Take, for example, speaking and listening standard 1 in grades 9 and 10 (see Figure 6.1). At this level, students are expected to participate in collaborative discussions as part of a whole class, small group, and with a partner on a variety of topics, texts, and issues. There are other expectations as well, including (1) coming prepared to participate in a discussion by having read the text in advance; (2) working with peers to set clear rules, goals, and roles for participants to abide by throughout the discussion; (3) propelling conversations by questioning and responding, incorporating others into discussion, and evaluating others' ideas; and (4) responding to others' views while supporting one's own views with reasons and evidence.

These expectations are undoubtedly aggressive, but they are also attainable. It is important to note that teachers should look at the standards for the grade level that they teach when planning classroom discussions. It is also important

Comprehension and Collaboration	
1	Initiate and participate effectively in a range of collaborative discussions (one-on-one, in groups, and teacher-led) with diverse partners on grades 9–10 topics, texts, and issues, building on others' ideas and expressing their own clearly and persuasively.
1.A	Come to discussions prepared, having read and researched material under study; explicitly draw on that preparation by referring to evidence from texts and other research on the topic or issue to stimulate a thoughtful, well-reasoned exchange of ideas.
1.B	Work with peers to set rules for collegial discussions and decision making (e.g., informal consensus, taking votes on key issues, presenting alternate views), clear goals and deadlines, and individual roles as needed.
1.C	Propel conversations by posing and responding to questions that relate the current discussion to broader themes or larger ideas; actively incorporate others into the discussion; and clarify, verify, or challenge ideas and conclusions.
1.D	Respond thoughtfully to diverse perspectives, summarize points of agreement and disagreement, and, when warranted, qualify or justify their own views and understanding and make new connections in light of the evidence and reasoning presented.

FIGURE 6.1. CCR speaking and listening standard 1 in grades 9 and 10.

to note that we have chosen to situate text-based discussion as an after-reading activity following the building of background knowledge before reading and the use of a supportive during-reading framework to promote comprehension. This instructional choice will go a long way toward ensuring that students come to discussions prepared. The discussion formats we have selected for this chapter will ensure that students are actually able to participate. Before we get to those, however, we address two important decisions teachers will have to make when approaching text-based discussions.

TEXT-BASED DISCUSSION APPROACHES

In a review of the research on text-based discussion, Wilkinson and Son (2011) identified two characteristics that distinguish different approaches from each other: the degree of control between teacher and students and the stance toward the text. We view these characteristics as equally important decisions that should be tied to teachers' instructional objectives.

The first question is a matter of who is controlling the discussion—the teacher or the students. A number of factors are at play here, including who decides on the topic and the text that will serve as the basis of discussion, who has the authority in terms of interpreting the meaning of the text, and who controls the order and timing of participants' turns (Lawrence & Snow, 2011; Wilkinson

FIGURE 6.2. Degree of control in discussions.

& Son, 2011). The degree of control can be thought of as a continuum, with teacher-controlled discussions at one end, student-controlled discussions at the other end, and shared control in the middle (see Figure 6.2). Another way of thinking about this is a choice between whole-class discussions on one end and small-group discussions on the other.

There are benefits and drawbacks to each approach. Teacher-led, whole-class discussions might be easier to manage, but students might not have as many opportunities to participate, as in the example discussion at the beginning of the chapter. Student-led, small-group discussions allow the teacher to serve as more of a facilitator while students play a larger role in discussion, but with that arise concerns about classroom management. Yet another approach is shared control in which the teacher takes primary responsibility for some decisions, while students take responsibility for other aspects of the discussion. As you will see in the following sections, the instructional strategies we have selected take a clear position on who controls the discussion.

The other question regards the purpose of the discussion, or what stance is taken toward the text: an expressive stance, an efferent stance, or a critical–analytic stance (Murphy, Wilkinson, Soter, Hennessey, & Alexander, 2009; Wilkinson & Son, 2011). These three approaches to text-based discussion are represented in Figure 6.3. An *expressive* stance toward the text, also referred to as an aesthetic stance, is based on Rosenblatt's (1978) reader-response theory. The focus of discussion is for readers to express their affective response or emotional connections to a work of literature. An *efferent* stance, also based on the work of Rosenblatt (1978), focuses on readers acquiring and retrieving information from the text. Finally, a *critical–analytic* stance leads to discussions focused on "interrogating or querying the text in search of the underlying arguments, assumptions, worldviews, or beliefs" (Murphy et al., 2009, p. 742). As you can see in Figure 6.3, these stances can be represented along the same continuum as degree of control, with teachers largely controlling efferent discussions, students controlling expressive discussions, and teachers and students sharing control in critical-analytic discussions (Wilkinson & Son, 2011).

FIGURE 6.3. Stances toward text in discussions.

At this point you might be wondering which approach to text-based discussion is best. Research shows that efferent approaches were the most effective for improving literal- and inferential-level comprehension, and critical–analytic approaches were the most effective for improving critical thinking, reasoning, and argumentation skills, especially for students with reading difficulties (Murphy et al., 2009; Wilkinson & Son, 2011). What about expressive discussions? Alexander and Fox (2011) argue that although student-controlled approaches such as Book Clubs (Raphael & McMahon, 1994) and Literature Circles (Daniels, 2002) have the potential to increase student talk (e.g., Maloch, 2002), there is little evidence of their effectiveness in improving comprehension. The research shows that simply increasing the amount of student talk does not necessarily lead to increased comprehension (Murphy et al., 2009). Further, at least one study suggests that Literature Circles might not be an effective approach for improving comprehension for students with reading difficulties (Marshall, 2006).

Although adopting a critical–analytic stance and taking shared control of the discussion have clear advantages, we acknowledge that this approach can be challenging to implement. There are also instances in which teachers might want to adopt more of a teacher-controlled or student-controlled discussion format. In the following sections, we present instructional strategies for conducting different types of discussions that vary in how much control is given to the teacher or to the students. However, we think it is helpful to first provide an example of a large-scale effort to promote high-level comprehension through small-group discussion.

Quality Talk

To illustrate how text-based discussion can support higher levels of comprehension, we want to introduce you to an intervention called Quality Talk (QT). Although QT was first developed to improve comprehension in upper-elementary ELA classes (Li et al., 2016; Murphy et al., 2018b), it has also been shown to improve critical–analytic thinking and written argumentation in high school science (Murphy et al., 2018a). Like CSR (see Chapter 5), QT is an instructional model that uses a B-D-A framework to support students as they engage in critical–analytic, text-based discussions in small groups. The four components of the QT instructional model are represented in Figure 6.4.

The first component of QT is the *instructional frame*, which is built around shared control between the teacher and students. The teacher chooses the text and topic and builds students' background knowledge before the discussion. During the discussion, the teacher facilitates as students engage in small-group discussion, encouraging them to adopt expressive, efferent, and critical–analytic stances (Murphy et al., 2018b). It is important to note that students are grouped heterogeneously by ability level. Research on QT showed that heterogeneous groups were more effective than homogeneous groups at promoting higher levels

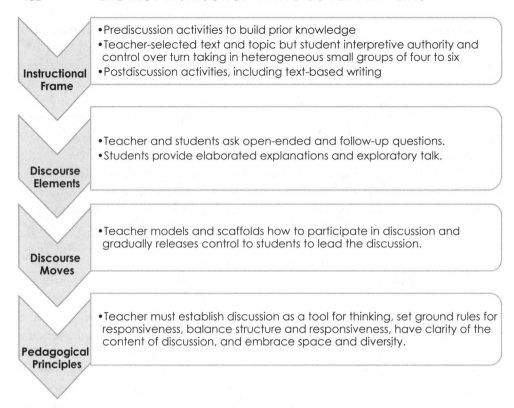

Instructional Frame
- Prediscussion activities to build prior knowledge
- Teacher-selected text and topic but student interpretive authority and control over turn taking in heterogeneous small groups of four to six
- Postdiscussion activities, including text-based writing

Discourse Elements
- Teacher and students ask open-ended and follow-up questions.
- Students provide elaborated explanations and exploratory talk.

Discourse Moves
- Teacher models and scaffolds how to participate in discussion and gradually releases control to students to lead the discussion.

Pedagogical Principles
- Teacher must establish discussion as a tool for thinking, set ground rules for responsiveness, balance structure and responsiveness, have clarity of the content of discussion, and embrace space and diversity.

FIGURE 6.4. QT components.

of comprehension, especially for students with reading difficulties (Murphy et al., 2017). Students engage in text-based writing activities after the discussion, which not only promotes comprehension but also improves written argumentation (Firetto et al., 2019; Murphy et al., 2018a; Wei et al., 2019).

The *discourse elements* that teachers and students use when participating in discussion are the second component of QT. Murphy and colleagues (2018b) refer to these as "tools for facilitating critical–analytic thinking" (p. 1121). The discourse elements constitute different types of open-ended questions and responses that participants are expected to produce. Teachers model how to use these tools until students are able to use them on their own. Here is a list of the discourse elements used in the QT model (Murphy et al., 2018b):

- *Authentic question:* The asker does not know how the responder will answer.
- *Test question:* The asker expects the responder to provide a specific answer.
- *Uptake question:* The asker follows up on a responder's contribution to the discussion.
- *High-level thinking question:* The asker expects the responder to generalize or analyze.

- *Speculation question:* The asker expects the responder to consider potential options.
- *Affective question:* The asker expects the responder to share his or her feelings or experiences.
- *Intertextual question:* The asker expects the responder to make a text-to-text connection.
- *Shared knowledge question:* The asker expects the responder to refer to prior knowledge.
- *Elaborated explanation:* The responder states a claim supported by reasons and evidence.
- *Exploratory talk:* Two or more responders co-construct understanding together.

The third component is the *discourse moves* that teachers use when leading small-group discussions. The teacher initially controls the discussion through use of specific moves but then gradually employs them less frequently as students begin to learn how to participate in a QT discussion on their own (Murphy et al., 2018b). Wei, Murphy, and Firetto (2018) synthesized the research on small-group discussions, providing the following list of effective discourse moves:

- *Backchanneling:* The teacher lets students know that he or she is listening using a few words.
- *Challenging:* The teacher encourages students to consider a different point of view.
- *Checking:* The teacher makes sure that students have a literal understanding of the text.
- *Clarifying:* The teacher refines a student's response and asks the student to state it more clearly.
- *Debriefing:* The teacher summarizes students' performance at the end of the discussion.
- *Instructing:* The teacher provides explicit instruction on discussion skills or text content.
- *Marking:* The teacher points out and praises a student's use of a discourse element.
- *Modeling:* The teacher explicitly shows students how to use a discourse element.
- *Procedural:* The teacher manages the focus and flow of the discussion (e.g., turn taking).
- *Prompting:* The teacher helps a student provide an elaborated explanation.
- *Reading:* The teacher reads a portion of the text aloud to reference in the discussion.
- *Summarizing:* The teacher provides an overview of students' responses in the discussion.

The fourth component of the QT model is a set of *pedagogical principles*. Murphy and colleagues (2018b) suggest five principles by which to abide when leading discussions: (1) communicate that discussion is a tool for thinking, (2) establish a set of ground rules for responsiveness (e.g., no need to raise hands and respect the opinions of other participants), (3) maintain a balance of structure and student responsiveness through discourse moves, (4) ensure that the teacher has clarity of the content and is prepared to ask questions, and (5) embrace space and diversity by encouraging students to discuss their own backgrounds and experiences.

These four components, which are embedded within professional development and mini lessons on questioning and argumentation, constitute the QT model. We encourage you to visit their website (*www.qualitytalk.psu.edu*), which provides a description of the project, as well as videos, lesson plans, and publications, to learn more about the program. We understand that many teachers will not implement the full program. However, we describe QT here because we feel that it provides the best instructional model for implementing text-based discussions. You will see that many of the components of the QT approach can be easily integrated within the instructional strategies we have chosen for this chapter. Next, we describe different approaches to text-based discussions that can be readily implemented in secondary classrooms.

Reciprocal Questioning

The first strategy we have chosen should be fairly easy to implement for teachers who are just getting their feet wet with different discussion formats. Although the teacher maintains control of the discussion, the tables are turned by having students ask the questions. The strategy, Reciprocal Questioning (ReQuest), was originally developed and tested by Manzo (1969) in one-on-one tutoring sessions, but it has also been used in whole-class and small-group formats (Kay, Young, & Mottley, 1986; Manzo, 1973, 1985). If you are thinking that the name sounds familiar, Manzo's (1969) research on the ReQuest procedure led to the development of Reciprocal Teaching (RT; Palincsar & Brown, 1984), which we discussed in Chapter 5.

The ReQuest procedure has five steps (Manzo, 1969). They are represented as a cycle in Figure 6.5. First, the teacher and students read a text segment silently. The segment could be as brief as a single sentence or as long as a few paragraphs. After reading, students take turns asking the teacher questions about the text. Some students will likely try to "stump" the teacher by asking difficult questions. In the third step, the teacher answers the students' questions without looking back at the text. We hope you can predict why it is especially important for the teacher to read the text ahead of time and be prepared for the discussion! In the fourth step, the roles are reversed. In a true reciprocal fashion, the teacher now asks questions of the students. In the final step, students answer the questions

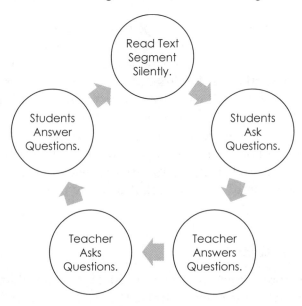

FIGURE 6.5. ReQuest cycle.

without looking back at the text. This cycle is repeated with each successive text segment until the teacher and students discuss the entire text.

In order to prevent ReQuest from becoming a rapid-fire exchange of literal-level questions, teachers have to model and scaffold how to ask good questions. The work of Alison King on guided reciprocal peer-questioning with students in fourth grade through college provides an example of the types of questions students should be taught to generate. Her research shows that teaching students how to ask questions with the aid of question stems led them to generate more critical thinking questions and respond with more elaborated explanations, as well as higher levels of comprehension (King, 1990, 1994). Teachers might choose to display the following question stems from King and Rosenshine (1993, p. 134) to help students ask questions:

- "Explain why. . . ."
- "Explain how. . . ."
- "How does . . . affect . . . ?"
- "Why is . . . important?"
- "How are . . . and . . . similar?"
- "How do . . . and . . . differ?"
- "Describe. . . ."
- "What does . . . mean?"
- "What is a new example of . . . ?"
- "What do you think would happen if . . . ?"
- "Why is . . . better than . . . ?"

ReQuest has the potential to be a powerful alternative to teacher-led IRE discussions, but we have found that it can easily fall into some of the same traps. However, these traps can be avoided with deliberate instructional choices. If you find that one or more students dominates the conversation, for example, you can increase student participation by having them ask and answer questions of each other. While ReQuest can be implemented with a whole class, it can also be used in small groups or pairs. Students can engage in a ReQuest discussion in heterogeneous groups following RT or in collaborative pairs following PALS (see Chapter 5), with each student taking turns role-playing as the teacher. It is hard to imagine another discussion framework that can be used in as many situations as ReQuest.

Questioning the Author

Questioning the Author (QtA) is another effective instructional strategy for teachers who would prefer to maintain control over the discussion. QtA (Beck, McKeown, Hamilton, & Kucan, 1997; Beck, McKeown, & Sandora, 2021; McKeown, Beck, & Worthy, 1993) is similar to ReQuest in that its goal is to teach students how to answer questions about texts. QtA engages readers through open-ended *queries* posed to the author of a text. Although it was originally developed and tested in fourth-grade ELA and social studies classes (Beck, McKeown, Sandora, Kucan, & Worthy, 1996), QtA has been implemented in grades 3–9 (Beck & McKeown, 2001; Sandora et al., 1999).

QtA comprises four instructional features. First, the teacher has to communicate to students that text is "the product of a fallible author, as someone's ideas written down" (Beck & McKeown, 2001, p. 229). In other words, comprehending is not just about understanding the words that a *fallible author* writes but also the ideas they attempt to communicate. Instead of putting authors on a pedestal, teachers need to help students to understand that, like other human beings, authors make mistakes and sometimes fail to effectively communicate their ideas.

The second feature of QtA is a set of *open-ended queries* that the teacher asks periodically while reading a text (see Figure 6.6). The teacher decides how to chunk a text during reading, pausing to pose initiating queries to help students think critically about the text. Initiating queries usually begin with the words "What is the author . . . ?" Although teachers might use the question stems in Figure 6.6 when first trying QtA, they can devise their own initiating queries that prompt students to discuss the author's message. When students respond to an initiating query, the teacher encourages elaborated explanations by asking follow-up queries that prompt them to integrate and connect two or more ideas in the text or ideas in the text with their background knowledge. Follow-up queries like "Does this make sense with what the author told us before?" help students to build meaning based on previously understood ideas (Beck et al., 1997, p. 38). While the initial and follow-up queries are flexible enough to use with

Initiating Queries
• "What is the author trying to say here?" • "What is the author's message?" • "What is the author talking about?"
Follow-Up Queries
• "What does the author mean here?" • "Did the author explain this clearly?" • "Does this make sense with what the author told us before?" • "How does this connect with what the author has told us before?" • "Does the author tell us why?" • "Why do you think the author tells us this now?"
Narrative Queries
• "How do things look for this character now?" • "How has the author let you know that something has changed?" • "How has the author settled this for us?" • "Given what the author has already told us about this character, what do you think he's up to?"

FIGURE 6.6. QtA queries. Adapted with permission from Beck, McKeown, and Sandora (2021). Copyright © 2021 The Guilford Press.

narrative and informational texts, QtA also includes a set of follow-up queries that are specific to the purpose and structure of narrative texts (see Figure 6.6).

Before continuing with the remaining features, let's take a look at an example of how QtA differs from a traditional teacher-led IRE sequence. To illustrate, we will return to the example of John's ninth-grade ELA class at the beginning of the chapter. Consider the opening paragraphs of "The Most Dangerous Game," a short story by Richard Connell:

> "Off there to the right—somewhere—is a large island," said Whitney. "It's rather a mystery—"
>
> "What island is it?" Rainsford asked.
>
> "The old charts call it Ship-Trap Island," Whitney replied. "A suggestive name, isn't it? Sailors have a curious dread of the place. I don't know why. Some superstition—"
>
> "Can't see it," remarked Rainsford, trying to peer through the dank tropical night that was palpable as it pressed its thick warm blackness in upon the yacht.
>
> "You've good eyes," said Whitney, with a laugh, "and I've seen you pick off a moose moving in the brown fall bush at four hundred yards, but even you can't see four miles or so through a moonless Caribbean night."
>
> "Nor four yards," admitted Rainsford. "Ugh! It's like moist black velvet."

Now consider how John's whole-class discussion would have differed by using QtA:

JOHN: Let's figure out the author's message in the opening paragraphs of "The Most Dangerous Game." Look at when Whitney says, "and I've seen you pick off a moose moving in the brown fall bush at four hundred yards, but even you can't see four miles or so through a moonless Caribbean night." What is the author trying to say here? (*Malik raises his hand, and John calls on him to answer.*)

MALIK: He's trying to say that Rainsford could pick off a moose in the woods, but he couldn't see four miles in the moonless Caribbean night.

JOHN: Yes, Malik. That's what the author says, but what does the author mean here? (*Malik raises his hand again. Lauren is looking in the text for the answer.*)

MALIK: Well, maybe he means that it's really dark out because there's no moon?

JOHN: Is that it? Is that all the author wanted us to know? What do you think, Lauren?

LAUREN: No, he also wants us to know that Rainsford has good eyes. He wants us to know that Rainsford could shoot a moose in the woods from far away.

JOHN: That's right. Why do you think the author tells us this now? Malik?

MALIK: I think he's trying to tell us two things. Rainsford is a good hunter because he has good eyes, and it's so dark and foggy that even he can't see Ship-Trap Island.

LAUREN: So, he's trying to tell us something about Rainsford as a character and the setting?

JOHN: That's right, Lauren and Malik. The author didn't tell us that Rainsford was a good hunter or that it was foggy, but you figured that out from his words. Let's read on to see what else the author tells us about Rainsford and Ship-Trap Island.

This QtA discussion was certainly a different experience than what actually occurred in John's classroom as a first-year teacher. Instead of asking surface-level questions about story elements in this example, he queried his students about a specific sentence in the text. Malik responded to the initial query by restating literal details from the story, but John posed a follow-up query to challenge Malik and Lauren to think about the meaning of the text. Through additional follow-up queries, he built more of a discussion about the two ideas Connell conveyed, as well as the narrative elements established in the beginning of the story. We admit that QtA, in our own experiences, can be difficult to implement well. However, we hope that you see that staying close to the text and asking questions about the author's intent can lead to rich discussion.

The third instructional feature of QtA, as you likely noticed in the previous example, is that it occurs *during reading,* going back and forth from reading a text segment to discussion (Beck & McKeown, 2001). This is one way in which QtA differs from the postreading discussions that we present in the following sections of the chapter. However, like ReQuest, we see no reason why teachers couldn't use a supportive during-reading framework like RT or PALS and then lead a QtA discussion while strategically rereading important text segments.

The last feature of QtA is that it is a *discussion* for the purpose of constructing meaning (Beck & McKeown, 2001). In addition to the queries that teachers pose, QtA includes six teacher discussion moves to help students construct understanding of a text (Beck et al., 1997):

1. *Marking:* The teacher points out important ideas in a student's comment.
2. *Turning back:* The teacher turns the discussion back to the students' ideas or to the text.
3. *Revoicing:* The teacher rephrases a student's ideas that are not expressed clearly.
4. *Modeling:* The teacher shows students how skilled readers make sense of text.
5. *Annotating:* The teacher adds missing information to help students understand the text.
6. *Recapping:* The teacher summarizes the ideas in a text segment before moving on.

Earlier we mentioned that effective classroom discussions require thoughtful planning. Indeed, planning a QtA discussion takes a considerable amount of time and effort. Beck and colleagues (1997) describe three steps: (1) identify important ideas in the text and anticipate potential difficulties students will have comprehending the text, (2) segment the text into logical chunks based on important ideas, and (3) develop queries to help students understand the important ideas. It is also true that, between queries and discussion moves, the teacher is doing a lot of the talking. Despite increasing teacher talk, QtA is one of the most effective whole-class discussion approaches for improving students' comprehension (Beck et al., 1996; Murphy et al., 2009). We think the time spent planning and conducting a QtA discussion is worth it. However, we now turn to small-group discussion formats in which students do most of the talking.

Collaborative Reasoning

Collaborative Reasoning (CR) is an effective approach for facilitating small-group discussions that promote students' oral argumentation skills. Although CR was originally developed and tested in upper-elementary grades (Chinn, Anderson, & Waggoner, 2001; Waggoner, Chinn, Yi, & Anderson, 1995), it has also proven effective in middle school (Coker & Erwin, 2011). CR takes a critical–analytic stance toward the text, with discussions that enable students to consider a controversial issue from multiple perspectives (Waggoner et al., 1995). Therefore, the only requirement for conducting a CR discussion is that the text must allow for students to take two or more positions on a central question related to the topic.

CR is a relatively easy strategy to implement. The seven steps for facilitating a CR discussion are presented in Figure 6.7. First, students read a text silently and form small groups (Chinn et al., 2001; Clark, Anderson, & Kuo, 2003). As in QT, we recommend forming heterogeneous small groups composed of students of mixed ability levels (Murphy et al., 2017). Teachers can use the same procedures to create small groups that we outlined for forming RT groups in Chapter 5. In addition, like ReQuest and QtA, we think that teachers can use a supportive during-reading framework like RT or PALS in place of silent reading. When small groups are formed, the teacher lays out five ground rules for a CR discussion (Clark, Anderson, & Kuo, 2003, pp. 184–185):

1. Stick to the topic.
2. Do not talk when others are talking.
3. Try to look at both sides of the issue.
4. Make sure everyone has a chance to participate.
5. Respond to the idea and not the person.

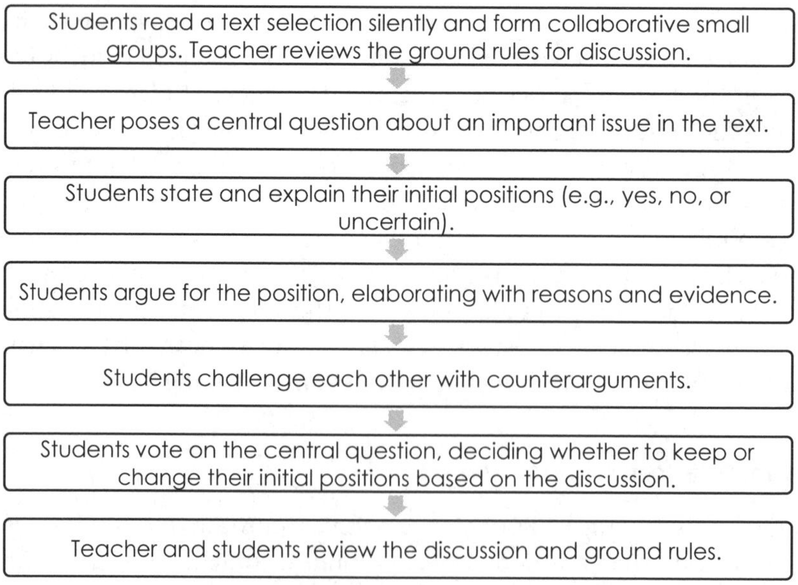

Students read a text selection silently and form collaborative small groups. Teacher reviews the ground rules for discussion.

Teacher poses a central question about an important issue in the text.

Students state and explain their initial positions (e.g., yes, no, or uncertain).

Students argue for the position, elaborating with reasons and evidence.

Students challenge each other with counterarguments.

Students vote on the central question, deciding whether to keep or change their initial positions based on the discussion.

Teacher and students review the discussion and ground rules.

FIGURE 6.7. Steps for facilitating CR.

The purpose of these ground rules is to promote open participation. During the CR discussion, students do not raise their hands to speak (Chinn et al., 2001; Clark et al., 2003). To start the conversation, the teacher poses a central question on which students take an initial position. For example, if John's ninth-grade ELA class engaged in a CR discussion after reading "The Most Dangerous Game," he might have posed the question "Do you think that Rainsford's views on hunting have changed as a result of the events in the story?" In their small groups, students would state and explain their initial position on the central question, whether it be "yes," "no," or "uncertain." Students take turns arguing for their position, providing reasons and evidence from the text, as well as their own experiences, to elaborate upon their explanations (Waggoner et al., 1995). In addition, students take turns challenging their groupmates' positions by forming counterarguments and rebuttals (Clark et al., 2003). While students engage in discussion, the teacher primarily takes the role of a facilitator. However, the teacher can also join the small groups and use discourse moves to promote discussion such as prompting, modeling, asking for clarification, challenging, encouraging, and summing up (Waggoner et al., 1995).

At the end of a CR discussion, the teacher reconvenes the small groups in a whole-class format. First, the teacher takes a final poll in which students vote on the central question (Clark et al., 2003). Importantly, students can decide whether to stick with their initial position or change it based on the persuasiveness of the reasons and evidence presented in their small-group discussion (Chinn et al., 2001). To conclude the discussion, the teacher reviews the results of the discussion and whether students followed the ground rules. Then the teacher provides students with suggestions for how to improve the quality of future discussions (Clark et al., 2003).

Planning a CR discussion is easier than planning other discussion formats, but there are still important decisions to make in advance. Zhang and Dougherty Stahl (2011) provide three tips for planning: (1) select a complex text about a controversial issue that is important to students, (2) design a central question that requires a yes–no answer or multiple questions for different text segments, and (3) prepare an argument outline of the possible positions, reasons, and evidence to help facilitate discussion. These tips are straightforward enough that CR can potentially be used with any content-area text. In addition, CR is one of the most effective approaches for increasing student talk and improving their oral and written argumentation skills (Chinn et al., 2001; Morris et al., 2018; Murphy et al., 2009; Reznitskaya et al., 2001), making it an excellent choice for a postreading activity prior to text-based argumentative writing (which we cover in Chapter 7).

Discussion Web

The final strategy we have chosen to highlight is one of our personal favorites to use in our own secondary teaching. Like CR, Discussion Web (Alvermann,

1991) is an approach that encourages students to take a position on a central question or issue. Discussion Web has been shown to improve the ability of high school students to engage in reasoned argument about literature as well as learning about science content (Alvermann, Hynd, & Qian, 1995; Heron-Hruby, Trent, Haas, & Allen, 2018). Not only is Discussion Web one of our favorites, it is also perceived as one of the most effective strategies among preservice social studies teachers (Sewell, 2013).

Two characteristics of Discussion Web distinguish it from other strategies. First, students participate in a range of collaborative discussions throughout the activity, moving from a one-on-one discussion with a partner to a student-led, small-group discussion and ending with a teacher-led, whole-class discussion. Second, students are aided in their postreading discussion through the completion of a graphic organizer (see Figure 6.8). As a result, students engage in reading, writing, speaking, and listening throughout the activity (Alvermann, 1991).

Implementing the Discussion Web strategy is as easy as following a five-step procedure (see Figure 6.9). Like QT, the Discussion Web procedure uses a B-D-A framework. First, the teacher builds background knowledge, previews vocabulary, and sets a purpose for reading a content-area text (Alvermann, 1991). We recommend using the before-reading strategies described in Chapter 4 during this step. In addition, we suggest using one of the during-reading strategies described in Chapter 5 to accomplish the reading portion of the activity.

The second step for implementing Discussion Web is to pose a central question about the text and introduce the graphic organizer (Alvermann, 1991). Like CR, this is often a yes–no or a pro–con question that requires students to consider two positions. For this step, the teacher places students in collaborative pairs. Students write the question in the center of the graphic organizer and then list an equal number of reasons in the "yes" and "no" columns with their partner. It is important to note that students should only list key words and phrases in the graphic organizer, not complete sentences. However, their reasons should be based on textual evidence.

After students have had time to list reasons, each pair joins another pair to complete the third step of the Discussion Web activity (Alvermann, 1991). This newly formed small group of four students works together to compare their graphic organizers. Group members should share their reasons for and against the central question or issue. Then the group is asked to reach a group consensus, or general agreement, which they write in the graphic organizer. Their conclusion does not have to be unanimous, as any dissenting views are shared in the next step.

For the fourth step of the Discussion Web strategy, the teacher reconvenes the small groups for a whole-class discussion (Alvermann, 1991). Each group nominates a spokesperson, who has approximately 3 minutes to share the group's consensus and the best reason that supports their position. It is important that students only share one reason not only for the sake of time but also to ensure

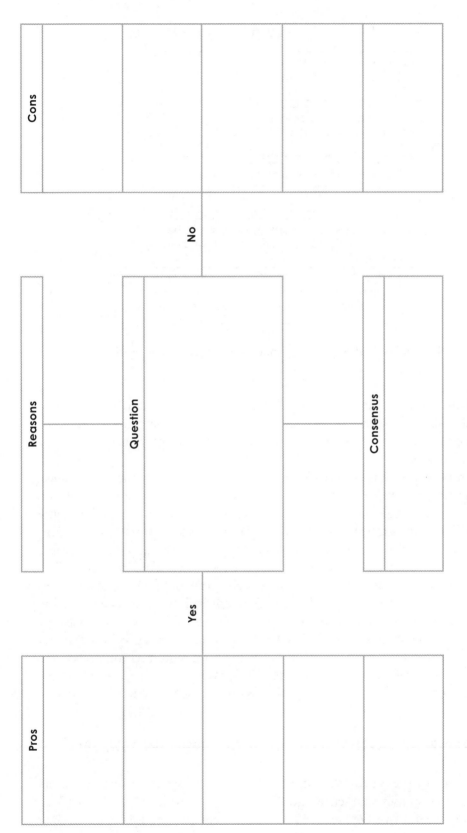

FIGURE 6.8. Discussion Web graphic organizer.

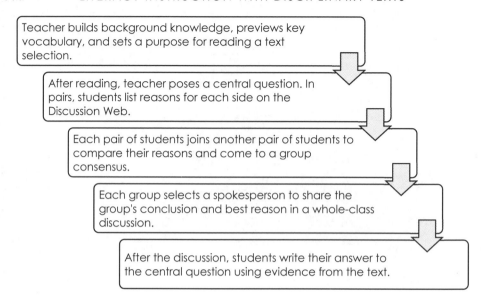

FIGURE 6.9. Procedure for implementing Discussion Web.

that each group has a reason to share that has not yet been heard. The spokesperson also shares any dissenting views held by one of the group's members. The teacher is encouraged to move beyond students sharing out to promoting a whole-class discussion.

The final step in Discussion Web is for students to answer the central question in writing (Alvermann, 1991). They do not have to argue for the position that their group initially chose. Students are encouraged to use textual evidence shared by any of the groups when completing their written response. We encourage you to follow up on a Discussion Web activity by having students write a text-based argument using the CSET strategy, which we discuss in Chapter 7.

We hope you see now why Discussion Web is one of our favorite strategies to use. It fits in seamlessly into the B-D-A framework we have been utilizing throughout this book. In our own experience, we have found, consistent with the research, that having students engage in a discussion aided by a graphic organizer before writing does the double duty of improving both high-level comprehension and written argumentation (Firetto et al., 2019; Wei et al., 2019). We turn now to describing how to use after-reading discussion strategies within quad text sets.

AFTER-READING DISCUSSIONS IN DISCIPLINARY TEXT SETS

Now that we have presented several options for conducting discussions, let's revisit the ELA, social studies, and science quad text sets we introduced in Chapter 3. In this section, we describe how teachers in each content area can follow up on their before- and during-reading strategies with effective text-based discussions. Note that we only describe some of the after-reading strategies in this chapter. The rest are text-based writing strategies covered in Chapter 7.

English Language Arts

Figure 6.10 shows the discussion strategies chosen for the ELA quad text set. After building background knowledge and then viewing the visual text, a contemporary film version of Act I, Scene i, of *Romeo and Juliet,* the teacher leads a QtA discussion about Shakespeare's decisions for establishing the characters and conflicts in the play. Because the scene is relatively brief, the teacher plays it again, pausing to pose initial and follow-up queries about the text (see Figure 6.6). For example, she asks what Shakespeare's possible message about young women in Elizabethan England is, based on how Juliet is introduced through dialogue, as well as his message about young men based on Romeo's thoughts and actions at the end of the scene. She uses discussion moves to engage her students in a robust whole-class discussion after viewing.

Although the teacher chooses to use text-based writing strategies after reading the informational and target texts, which we describe in Chapter 7, she decides to use a modified Discussion Web after reading the accessible text, selected chapters from *Eleanor and Park.* Instead of answering "yes" or "no," the teacher asks students to consider which character is more of an outsider or is considered "different" based on gendered expectations, Eleanor or Park. Students work in pairs to list textual evidence about each character in the Discussion Web graphic organizer (see Figure 6.8) before joining another pair and coming to a group consensus. Each group nominates a spokesperson to share which character was more of an outsider and why, as well as any dissenting views held by group members, as part of a whole-class discussion.

Social Studies

The discussion strategies for the social studies quad text set are shown in Figure 6.11. After previewing and then viewing the video text, "Kids Talk about Segregation," the teacher conducts a postviewing discussion. Because students have already taken notes in a small group when completing a Collaborative Listening–Viewing Guide (CLVG), which we discussed in Chapter 5, the teacher has them engage in a CR discussion (see Figure 6.7) in their small groups. She sets the ground rules for discussion and then asks students a central question: "Are the reasons for why schools are segregated provided by the kids in the video convincing?" Students explain their initial positions, as well as their reasons and evidence from their notes in their small groups. Students then challenge their group members with counterarguments before the teacher asks students to vote on the central question and reviews their positions in a whole-class discussion.

	Instructional Objective(s): Analyze how characters develop over the course of a text, interact with other characters, advance the plot, and develop the theme.	
	Visual Text: Video of Act I from contemporary film version of *Romeo and Juliet*	
Instructional Strategies	**Before Reading:** Listen–Read–Discuss	
	During Reading: Collaborative Listening–Viewing Guide	
	After Reading: Questioning the Author	
	Informational Text(s): Article on gender roles and power in Elizabethan England	
Instructional Strategies	**Before Reading:** Concept of Definition	
	During Reading: Reciprocal Teaching	
	After Reading:	
	Target Text: Act I of Shakespeare's *Romeo and Juliet*	
Instructional Strategies	**Before Reading:** K-W-L strategy	
	During Reading: Reading Guide	
	After Reading:	
	Accessible Text: Selected chapters from *Eleanor and Park* by Rainbow Rowell	
Instructional Strategies	**Before Reading:** Prereading Plan	
	During Reading: Collaborative Strategic Reading	
	After Reading: Discussion Web	
	Extended Writing:	

FIGURE 6.10. ELA quad text set with after-reading discussion strategies.

	Instructional Objective(s): Analyze historical materials to trace the development of an idea over time and explain patterns of continuity and change; determine the central idea of a primary source and accurately summarize the central idea and key details.
	Visual Text: "Kids Talk about Segregation" video
Instructional Strategies	**Before Reading:** Prereading Plan
	During Reading: Collaborative Listening–Viewing Guide
	After Reading: Collaborative Reasoning
	Informational Text(s): Article on the history of racial segregation in the United States
Instructional Strategies	**Before Reading:** Semantic Feature Analysis
	During Reading: Reciprocal Teaching
	After Reading: Discussion Web
	Target Text: *Brown v. Board of Education* decision
Instructional Strategies	**Before Reading:** Listen–Read–Discuss
	During Reading: PALS (Paragraph Shrinking)
	After Reading:
	Accessible Text: Article on racial disparities in modern U.S. public schools
Instructional Strategies	**Before Reading:** Concept of Definition
	During Reading: Reading Guide
	After Reading:
	Extended Writing:

FIGURE 6.11. Social studies quad text set with after-reading discussion strategies.

The next text in the quad text set, an informational text about the history of racial segregation in the United States, was selected to build knowledge about the differences between *de jure segregation* and *de facto segregation*. The teacher decides to use a modified Discussion Web to conduct a postreading discussion, asking students which of the two types of segregation was most responsible for America's racially segregated cities. Students work in pairs with one of their group members from their RT group to list evidence about each type of segregation in the Discussion Web graphic organizer (see Figure 6.8). Each pair meets with the other pair in their RT group to compare their evidence and come to a group consensus. The spokesperson in each group shares their position and reasons, as well as dissenting opinions, in a whole-class discussion. The teacher decides to have her students engage in text-based writing activities after reading the final two texts in this quad text set, which are presented in Chapter 7.

Science

The after-reading discussions for the quad text set on climate change are represented in Figure 6.12. The teacher decides to follow up on the Bill Nye video with a text-based summary that is described in Chapter 7. For the second text, an interactive digital text about climate change, the teacher chooses to conduct a CR discussion (see Figure 6.7) after students read the text with a reading guide in small groups. Because each student read different sections of the text and then met in new "jigsaw groups" (see Chapter 5), students are able to draw on different evidence to argue for and against their position on a central question. The teacher poses the controversial question "Is human activity a contributor to climate change?" Students state and explain their initial positions in their small groups using evidence from the text before challenging their group mates with counterarguments. At the end of the discussion, students vote on the central question. and the teacher leads a whole-class discussion to review the evidence.

For the third text, a chapter in Paulo Bacigalupi's dystopian novel *Ship Breaker,* the teacher chooses to conduct a QtA discussion. He asks students to reread particular sections of the text. He pauses to ask initiating and follow-up queries (see Figure 6.6) that prompt his students to think about what the author is trying to say about climate change when describing the setting of his fictional world. He also uses discourse moves to engage students in whole-class discussion.

The target text presents different ways to curb climate change. Because the teacher plans to have his students write an extended argument, which we describe in Chapter 8, he decides to use a modified Discussion Web after reading. The teacher asks students to select two of the five actors described in the article (individuals, businesses, cities, nations, and the world) and to determine which is more likely to make a difference in mitigating the effects of climate change. Students work in pairs to complete a Discussion Web graphic organizer (see Figure 6.8), which they fill in with evidence for each of the actors they selected. Student

	Instructional Objective(s): Construct an argument supported by evidence (e.g., patterns in graphs, charts, and images) for how humans impact Earth's systems; integrate technical information expressed in words in a text with a visual representation of that information.

Visual Text: "Climate Change 101" video with Bill Nye

Instructional Strategies	**Before Reading:** Prereading Plan
	During Reading: Collaborative Listening–Viewing Guide
	After Reading:

Informational Text(s): "Climate Change: How Do We Know?" website

Instructional Strategies	**Before Reading:** Listen–Read–Discuss
	During Reading: Jigsaw Groups with Reading Guide
	After Reading: Collaborative Reasoning

Accessible Text: Chapter 1 of *Ship Breaker* by Paolo Bacigalupi

Instructional Strategies	**Before Reading:** K-W-L strategy
	During Reading: PALS (Paragraph Shrinking)
	After Reading: Questioning the Author

Target Text: "5 Ways to Curb Climate Change" articles

Instructional Strategies	**Before Reading:** Semantic Feature Analysis
	During Reading: Reciprocal Teaching
	After Reading: Discussion Web

Extended Writing:

FIGURE 6.12. Science quad text set with after-reading discussion strategies.

pairs join another pair to compare their evidence and reach a group consensus. Each group nominates a spokesperson to share their position, evidence, and any dissenting views in a whole-class discussion.

FINAL THOUGHTS

Most secondary teachers will likely tell you that they spend a lot of time trying to get students to stop talking in class. In this chapter, we described approaches to get them to talk more. Adolescents are developmentally primed for discussion. They are cognitively able to communicate their ideas and consider issues from multiple perspectives. In order to promote high levels of comprehension after reading and to prepare students for writing, teachers could do a whole lot worse than make time for discussion. The approaches in this chapter were selected to help teachers move away from leading the IRE sequences that so many of us have had to sit through and toward conducting a range of paired, small-group, and whole-class discussions. We hope that you found something in this chapter to keep you from falling into the same old traps.

CHAPTER 7

Text-Based Writing
to Promote Comprehension

When Bill teaches his preservice teachers about summary writing, he often shares the troubles he had with this genre when he was a student in middle and high school. Back in those days, Bill "summarized" text by copying one line from the first part of the reading assignment, one from the middle, and one from the end. He then misspelled a few words so the teacher would believe that it was he who wrote the text. Although this "copy–delete" method commonly employed by some adolescent students (Brown & Day, 1983, p. 2) can be loosely considered a summary writing "strategy," it is certainly not an effective one! Besides being ineffective, this approach does not allow students to experience the true benefits of writing about the texts they read. Writing after reading provides the opportunity to synthesize key textual details in a way that significantly improves comprehension of disciplinary texts (Graham & Hebert, 2010).

It is not surprising that Bill had issues with postreading summary writing in secondary school. Although secondary students are often asked to write summaries about what they read, teachers rarely *teach* this skill to their students (Asaro-Saddler, Muir-Knox & Meredith, 2018; Kiuhara et al., 2009). And although teachers may feel that summary writing is a fairly simple and straightforward classroom activity, it actually requires balancing and organizing multiple cognitive processes that can challenge adolescent students, particularly those with writing difficulties (Mason, Kubina, Valasa, & Cramer, 2010). Students must not only comprehend the texts they read, but they must also identify key ideas and details, discard ideas that are not important, and then translate and connect textual elements in a factually accurate paraphrase that avoids the word-for-word copying that was the hallmark of Bill's early—and unsuccessful—efforts (Asaro-Saddler et al., 2018; Troia, 2014). Summarizing is hard, but its benefits lie in the cognitive effort needed to synthesize key ideas and details into a meaningful whole. As the National Commission on Writing (2003) puts it, "If students are to make knowledge their own, they must struggle with the details, wrestle with the facts, and rework raw information and dimly understood concepts into language they can communicate to someone else. In short, if students are to learn, they must write" (p. 9).

Students can only benefit from summary writing if they are *taught* how to do it. Fisher and Frey (2003) argued that teachers are more likely to "cause writing to happen" than to teach the processes and genre characteristics that develop proficient writing skills (p. 396). That is why we have dedicated two chapters of this book to writing instruction. This chapter focuses on teaching students how to produce shorter text-based written responses that can easily be worked into a B-D-A reading framework. Chapter 8 is dedicated to teaching extended writing strategies that encourage students to plan, draft, and revise longer compositions.

The goal of this chapter is to provide a menu of after-reading strategies that will not only teach students how to write but also enhance their comprehension and ability to share important disciplinary concepts with others. We begin this chapter by highlighting the kinds of writing activities that improve students' comprehension and showing why a shared responsibility for writing across content areas is so important for students' literacy development and learning. We then describe several summary writing strategies that help students to synthesize their understanding of the texts they read. Additionally, because argumentation is at the forefront of college and career readiness standards (NGA & CCSSO, 2010) and integral to learning and communicating in the disciplines (Monte-Sano & Allen, 2019; Shanahan & Shanahan, 2008), we present a strategy for composing concise text-based arguments (Lewis et al., 2014). We end the chapter by applying these strategies to our quad text sets introduced in Chapter 3.

WHY TEXT-BASED WRITING?

Although some secondary teachers believe that writing instruction is the sole purview of the ELA teacher (Asaro-Saddler et al., 2018), we want to encourage teachers of *all* content areas to include writing in their after-reading instruction. There are good reasons why you should consider this. First, students' ability to read, comprehend, *and write* about content-area material in science, social studies, and ELA is an increasingly important element of academic success in secondary school and beyond (Reynolds & Perin, 2009).

Second, as students move through their secondary programs, their progress increasingly depends on more specialized and discipline-specific ways of reading, thinking, and writing (Shanahan & Shanahan, 2008, 2012). For instance, a student who is writing a character analysis of Juliet in an ELA class is going to use different reading, writing, and evidence-gathering processes than a student in a social studies class who is analyzing segregation in contemporary school systems.

A student in an earth science class who is using data charts and graphs to analyze patterns of climate change will use processes and skills that are different from those of a student in a math class who is explaining how a mathematical function can determine a tree's age in relation to its height. If we want students to read, think, and write like experts in the disciplines, teachers need to be explicit about the ways that disciplinary experts make sense of texts and share their understanding with others. Content-area teachers are uniquely situated to teach these disciplinary skills because they are the experts in the ways of communicating in their discipline.

There is a third and equally important reason teachers should want to engage students in a higher volume of writing activities—adolescent students in the United States have impoverished writing skills. In the most recent National Assessment of Educational Progress (National Center for Education Statistics [NCES], 2012), only 27% of 8th and 12th graders scored at or above proficient in writing. Maybe more concerning is the high percentage of students who scored "below basic," with 20% of 8th graders and 21% of 12th graders achieving this lowest level of achievement. Since writing proficiently and flexibly is critical to students' success in college and the workplace (Ferretti & Graham, 2019; Graham & Perin, 2007) and important to their ability to deepen and extend their content knowledge (Shanahan & Shanahan, 2008, 2012), secondary teachers need to think hard about how to include more writing opportunities in every classroom. Just as designing quad text sets can provide students with a higher *reading* volume, teachers also need to plan instruction that provides students with a high volume of connected *writing* experiences. This volume can only be achieved if all content-area teachers include writing in their classrooms as an integral part of their B-D-A framework.

Finally, although our previous chapters have focused on before-, during-, and after-*reading* strategies, the Carnegie Corporation's *Writing to Read* report (Graham & Hebert, 2010) indicates that some *writing* activities are actually more effective than some well-accepted reading strategies for improving students' reading comprehension. In their report, Graham and Hebert (2010) determined that four categories of writing activities have demonstrated positive effects on reading comprehension. These activities are represented in Figure 7.1.

Although all four of these activities have positive impacts on comprehension, in this chapter we focus on the two activities that we believe all content-area teachers should commit to as an integral part of their daily routines: summary writing and text-based argumentative writing, which fall under "analysis and interpretation." These types of writing have the largest effects on comprehension (Graham & Hebert, 2010), and they can also improve students' writing quality when paired with strategic instruction that teaches students how to write these types of texts (Graham & Perin, 2007). For time-strapped teachers who are looking to improve students' literacy skills while also making sure they comprehend content-area material, these two writing activities are an efficient and effective use of instructional time.

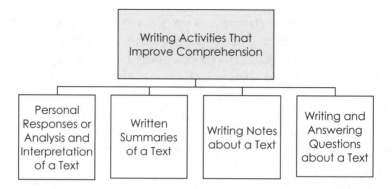

FIGURE 7.1. Writing activities that improve comprehension.

SUMMARY WRITING STRATEGIES

As you have seen, making time for summary writing has obvious benefits, but one important question remains: What strategies are best for teaching students to summarize? This is a complex question, as the research base for writing instruction is not nearly as extensive as research about building students' background knowledge or supporting comprehension during and after reading. Since one of our goals in writing this book is to ensure that all the strategies we recommend are firmly grounded in empirical research, this puts us in a bit of a quandary.

Although the individual strategies we have chosen have not been extensively studied, research into the impact of summary writing on reading comprehension provides us with a principled way to choose effective strategies for teaching this skill and then using it to support content learning. Seminal studies from the 1980s demonstrate that there are specific activities that are the hallmarks of effective summary strategy instruction (Brown & Day, 1983; Rinehart, Stahl, & Erickson, 1986). Brown and Day (1983) call these activities "macrorules" (p. 1). These rules, which we can use to guide our strategic decision making, are represented in Figure 7.2.

In a nutshell, effective summary writing strategies are those that encourage students to *select* only the most important information from a passage and then *synthesize* that information into a concise composition that captures the gist of what was read. Each of the strategies that we have chosen for this chapter is based on these summarization rules.

Magnet Summaries

One of the most effective strategies that we have used in our work in secondary schools is Magnet Summaries (Buehl, 1993, 2014). However, it is important to note that when explicitly teaching this strategy to your students (or any strategy in this chapter), we suggest following a *gradual release of responsibility* model of instruction (Pearson & Gallagher, 1983), which in the field is simply called the "I

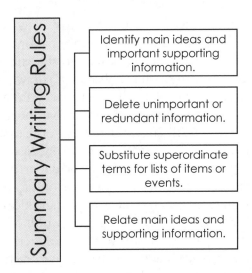

FIGURE 7.2. Rules for summary strategies.

do, we do, you do" approach (Webb, Massey, Goggans, & Flajole, 2019). In this case, the teacher first explains the importance of the strategy, explicitly teaches its steps, and models the use of the strategy on sample reading passages (I do). Next, the teacher provides opportunities for students to engage in collaborative practice (we do). Finally, the teacher slowly transfers responsibility for independent use of the strategy to students (you do). Writing researchers suggest adding one more item to the "you do" step—reflection (Graham et al., 2016). While students take on increasing responsibility for independently using a strategy, they must also be given time to reflect on and evaluate the effectiveness of that strategy.

The Magnet Summaries strategy is presented in Figure 7.3. To begin teaching the strategy using explicit instruction, first follow Buehl's (2014) advice by

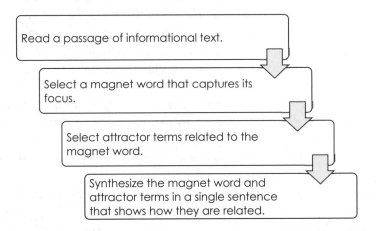

FIGURE 7.3. Procedure for implementing Magnet Summaries.

introducing students to the idea of "magnet words" after reading an informational text. These are the main idea words from a passage that "attract" other supporting ideas to them. At this stage, explain to students that magnet words are often found in titles, headings, and subheadings, drawing their attention to the important text features included in what they read. Also inform students that some texts might not have explicit text features or that the magnet words might not always be found there (Buehl, 2014). Therefore, more careful examination of the text will be needed to determine the magnet word from these types of passages. After explaining this step, model and provide opportunities for students to practice identifying magnet words in short passages of informational text.

Next, explain to students that the most important ideas in the passage are most clearly related, or "attracted," to the magnet word. Model how to choose attractor terms in sample passages, explain why these terms are related to the magnet word, and then provide students collaborative practice opportunities to identify attractor terms in other sample passages. At this stage we suggest limiting students to three to five attractor terms because it forces them to select only the most important supporting information, leaving the least important information behind.

The next step is the most beneficial and also the most important. Using both the magnet word and attractor terms, teach students how to combine all the terms into a summary statement that expresses the gist of the text. At this stage it is crucial that you model the process for students, clearly explaining how you are relating each of the important ideas in the passage and synthesizing them into a meaningful whole. This is important because without careful modeling and discussion, students often create summary statements that list each of the terms one after another with no attempt to meaningfully connect them (except for the use of an occasional comma or an *and*). In order to benefit from the strategy, students must write sentences that clearly demonstrate the relationship between the magnet word and attractor terms.

You have probably noticed that the instructional segment we just described adheres to most of the summary writing rules (Brown & Day, 1983; Rinehart et al., 1986). By teaching students how to select a magnet word and attractor terms, you help them to identify main ideas and important supporting information. By limiting the number of attractor terms, you encourage them to delete (or ignore) unimportant or redundant information. By writing a summary statement that combines the magnet word and attractor terms, you nurture their ability to relate main ideas and supporting information in a single sentence that captures the gist of the text. By discussing the summaries that you and your students produce, you are also engaging them in a reflection process that contributes to an improvement in writing quality (Graham et al., 2016).

To show how the Magnet Summaries strategy can be used with content-area material, let's revisit our science teacher who is designing a unit around climate change. As you recall, the teacher chose the informational text, "Climate Change: How Do We Know?" (NASA, 2019) as an informational text to build background knowledge in his quad text set. The introduction to that text is represented in Figure 7.4.

Once students have learned how to use the strategy with sample passages, our teacher uses Magnet Summaries in his quad text set by having students look for a magnet word after reading the passage that represents its content. In this case, "climate change" is featured prominently in the title of the selection, and the idea of a changing climate is repeated several times throughout. Therefore, by just paying attention to the text features of this passage, his students are able to quickly identify *climate change* as the magnet word. At this point, the teacher writes the magnet word on the board to focus student attention on the central idea of the passage. He instructs his students to write the word in the center of a page of notes or on an index card.

Our teacher would then direct his students to reread the passage to select the attractor terms that are most clearly related to climate change. We remind you that when first using this strategy, we recommend that students choose no more than three to five words or short phrases that are "attracted" to the magnet word. This helps them to choose the most important words, and it also makes the summary statement easier to construct. We also suggest that you engage

---

Climate Change: How Do We Know?

The Earth's climate has changed throughout history. Just in the last 650,000 years there have been seven cycles of glacial advance and retreat, with the abrupt end of the last ice age about 7,000 years ago marking the beginning of the modern climate era—and of human civilization. Most of these climate changes are attributed to very small variations in Earth's orbit that change the amount of solar energy our planet receives.

The current warming trend is of particular significance because most of it is extremely likely (greater than 95 percent probability) to be the result of human activity since the mid-20th century and proceeding at a rate that is unprecedented over decades to millennia.

Earth-orbiting satellites and other technological advances have enabled scientists to see the big picture, collecting many different types of information about our planet and its climate on a global scale. This body of data, collected over many years, reveals the signals of a changing climate.

The heat-trapping nature of carbon dioxide and other gases was demonstrated in the mid-19th century. Their ability to affect the transfer of infrared energy through the atmosphere is the scientific basis of many instruments flown by NASA. There is no question that increased levels of greenhouse gases must cause the Earth to warm in response.

Ice cores drawn from Greenland, Antarctica, and tropical mountain glaciers show that the Earth's climate responds to changes in greenhouse gas levels. Ancient evidence can also be found in tree rings, ocean sediments, coral reefs, and layers of sedimentary rocks. This ancient, or paleoclimate, evidence reveals that current warming is occurring roughly ten times faster than the average rate of ice-age-recovery warming.

FIGURE 7.4. Informational text on climate change (NASA, 2019).

your students in conversations about the attractor terms they choose, encouraging them to provide rationales for their choices and helping them to understand how some choices of attractors might be better than others. For instance, in the sample science passage students could choose *cycles, warming trend, human activity, technological advances,* and *carbon dioxide* as attractor terms that are all clearly related to climate change. However, it may be the case that a student might also pick *Earth's orbit* or *instruments flown by NASA* as their attractor terms. Although these terms can be used in a summary sentence, they are not as clearly related to climate change that is caused by human activity, the key focus of this article. Encouraging students to reflect on their choices can lead to improved summary sentences.

After his students identify their attractor terms, the science teacher writes those terms on the board around the magnet word while students do the same thing on their index cards. See Figure 7.5 for an example of what this can look like.

Now that students have identified the magnet word and attractor terms and written them on their cards, the summarizing and synthesis of ideas can begin. Here the teacher encourages students to combine the magnet word and attractor terms in a single sentence that demonstrates relationships between the words *and* captures the gist of the passage. As we stated previously, this is the most difficult (and most beneficial) aspect of the strategy. Therefore, the teacher first introduces Magnet Summaries to his students and can support them by "thinking aloud" about his own synthesizing processes. By thinking aloud for his students about how he combines the terms into a meaningful whole, they are more likely to adopt that kind of strategic thinking when they write.

Thinking Aloud during Strategy Instruction

In our work in schools, we have found that secondary teachers often have trouble "thinking aloud" to their students. Think-alouds are an effective instructional activity in which the teacher models how she or he, as a proficient reader, uses

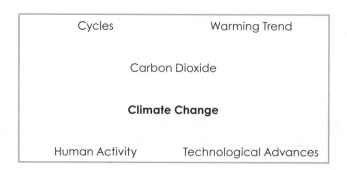

FIGURE 7.5. Sample index card with magnet word and attractor terms.

strategic knowledge to read and write about texts (Fisher, Frey, & Lapp, 2011). Instead of talking about how they make sense of texts *themselves,* however, we find that teachers often want to tell students about what *students* should be doing during these instructional activities. When using think-alouds in your instruction, we would encourage you to use *I-statements* that focus on your processes, instead of *You-statements* that focus on student activity (Gordon, 1980). To illustrate how to think aloud during the summarization process, let's take another look at our science teacher thinking aloud to his students while he constructs a summary statement on the climate change text. We suggest that as you think aloud you write your sentence on the board while students write it on the back of their index cards (see Figure 7.6). Here is his think-aloud:

"Since **climate change** is the magnet word, I think that I am going to start my summary statement with that. Now I will look for an attractor term that I can connect to it. Since science is often concerned with causes and effects, I am going to start with a cause of climate change, greater levels of **carbon dioxide**. There is more carbon dioxide in the atmosphere because of **human activity**, and that is causing climate change. Great! I have the first part of my sentence complete: *Climate change is caused by increased levels of carbon dioxide in the atmosphere brought on by human activity.* . . .

"Next, I need to think about how to include another attractor term in my summary statement. The reason we know more about climate change is because of **technological advances**. Maybe I can add that information before what I just wrote. Let's see: *Because of technological advances, scientists have been able to definitively measure climate change, which is caused by increased levels of carbon dioxide in the atmosphere and brought on by human activity.* That works!

"Now I need to think about what term to include next. Since climate change can be seen in the dangerous **warming trends** across the globe, I think that I can put that next: *Because of technological advances, scientists have been able to definitively measure climate change, which is caused by increased levels of carbon dioxide in the atmosphere brought on by human activity and has led to a sustained and dangerous warming trend.* I like that!

> Because of **technological advances**, scientists have been able to definitively measure **climate change**, which is caused by increased levels of **carbon dioxide** in the atmosphere brought on by **human activity** and has led to a sustained and dangerous **warming trend** that is much different from the natural warming and cooling **cycles** of the past.

FIGURE 7.6. Sample index card with summary statement using magnet word and attractor terms.

"But I still have the word **cycle** left. That word seemed important at first, but now I am not sure. Let's see, how does **cycle** fit with what came before? Well, the current warming trend is different than the warming and cooling cycles that happened long ago. That's why I chose that attractor term. I'll add that to the end of the sentence: *Because of technological advances, scientists have been able to definitively measure climate change, which is caused by increased levels of carbon dioxide in the atmosphere brought on by human activity and has led to a sustained and dangerous warming trend that is much different from the natural warming and cooling cycles of the past.*"

This summary statement is a long one (although, as former ELA teachers, we assure you that it is grammatically correct!). However, the key to a successful summary statement is not the relative length or brevity of what students write; it is the ability to successfully synthesize the key terms and capture the gist of the passage. Because an accurate gist statement is our goal, it is important to guide students to reflect on the summary statements they produce and to make sure that what they write is accurate. For instance, as part of her summary statement, a student might write: *Climate change is part of the natural warming and cooling cycles of the Earth.* Although this part of the statement combines both terms, it does not capture the gist of the passage, which focuses on how our current climate patterns are *much different from* the natural cycles of the past. Reflecting on and discussing these statements, therefore, provides teachers the opportunity to teach content at the same time as they are teaching students how to write summaries. After modeling this synthesis process for students, we suggest that you gradually release more responsibility to students by having them practice summarizing shorter passages in pairs or small groups before progressing to constructing Magnet Summaries of their own.

Expanding on Magnet Summaries

Once students have the basic strategy firmly in place, we can expand its use to summarize longer pieces of text or textbook chapters. This is an important element of the Magnet Summaries strategy since secondary students are required to read and comprehend increasingly longer and more complex passages as they move through secondary school and into college (NGA & CCSSO, 2010). And longer texts require more space than can be easily accommodated in one sentence. Let's use an example from social studies to demonstrate how we can expand the strategy to accommodate longer texts.

As you recall, for her quad text set on segregation, our social studies teacher chose a longer informational passage on the history of segregation in American cities. This informational text provides important historical context and background knowledge for reading her target text, the *Brown v. Board of Education* decision. However, although this 24-paragraph essay is aligned to her objectives, the text does not contain headings or subheadings that separate the text into meaningful "chunks" that can help students to more easily identify magnet words. Therefore, the teacher decides to break this text into five separate sections and write in her own headings that convey what each section is about. Now that the text is effectively chunked for instruction, she can place students into RT groups (see Chapter 5) to read each of the sections, identify the magnet word and attractor terms, and then collaboratively create summary statements for each section on the back of index cards. Once students have completed their five summary statements, they can then arrange the cards in an order that makes sense, discuss transitional phrases that link the sentences, and then collaboratively write a summary paragraph about the whole text. Writing summaries of informational texts is difficult (Taylor, 1986; Winograd, 1984). However, when students are taught how to develop individual summary statements from smaller chunks of text, the natural next step for teachers is to encourage them to combine them to produce summary paragraphs for longer passages of text or textbook chapters.

Magnet Summaries with Academic Vocabulary

We have found another helpful way to use the sentence composing element of the Magnet Summaries strategy to teach academic vocabulary. In this variation, teachers—not students—choose four to six key academic vocabulary words (see Chapter 4) from an assigned reading or classroom lecture, followed by students composing summary statements using the teacher-chosen terms. We have found this variation to be a quick and effective assessment of student comprehension and a useful introduction activity or "exit slip" (Marzano, 2012). Additionally, this variation provides us with control over the academic vocabulary terms with which we want students to engage.

For instance, when one of our ELA colleagues teaches his students about literary devices that authors use to compare one thing to another, he provides them with five key academic vocabulary terms drawn from the day's lecture (simile, metaphor, analogy, allegory, comparison) which they copy onto index cards. Before students leave class, he has them work as partners to collaboratively produce a single summary statement that synthesizes the academic vocabulary. Not only does this force students to collaboratively construct meaning from the lecture, but the teacher is also able to quickly assess if students understand the concept of literary comparison and can differentiate between the terms used to describe it. See Figure 7.7 for the academic vocabulary terms and sample summary statement derived from that activity.

Somebody Wanted But So

Unlike Magnet Summaries, which are especially useful when reading informational texts, the Somebody Wanted But So (SWBS) strategy (Macon, Bewell, &

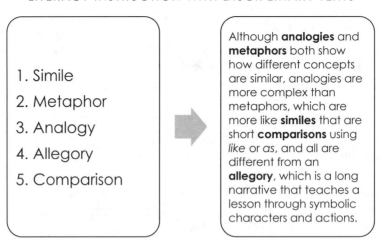

FIGURE 7.7. Sample summary statement from teacher-chosen academic vocabulary.

Vogt, 1991) was designed to help students produce concise summaries of *narrative* texts. By including a clear mnemonic scaffold, this strategy encourages students to identify the main actors in a narrative text (the *somebody*); determine their goals, motivations, or desires (what they *wanted*); identify the conflicts or barriers to achieving those goals (the *but*); and explain how these conflicts are resolved (*so* what happened?). Figure 7.8 displays a blank SWBS graphic organizer.

To illustrate, let's revisit our ELA teacher who wants her students to summarize Act I, Scene i, of *Romeo and Juliet* as part of her quad text set. She knows that this scene is important because it provides critical background knowledge about the play's main characters and the feud that serves as its backdrop. As you might recall, this scene begins with two Capulet servants provoking two Montague servants into a fight with a rude gesture which quickly escalates into an all-out street brawl. This fight eventually expands to include multiple family members and eventually the Prince of Verona himself, who brings the conflict to an end. The scene ends with Benvolio speaking with our hero, the heartbroken Romeo.

Somebody	Wanted	But	So
The main actor	The motivation or goal	The conflict or problem	How it was resolved

FIGURE 7.8. SWBS graphic organizer.

The teacher chose the SWBS strategy to focus her students on the characters' motivations when summarizing the scene. In the completed SWBS graphic organizer represented in Figure 7.9, the teacher filled in each of the "Somebody" boxes so that students would focus on these individual characters or groups of characters. The students were then responsible for completing the "Wanted," "But," and "So" boxes. To differentiate instruction, she might have also chosen to fill in more boxes for students who needed additional support and scaffolding. After students are familiar with the SWBS strategy, she may choose to not fill in any boxes at all and give students total responsibility for completing all of the boxes after reading subsequent scenes of the play.

Like Magnet Summaries, the SWBS strategy closely adheres to Brown and Day's (1983) rules of summary writing. First, providing students with the SWBS mnemonic guides them to choose only the most important details about each character's actions and motivations. Second, limiting students to a single sentence encourages them to delete extraneous or redundant information and to synthesize the details into a meaningful whole.

Although SWBS is most often used for summaries of narrative texts, we have found that the strategy can work equally well for informational texts that have a clear chronological or problem–solution text structure, especially those featuring individuals or organizations attempting to achieve goals. Additionally, math teachers have found this strategy helpful for encouraging their students to explain their problem-solving processes. Figure 7.10 offers a few SWBS examples drawn from multiple content areas, including mathematics.

Somebody	Wanted	But	So
Capulet Servants	To provoke the Montague servants into a fight	They do not want to break the law, which prohibits street violence.	One of the servants "bites his thumb," an insulting but nonviolent gesture.
Montague Servants	To maintain their honor	The Capulet servants provoked them.	They had to fight.
Benvolio	To maintain the peace	Tybalt said he hated peace and continued the brawl.	Benvolio had to continue to fight.
Tybalt	To kill all Montagues	Benvolio tried to break up the fight.	He jumped in and said he hated peace as much as he hated Montagues.
Prince Escalus	To maintain the peace of Verona	The Montagues and Capulets continued to feud and kill each other.	He made a decree that anyone caught fighting would be tortured to death.
Romeo	To marry Rosaline	She did not return his love.	Benvolio told Romeo to forget her by looking at other beautiful women.

FIGURE 7.9. SWBS graphic organizer for *Romeo and Juliet,* Act I, Scene i.

Content Area	Somebody	Wanted	But	So
Earth Science	Scientists	To prove that human activity is related to climate change	There is no climate data from before the industrial revolution.	They decided to carefully track current global temperature patterns, glacier mass, and carbon output using computers and satellites.
World History	Henry Hudson	To find an easterly passage to Asia	His crew eventually mutinied in Hudson Bay.	He was put on a small boat with loyal crew members and was never seen again.
Mathematics	A student	To find the height of a tree	But the tree was too big to physically measure.	He determined his distance from the tree, his angle of sight to the top, and then used the tangent function to figure out the tree's height.
American Literature	The narrator of "The Raven"	To know if he would ever see his dead lover again	The raven kept saying the word nevermore to all of his questions about her.	The narrator lost his mind, screamed at the raven, and ended up sitting in pain and anguish at the end of the poem.

FIGURE 7.10. SWBS examples for different content areas.

Although the SWBS strategy is easy to use and remember, we encourage you to employ the same gradual release of responsibility model that we recommended using with the Magnet Summaries strategy. This includes direct explanation of the use of the strategy, teacher modeling, collaborative and individual practice, and student reflection. Otherwise, students might produce summaries that use all of the elements of the SWBS mnemonic but are still of low quality. Take the last example in Figure 7.10. Here the student has written a robust SWBS summary that includes important details about the poem's narrator and the pain the he feels about his lost love. However, the student could just as easily have produced something like we see in Figure 7.11.

Although the student has used all of the elements of the mnemonic and has provided an accurate summary of the basic plot of this narrative poem, this summary addresses neither the narrative context nor the emotional turmoil that

Somebody	Wanted	But	So
The narrator of "The Raven"	To know who was knocking at his door	He opened it and a raven came in.	He decided to ask it questions.

FIGURE 7.11. Low-quality SWBS example.

is critical to understanding the work as a whole. Providing time for students to reflect on their summaries and evaluate which elements lead to a higher-quality product will improve their summary writing abilities (Graham et al., 2016).

RAFT Strategy

We have left the RAFT strategy for last because, unlike the previous two strategies, RAFT summaries do not require explicitly teaching students how to select the most important information from a reading or synthesize that information into a meaningful whole. Instead, RAFT summaries allow teachers to creatively engage students in various writing tasks that encourage—but don't necessarily teach—them to synthesize what they have read (Santa, 1988; Santa, Havens, & Valdes, 2004). However, an important benefit of the strategy is that it provides students with opportunities to write for different purposes and to different audiences, a key writing goal of college and career readiness standards (NGA & CCSSO, 2010). For teachers who want to develop flexible summary writing skills in their students, the RAFT strategy (Buehl, 2014) is an efficient and effective means of accomplishing this goal.

Like SWBS, the RAFT strategy is based on a simple mnemonic. After students read a text, teachers encourage them to summarize their understanding of the passage by taking on a specific *role* (R) as they write to a particular *audience* (A) in a particular *form* of writing (F) and about a specific *topic* (T) related to their reading (see Figure 7.12 for a sample RAFT strategy sheet). It is important to note that when first using this strategy it is teachers, not students, who are choosing the prompt for this writing activity. After reading, teachers assign the role, audience, format, and topic students are writing about in order to best meet the instructional objectives. Later, when students gain experience with the

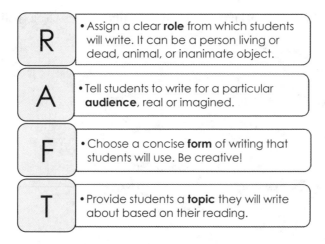

FIGURE 7.12. RAFT strategy mnemonic.

strategy, they can begin to choose their own RAFTs that are aligned to the texts they read.

Let's think about how this strategy could be used in an earth science class to help students to synthesize a short informational text passage on tsunamis from the United States Geological Survey (n.d.). The teacher chose this text to furnish his students with a clear definition of what a tsunami is and to provide them background knowledge about the causes and effects of this ocean phenomenon. For an excerpt from the passage, see Figure 7.13.

After reading this passage, the teacher decides to assign them a RAFT as an "exit slip" to assess their comprehension of the passage. Considering his adolescent students' experience with social media and wanting to engage them creatively, he assigns the RAFT prompt in Figure 7.14.

What Are Tsunamis?

Tsunamis are ocean waves triggered by large earthquakes that occur near or under the ocean, volcanic eruptions, submarine landslides, and by onshore landslides in which large volumes of debris fall into the water. Scientists do not use the term "tidal wave" because these waves are not caused by tides. Tsunami waves are unlike typical ocean waves generated by wind and storms, and most tsunamis do not "break" like the curling, wind-generated waves popular with surfers. Tsunamis typically consist of multiple waves that rush ashore like a fast-rising tide with powerful currents. Tsunami waves can travel much farther inland than normal waves. When tsunamis approach shore, they behave like a very fast moving tide that extends far inland. If a tsunami-causing disturbance occurs close to the coastline, a resulting tsunami can reach coastal communities within minutes. A rule of thumb is that if you see the tsunami, it is too late to outrun it. Even small tsunamis (for example, 6 feet in height) are associated with extremely strong currents, capable of knocking someone off their feet. As a result of complex interactions with the coast, tsunami waves can persist for many hours.

FIGURE 7.13. Informational text on tsunamis (United States Geological Survey, n.d.).

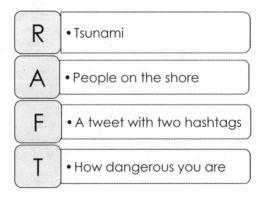

FIGURE 7.14. Sample RAFT prompt for tsunami passage.

In response to this RAFT prompt, students might produce something like this:

> A big earthquake got me on my way this morning, and my powerful waves and fast-rising tides are going to DESTROY your coast in a matter of minutes! Don't try to run if you see me! #InlandDestruction #NotATypicalWave

The 280-character limit of the tweet format forces students to choose only the most important ideas from the informational passage, jettison the least important, and then connect the main and supporting ideas in a new (and creative!) form. Thus, the RAFT strategy also adheres to the summary writing rules that have guided our strategic choices in this section (Brown & Day, 1983). Because we want students to be thoughtful about the information they include, we suggest that you choose a format that can be completed in a single sitting. Although you might choose to have students write a RAFT in the form of a poem or a 30-second infomercial, we would *not* suggest that you assign a RAFT that takes the form of a five-paragraph essay. Essays can be appropriate postreading assignments; however, the RAFT strategy does not provide the scaffolded support that students need to compose longer writing assignments. We discuss strategies for planning, revising, and editing longer compositions in Chapter 8.

It is also important to note that although adolescents will generally be familiar with the tweet format, other forms of writing might need more specific instruction and scaffolding. Doug Buehl (2014) suggests that when using the RAFT strategy, teachers should provide examples of the text formats that we want students to produce and engage them in a discussion of their salient features. For example, Figure 7.15 shows several RAFT prompts that were designed by teachers in science, mathematics, ELA, and social studies. These RAFTs were

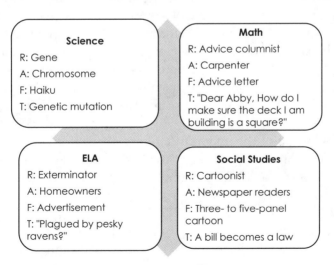

Science
R: Gene
A: Chromosome
F: Haiku
T: Genetic mutation

Math
R: Advice columnist
A: Carpenter
F: Advice letter
T: "Dear Abby, How do I make sure the deck I am building is a square?"

ELA
R: Exterminator
A: Homeowners
F: Advertisement
T: "Plagued by pesky ravens?"

Social Studies
R: Cartoonist
A: Newspaper readers
F: Three- to five-panel cartoon
T: A bill becomes a law

FIGURE 7.15. Sample RAFT prompts for different content areas.

designed based on a brief science video on gene mutation, a math textbook chapter about the Pythagorean theorem and its applications, the poem "The Raven," and a social studies textbook chapter on how a bill becomes a law. Although students probably have some experience with each of the formats in these RAFT prompts, having authentic examples on hand can give students the additional support they need to successfully complete their RAFT summaries.

Students can also sometimes have difficulty assuming the role teachers want them to take. In the RAFTs represented in Figure 7.15, students will probably not have much trouble taking the role of an advice columnist or cartoonist. However, asking them to take on the role of a gene or a tsunami can be a much more difficult task! Therefore, when using RAFTs for content-area learning, we agree with Buehl's (2014) suggestion that teachers provide students with opportunities to brainstorm their roles with other students; determine their role's traits, feelings, and beliefs; and identify the key information that their role needs to convey in the writing assignment, even if that character is an inanimate 60-foot wall of water.

ARGUMENTATIVE WRITING: THE CSET STRATEGY

The Common Core State Standards (CCSS)—and other standards that are aligned with them—mandate that students become proficient in argumentative writing and should be able to create "logical arguments based on substantive claims, sound reasoning and relevant evidence" (NGA & CCSSO, 2010, p. 41). There is a good reason why argumentative writing has become a cornerstone of state writing standards. Gerald Graff (2003) argues that argument is the "hidden curriculum" (p. 3) of all academic work at the university level. Deborah Meier (2002) goes further to state that argumentation fuels intellectual growth and understanding and is a critical element in developing the habits of mind on which civic life and democratic engagement depend. Therefore, although summary writing is critical to student comprehension of text, instructing students in how to create text-based arguments that apply their content knowledge also needs to be a focus of secondary instruction across content areas (Ferretti & Graham, 2019).

As an illustration of the importance of argumentation, let's take a look at a text-based writing prompt from one of the highest-stakes tests out there for our high school students: the SAT. The sample prompt is highlighted in Figure 7.16, which students complete after reading a seven-paragraph informational text selection (College Board, n.d.).

As you can imagine, this is a very difficult writing assignment for high school students. Not only do they have to read a challenging informational text and effectively summarize the author's argument, but they also need to analyze the author's rhetorical choices and write an analytical argument of their own that

Write an essay in which you explain how Paul Bogard builds an argument to persuade his audience that natural darkness should be preserved. In your essay, analyze how Bogard uses one or more of the features in the directions that precede the passage (or features of your own choice) to strengthen the logic and persuasiveness of his argument. Be sure that your analysis focuses on the most relevant features of the passage.

Your essay should not explain whether you agree with Bogard's claims, but rather explain how Bogard builds an argument to persuade his audience.

FIGURE 7.16. Sample SAT text-based writing prompt (College Board, n.d.).

explains how these choices strengthen the persuasiveness of the passage. It is clear that if students are going to complete this cognitively complex task—and academic tasks like it—they will need to be given ample instruction and practice in writing and evaluating interpretive claims in their content-area classrooms (Ferretti & De La Paz, 2011; Ferretti & Graham, 2019). But the question remains about how best to teach this important, standards-based skill. We have found the CSET strategy (Lewis & Ferretti, 2011; Lewis et al., 2014) to be an effective method for teaching the basics of text-based argumentative writing.

Bill originally developed a version of the CSET strategy as a way to help students in his ELA classes develop text-based arguments and then support them with *relevant* and *sufficient* evidence drawn from their reading (NGA & CCSSO, 2010). Since adolescents are naturally argumentative, he found that students were often very good at making argumentative claims about literature: "Holden Caulfield, the main character in Salinger's *Catcher in the Rye,* is a big fraud," or "The narrator in Poe's 'The Tell-Tale Heart' is insane," or "The ending of *Mockingjay* in *The Hunger Games* trilogy by Suzanne Collins is stupid!" However, Bill also found they had a much more difficult time identifying relevant textual evidence or explaining how that evidence supported their claims. He was able to successfully employ this strategy to teach this skill, and since then we have used this strategy extensively in schools to help teachers support students' ability to write text-based arguments in all content areas.

Like the SWBS or RAFT strategy, the CSET strategy is based on a clear mnemonic that provides students the basic building blocks of an argument (see Figure 7.17). Because students' knowledge of genre-specific writing goals is predictive of argumentative writing quality (Ferretti & Lewis, 2019), we designed this strategy with a clear strategic scaffold that explicitly teaches students to produce the elements that are expected in an argumentative text. Using the CSET mnemonic, students are encouraged to (1) develop a clear claim (C) about what they have read, (2) find relevant evidence in support of the claim and then provide contextual information to "set up" (S) the evidence for the reader, (3) embed that evidence (E) in the text, and (4) "tie in" (T) their evidence by explaining

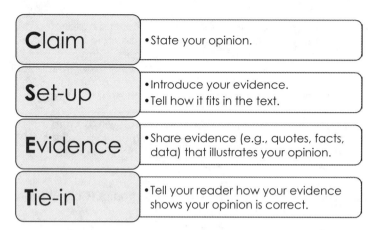

FIGURE 7.17. CSET strategy mnemonic. Adapted with permission from Lewis, Walpole, and McKenna (2014). Copyright © 2014 The Guilford Press.

how it supports their claim (Lewis et al., 2014). Like the other strategies in this chapter, we suggest that you follow a gradual release model of instruction by providing a clear rationale for using the strategy; explicitly teaching each of the CSET elements and posting the elements in your classroom; modeling the use of the strategy for students; providing students time for collaborative practice; and then gradually releasing responsibility until students can independently use the strategy for producing their own text-based arguments.

We also suggest that when introducing this strategy to students, you model and practice using the strategy with brief and easily comprehendible reading passages. In this way we can focus students on learning the *strategy* instead of bogging them down in the comprehension difficulties of a challenging disciplinary text. For instance, when John taught this strategy to his ninth-grade ELA students, he began his instruction with a fable from *The Aesop for Children* (1919), which is shown in Figure 7.18. He also gave students a simple argumentative writing prompt: "What is the moral or lesson of the fable 'The Ant and the Grasshopper'?" John was able to use this simple text and prompt to effectively model the use of the strategy, which he scaffolded with a graphic organizer (see Figure 7.19).

After modeling the strategy for students using the graphic organizer, John would use the same text but provide students the opportunity for collaborative practice using a different argumentative writing prompt: Were the Ants right to turn their backs on the Grasshopper? This time, students would complete their own graphic organizer with a partner. We provide a blank CSET graphic organizer in Figure 7.20. He chose this prompt for two reasons. First, this prompt encourages students to develop arguments based on the development of characters with conflicting motivations, an important standards-based ELA skill. Second, because the fable contains contradictory evidence, it provides students the freedom to support multiple interpretations of the text. For instance, some

The Ant and the Grasshopper

One bright day in late autumn a family of Ants were bustling about in the warm sunshine, drying out the grain they had stored up during the summer, when a starving Grasshopper, his fiddle under his arm, came up and humbly begged for a bite to eat.

"What!" cried the Ants in surprise, "haven't you stored anything away for the winter? What in the world were you doing all last summer?"

"I didn't have time to store up any food," whined the Grasshopper; "I was so busy making music that before I knew it the summer was gone."

The Ants shrugged their shoulders in disgust.

"Making music, were you?" they cried. "Very well; now dance!" And they turned their backs on the Grasshopper and went on with their work.

FIGURE 7.18. Sample passage for CSET instruction (*The Aesop for Children*, 1919).

Claim	The moral of the fable is to finish work before playing.
Set-up	In the middle of the story the Grasshopper says . . .
Evidence	"I didn't have time to store up any food" and "I was so busy making music that before I knew it the summer was gone."
Tie-in	Since there is usually a fixed amount of time to finish work, he had no time to store food for winter after playing music all summer.

The moral of the fable is to finish work before playing. In the middle of the story, the Grasshopper says that he "didn't have time to store up any food" because he "was so busy making music that . . . summer was gone." Since there is usually a fixed amount of time to finish work, the Grasshopper had no time to store food for winter after playing music all summer.

FIGURE 7.19. Completed CSET graphic organizer for sample passage.

Claim	
Set-up	
Evidence	
Tie-in	

FIGURE 7.20. CSET graphic organizer.

students might make the claim that the Ants were right to turn their backs on the Grasshopper because he was busy making music while they stored up grain during the summer. Others might argue that the Ants were wrong to shrug their shoulders in disgust and turn their backs on the starving Grasshopper who humbly asked for food. The point of this exercise is not that students make a specific claim; it is that they are able to practice supporting the claims that they do make with sufficient evidence and explanations.

Scaffolding the CSET Strategy

In the early stages of instruction, we have found that students often have the most difficulty producing effective *tie-in statements* that link their evidence to their claims. In argumentative terms, tie-ins are called *warrants* (Toulmin, 1958), statements that are commonsense rules or principles that reasonable people usually agree are true. For instance, in the sample CSET above, the teacher invokes the rule that there is generally a fixed amount of time to finish work, so reasonable people will agree that the Grasshopper should have finished work before playing. However, instead of explaining how their evidence supports their claims by invoking these commonsense rules, students often just restate or paraphrase their evidence when first learning how to produce tie-ins. Therefore, teachers need to work closely with students when teaching this important element of the mnemonic.

One way that we suggest you do this is by practicing tie-ins with easily found "picture mysteries" (Hillocks, 2011). These are visual texts that encourage students to solve a mystery by explaining how the evidence in the picture points to a solution. For example, in one picture mystery that Bill uses in his instruction, a detective is depicted contemplating a museum painting by a supposedly famous outdoor painter which the museum curator believes may be a fraud. The painting, called *Salmon Journey,* depicts a school of adult salmon swimming downstream with the current. Readers are asked to determine whether they believe that the painting is real. Using the same CSET organizer as with the fable, teachers can model and help students practice producing effective tie-in rules that link their evidence to claims (see Figure 7.21).

In this example, the tie-in actually includes two rules. The first is that adult salmon generally swim upstream, and the second is that famous outdoor painters would know this fact. Providing students this kind of evidentiary reasoning practice can be an entertaining and effective way to draw student attention to the link between evidence and claims, as well as improve their ability to write effective CSETs about content-area texts.

Expanding on the CSET Strategy

After you explicitly teach the strategy, model its use, and practice it with accessible texts, you are now able to use CSETs for creating arguments based on more challenging content-area material. For example, a science teacher may have students read an article that presents historical data about the number of tsunamis that have hit the east and west coasts, including damage figures, numbers of deaths, and wave height. After reading this text, he may have students construct a CSET

Claim	The painting is not real.
Set-up	In the painting we see . . .
Evidence	Adult salmon swimming downstream instead of upstream.
Tie-in	Since adult salmon swim upstream to spawn instead of downstream and a famous outdoor painter would know this important nature fact, this painting is probably a fake.

FIGURE 7.21. Sample CSET graphic organizer for picture mystery.

> More money should be spent on tsunami detection devices for the west coast of the United States. In the article the authors stated that there are more earthquakes in the Pacific Rim than in the Atlantic Ocean. Because earthquakes are a major cause of tsunamis, money should be funneled into areas that are more likely to experience earthquakes that cause tsunamis. Also, the article stated that on the east coast, "tsunami run-ups have been between 6 and 23 feet" (p. 3), with the west coast experiencing "tsunami run-ups as much as 33 to 55 feet" (p. 4). These water surges have killed many people in many west coast states. Because tsunami water heights are higher on the west coast and have been the cause of many deaths, more money should be funneled into the west coast where the potential for life-threatening tsunamis is more likely.

FIGURE 7.22. Sample CSET response for tsunami text.

that prompts them to argue for whether more money should be spent for tsunami detection on the west coast or the east coast. Figure 7.22 shows a sample CSET response written for this prompt.

This example shows that, with practice, students can flexibly apply the strategy to use multiple pieces of evidence in support of a claim. In the example, the student first offered paraphrased evidence about the likelihood of earthquakes, followed by quoted evidence about the relative size of tsunami heights. Both pieces of evidence were set up, and the student provided two clear tie-in statements that linked the evidence to their claims. So instead of answering this question with a simple CSET, the student expanded on the basic mnemonic to produce a CSET-SET that more thoroughly supported his point of view. By providing students additional modeling and practice, teachers can help them to use the CSET strategy to write more elaborated paragraph-length arguments or multiparagraph argumentative compositions.

TEXT-BASED WRITING IN DISCIPLINARY TEXT SETS

Now that we have a menu of text-based writing strategies that encourage students to summarize and synthesize their understanding of challenging disciplinary texts, let's revisit our quad text set examples in ELA, social studies, and science to see how teachers use text-based summary writing and argumentative writing strategies to achieve their instructional goals. Although we have already described some potential options throughout this chapter, we provide additional examples for using text-based writing within our quad text sets in this section.

English Language Arts

In the *Romeo and Juliet* text set, our teacher has decided to use text-based writing strategies after reading two of the texts (see Figure 7.23) and discussions for the

	Instructional Objective(s): Analyze how characters develop over the course of a text, interact with other characters, advance the plot, and develop the theme.		
	Visual Text: Video of Act I from contemporary film version of *Romeo and Juliet*		
Instructional Strategies	**Before Reading:** Listen–Read–Discuss		
	During Reading: Collaborative Listening–Viewing Guide		
	After Reading: Questioning the Author		
	Informational Text(s): Article on gender roles and power in Elizabethan England		
Instructional Strategies	**Before Reading:** Concept of Definition		
	During Reading: Reciprocal Teaching		
	After Reading: Magnet Summary		
	Target Text: Act I of Shakespeare's *Romeo and Juliet*		
Instructional Strategies	**Before Reading:** K-W-L strategy		
	During Reading: Reading Guide		
	After Reading: CSET Strategy		
	Accessible Text: Selected chapters from *Eleanor and Park* by Rainbow Rowell		
Instructional Strategies	**Before Reading:** Prereading Plan		
	During Reading: Collaborative Strategic Reading		
	After Reading: Discussion Web		
	Extended Writing:		

FIGURE 7.23. ELA quad text set with text-based writing strategies.

other two texts, which we described in Chapter 6. Remember that the teacher is helping students to trace the development of the main characters, including how they are impacted by the gendered expectations of their society, a key theme of the play. To achieve that goal, she has chosen an informational text on gender and power in Elizabethan England. Because of the text's clear headings and subheadings, she has students complete an extended Magnet Summary that can take advantage of these text features. Students work collaboratively in their RT groups assigned as a during-reading support to create summary sentences for each individual chunk of text. After reading the whole text, students combine those individual summary sentences into a multisentence summary paragraph using appropriate transitional phrases.

Now that students have a more comprehensive understanding of the gendered expectations of the era, they read Act I of the target text, *Romeo and Juliet,* with a scaffolded reading guide (which we discussed in Chapter 5). After reading this text, the teacher asks students to develop a text-based argument using the CSET strategy based on the following prompt: "Do you think that the gendered expectations of the Elizabethan era are partially responsible for Romeo and Juliet falling in love so quickly?" This assignment is not only aligned with the instructional objectives of the unit, but it also encourages students to make cross-textual connections as they draw from both the target and informational texts to support their arguments.

Social Studies

Our social studies quad text set encourages students to trace the development of American segregation over time (see Figure 7.24). In order to help students to achieve this objective, our teacher has built background knowledge through video and informational texts about the history and impacts of racial segregation, which were followed by the robust discussions of the ideas in those texts that we presented in Chapter 6.

After reading the target text, the *Brown v. Board of Education* decision, the teacher has chosen to use a modified Magnet Summary to encourage her students to synthesize the Supreme Court's decision. This strategy also provides a quick comprehension check of her students' understanding of the main idea of the text—that segregation of public schools was deemed illegal and "separate but equal" was no longer acceptable in U.S. public schools. To modify the Magnet Summary, she chooses the magnet word for her students: *Brown v. Board of Education.* Then she selects five attractor terms drawn from the text: separate but equal, public schools, equal protection, 14th Amendment, and segregation. Students work in their PALS pairs to write their summary by combining these terms into a single summary sentence that demonstrates the relationship between these words. The teacher encourages her students to read their summary sentences aloud and then leads a discussion about the accuracy and detail of their summaries.

Instructional Objective(s): Analyze historical materials to trace the development of an idea over time and explain patterns of continuity and change; determine the central idea of a primary source and accurately summarize the central idea and key details.		
Visual Text: "Kids Talk about Segregation" video		
Instructional Strategies	**Before Reading:** Prereading Plan	
	During Reading: Collaborative Listening–Viewing Guide	
	After Reading: Collaborative Reasoning	
Informational Text(s): Article on the history of racial segregation in the United States		
Instructional Strategies	**Before Reading:** Semantic Feature Analysis	
	During Reading: Reciprocal Teaching	
	After Reading: Discussion Web	
Target Text: *Brown v. Board of Education* decision		
Instructional Strategies	**Before Reading:** Listen–Read–Discuss	
	During Reading: PALS (Paragraph Shrinking)	
	After Reading: Magnet Summary	
Accessible Text: Article on racial disparities in modern U.S. public schools		
Instructional Strategies	**Before Reading:** Concept of Definition	
	During Reading: Reading Guide	
	After Reading: CSET Strategy	
Extended Writing:		

FIGURE 7.24. Social studies quad text set with text-based writing strategies.

The last text in this quad text set is a shocking report on the continued racial disparities in U.S. public schools and the reality of *de facto segregation* in many modern school systems. To encourage students to wrestle with continuity and change around the important concept of segregation, she assigns her students an argumentative writing prompt. Students write a text-based response using the CSET strategy and arguing whether the *Brown v. Board of Education* decision was effective in eliminating segregation from public schools, backing up their claims with evidence drawn from multiple texts in the quad text set.

Science

In our science quad text set (see Figure 7.25), students were asked to read and view a number of texts to investigate the impact of humans on Earth's systems. To build background knowledge about the subject, the teacher selected Bill Nye's "Climate Change 101" video and scaffolded their interaction with this text through a CLVG. As you will recall from Chapter 5, CLVGs encourage students to individually take notes on important concepts in video texts, combine and elaborate on individual notes in small groups, and then synthesize their notes in a whole-class discussion. The last element of a CLVG is to extend student understanding through writing or research.

To accomplish this, the teacher has his students complete a Magnet Summary, looking back through their notes to identify what they believe are the five most important attractor terms related to the magnet word (climate change). Students then write a summary sentence and share it with the class. For the three remaining texts in the quad text set, the teacher had students participate in a variety of text-based discussions, which we described in Chapter 6.

FINAL THOUGHTS

In order for students to synthesize their understanding of content-area texts and learn discipline-specific ways of sharing information with others, they must write! As we have argued, writing instruction need not be limited to either ELA classrooms or extended writing assignments that are assigned only once or twice per marking period. Just like reading, students must be provided a high volume of writing experiences that can only be accomplished through daily text-based written responses in all content-area classes. We hope that this chapter has given you a menu of strategies that you can use with your students to provide that writing volume.

Instructional Objective(s): Construct an argument supported by evidence (e.g., patterns in graphs, charts, and images) for how humans impact Earth's systems; integrate technical information expressed in words in a text with a visual representation of that information.		
Visual Text: "Climate Change 101" video with Bill Nye		
Instructional Strategies	**Before Reading:** Prereading Plan	
	During Reading: Collaborative Listening–Viewing Guide	
	After Reading: Magnet Summary	
Informational Text(s): "Climate Change: How Do We Know?" website		
Instructional Strategies	**Before Reading:** Listen–Read–Discuss	
	During Reading: Jigsaw Groups with Reading Guide	
	After Reading: Collaborative Reasoning	
Accessible Text: Chapter 1 of *Ship Breaker* by Paolo Bacigalupi		
Instructional Strategies	**Before Reading:** K-W-L strategy	
	During Reading: PALS (Paragraph Shrinking)	
	After Reading: Questioning the Author	
Target Text: "5 Ways to Curb Climate Change" articles		
Instructional Strategies	**Before Reading:** Semantic Feature Analysis	
	During Reading: Reciprocal Teaching	
	After Reading: Discussion Web	
Extended Writing:		

FIGURE 7.25. Science quad text set with text-based writing strategies.

CHAPTER 8

Teaching Extended Writing

There is an unfortunate truth about the extended writing instruction that many adolescents receive in school: There is not nearly enough of it! This is not to say that students aren't writing in school. Based on surveys of middle and high school teachers and observations of their classrooms, Applebee and Langer (2011) estimated that students wrote three or more pages per week in their content-area classes. Although teachers may have *assigned* these extended writing activities, they less often *taught* students the strategies needed to produce effective writing. On average, students received only 3 minutes of explicit instruction in writing strategies in a given class period, or about 2½ hours over the course of a 9-week grading period.

In a series of national surveys, Steve Graham and colleagues confirmed that the lack of writing instruction in secondary content-area classes is a matter of widespread concern. On average, middle and high school teachers assign brief writing activities at least once a week and extended writing activities, such as essays, around once per 9-week grading period (Gillespie, Graham, Kiuhara, & Hebert, 2014; Graham et al., 2014; Kiuhara, Graham, & Hawken, 2009; Ray, Graham, Houston, & Harris, 2016). In contrast to *assigning* writing, teachers only reported explicitly *teaching* evidence-based practices for writing several times per year, with ELA teachers responding that they taught writing more often than science and social studies teachers.

Please don't misunderstand us. We are not suggesting that teachers are completely to blame. As teacher educators, we feel partly responsible for the lack of adequate writing instruction in our nation's schools. Surveys show that most teachers reported receiving minimal or inadequate preparation for teaching writing in college or in professional development (Gillespie et al., 2014; Graham et al., 2014; Kiuhara et al., 2009; Ray et al., 2016). How can teachers be expected to teach their students something that they haven't been prepared to teach?

Another possible explanation for the lack of writing instruction in schools is how much time it takes to assign, teach, and assess extended writing. Most of the writing activities that content-area teachers report using frequently, including fill-in-the-blank worksheets and copying notes (Drew, Olinghouse, Faggella-Luby, & Welsh, 2017; Gillespie et al., 2014; Ray et al., 2016), take considerably less time than assigning multiparagraph compositions. Given limited instructional time, what should teachers prioritize when teaching extended writing? According to Graham (2019), two of the most important practices that receive minimal attention in classrooms are assigning argumentative and expository writing and teaching strategies for planning and revising. Keeping these instructional priorities in mind, the goals of extended writing instruction should be to make time for assigning discipline-specific *genres* of extended writing, assessing students' writing *skills,* and teaching *strategies* to engage in the writing process (Bazerman et al., 2017).

In the previous chapter, we introduced several strategies for teaching brief text-based arguments and written summaries to support comprehension after reading. In this chapter, we turn our attention to extended writing assignments that might be completed over several class periods for the purpose of demonstrating understanding of content. We begin by discussing the types of extended writing students are expected to produce according to next-generation learning standards, including argumentative and informative/explanatory essays in all content areas and narratives in ELA (NGA & CCSSO, 2010). Next, we focus on three evidence-based practices for teaching writing: (1) teaching strategies for planning and revising, (2) integrating reading and writing instruction, and (3) using assessments to inform instruction (Graham et al., 2016). As in previous chapters, we conclude the chapter by describing how to teach extended writing with our exemplar quad text sets introduced in Chapter 3 and updated throughout this book.

TYPES OF EXTENDED WRITING

Writers, by definition, work within writing communities in order to produce written products for specific purposes and for particular audiences (Graham, 2018). Outside of school, adolescents might take part in a writing community by sharing stories or details about their lives on social media with friends and relatives. In school-based communities of writers, secondary students will typically write to an audience of a teacher or peer(s) who will read and evaluate their composition. School-based purposes for writing in the United States, for better or worse, are defined by curricula, standards, and high-stakes assessments. On the National Assessment of Educational Progress (NAEP), middle and high school students are prompted to write for three purposes: (1) to *persuade* readers to take a position or point of view, (2) to *explain* a topic in order to inform readers and demonstrate understanding, and (3) to *convey experience* to readers in the form of real or imagined narratives (National Assessment Governing Board, 2017).

Like NAEP, the CCSS identify three types of writing that should be assigned in grades 6–12 (see Figure 8.1). The first type, argumentative writing, has received the most attention since the release of the CCSS in 2010 and subsequent adoption in many states. In their most basic form, as discussed in Chapter 7, arguments include a claim that is supported by relevant evidence and logical reasoning (Hillocks, 2011). However, what constitutes an acceptable claim and evidence varies by discipline. For example, literary arguments generally include an interpretative claim about a theme supported by evidence in the form of direct quotes (Newell, Bloome, Kim, & Goff, 2019). In scientific arguments, writers generally transform data into evidence to support their claims or explanations (Sampson, Enderle, Grooms, & Witte, 2013). In historical arguments, a claim is generally an interpretation of events based on differing perspectives that is supported by multiple pieces of evidence that have been sourced, contextualized, and corroborated (Monte-Sano & Allen, 2019). In addition to literary analysis, historical arguments, and scientific arguments, teachers might assign other genres of argumentative writing such as argumentative letters, five-paragraph essays, and document-based questions (Drew et al., 2017; Gillespie et al., 2014; Ray et al., 2016).

The second type of writing, what the CCSS call informative/explanatory, has traditionally been referred to as expository writing. Expository writing conveys information using different text structures, such as compare–contrast, problem–solution, or explanation, based on the writer's purpose (Raphael, Kirschner, & Englert, 1988). Although it has received less attention than argumentative writing in recent years, expository writing has long been considered an important type of writing in high school English (Norton, 1967), science (Koeller, 1982), and social studies (Welton, 1982). In general, expository writing includes an introduction, main ideas and elaboration of details, and a conclusion (Olinghouse,

Text Types and Purposes		
Writing Standard 1	**Writing Standard 2**	**Writing Standard 3**
Write arguments to support claims in an analysis of substantive topics or texts using valid reasoning and relevant and sufficient evidence.	Write informative/ explanatory texts to examine and convey complex ideas and information clearly and accurately through the effective selection, organization, and analysis of content.	Write narratives to develop real or imagined experiences or events using effective technique, well-chosen details, and well-structured event sequences.

FIGURE 8.1. CCR anchor standards related to writing types.

Graham, & Gillespie, 2015). Teachers might assign expository writing genres such as book reports, lab reports, research reports, newspaper articles, business letters, compare–contrast essays, problem–solution essays, step-by-step instructions, descriptions, procedural texts, and scientific explanations (Drew et al., 2017; Gillespie et al., 2014; Ray et al., 2016).

According to the CCSS, the third type of writing, narrative, is explicitly taught only in ELA. However, students might be expected to integrate elements of narrative writing in other content-area writing such as narrative accounts of historical events in social studies (NGA & CCSSO, 2010). Most narratives tend to follow a predictable structure and contain common elements: a setting (time and location), a main character (or protagonist), and a plot, including an initiating event, the protagonist's goal or reaction to the event, events or attempts to achieve the goal, the outcome of the attempts, and the ending or consequence of the event sequence (Fitzgerald & Teasley, 1986). In addition, writers of narratives include techniques such as dialogue, theme, point of view, style, and tone to convey experience (Olinghouse et al., 2015; Wolf & Gearhart, 1994). Teachers might assign narrative writing genres such as stories, personal narratives, poems, plays, social letters, autobiographies, and biographies (Gillespie et al., 2014; Ray et al., 2016).

EFFECTIVE WRITING INSTRUCTION

While the CCSS and other next-generation learning standards identify what types of writing should be assigned, they provide little guidance on how to teach extended writing. The most comprehensive guidance on secondary writing instruction is described in the Carnegie Corporation's *Writing Next* report (Graham & Perin, 2007). In their report, Graham and Perin (2007) list the 11 most effective instructional practices for teaching writing to adolescents. These practices are presented in Figure 8.2. On the left-hand side, they are listed in order from most effective to least effective. On the right-hand side, they are listed again in order from most to least frequently used according to a survey of middle school teachers (Graham et al., 2014).

The most important point to note about these writing practices is that they are all effective, though some are more effective than others. The two practices with the largest effects on adolescents' writing quality are teaching strategies for planning, revising, and editing and teaching summarization. You may recall that we have focused on summary writing and strategies for planning text-based arguments in Chapter 7 due to their effectiveness in promoting comprehension. In essence, these practices are doing double the work, promoting both reading and writing proficiency. Four writing practices have moderate effects on writing quality: having students work collaboratively to plan, draft, revise, and edit their writing; setting specific product goals for writing; having students write using

Most Effective Writing Practices	Most Frequent Writing Practices
1. Writing Strategies	4. Specific Product Goals
2. Summarization	7. Prewriting
3. Collaborative Writing	9. Process Writing Approach
4. Specific Product Goals	5. Word Processing
5. Word Processing	11. Writing for Content Learning
6. Sentence Combining	3. Collaborative Writing
7. Prewriting	2. Summarization
8. Inquiry Activities	1. Writing Strategies
9. Process Writing Approach	10. Study of Models
10. Study of Models	8. Inquiry Activities
11. Writing for Content Learning	6. Sentence Combining

FIGURE 8.2. Effective writing practices.

word processing software; and teaching students to write complex sentence structures by combining simple sentences (Graham & Perin, 2007). The remaining practices (having students engage in prewriting or inquiry activities, using a process approach to writing instruction, having students study and imitate models of good writing, and using writing as a tool to learn content) have smaller but still positive effects on students' writing quality. Notably absent from the list of effective writing practices is traditional grammar instruction, which actually has a negative effect on students' writing quality (Graham & Perin, 2007). Instead of grammar instruction that focuses on defining and providing examples of grammatical features, a better use of instructional time would be teaching students to apply grammatical rules within the context of their own writing through sentence combining (e.g., Saddler, 2012).

The other important point is the mismatch between which writing practices are most effective and which practices teachers report using most frequently. The numbering system used to list writing practices by effectiveness in the left-hand side of Figure 8.2 has been retained in the right-hand side to make this contrast more evident. On average, middle school teachers report having students engage in prewriting activities weekly and establishing specific goals for students' writing several times a week or more (Graham et al., 2014). They report using a process writing approach several times a month or more and teaching strategies for planning, revising, and editing (three components of the writing process) less frequently. Due to the effectiveness of writing strategies and their relative lack of frequency in content-area classes, we devote a great portion of this chapter to teaching strategies for planning, revising, and editing. One of the least frequently used writing practices, inquiry activities, is the subject of Chapter 9.

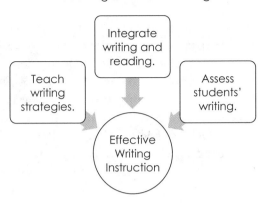

FIGURE 8.3. Effective writing instruction in secondary grades.

Although it is one of the most powerful approaches, there is more to teaching writing than teaching strategies. In the What Works Clearinghouse Practice Guide *Teaching Secondary Students to Write Effectively,* Graham and colleagues (2016) present three recommendations based on the best available research evidence on writing instruction. These recommendations are summarized in Figure 8.3. Unsurprisingly, teaching writing strategies is the first practice. In the sections that follow, we describe how to teach strategies for three components of the writing process (planning, revising, and editing) using a gradual release model of instruction. You will see that the strategies we selected also address the second recommendation by integrating writing and reading instruction when planning and revising argumentative, expository, and narrative texts. Third, we describe how to implement the final recommendation by using genre-specific rubrics to assess students' writing and inform subsequent instruction. We conclude the chapter by showing how these three practices can be used in our quad text sets.

TEACHING WRITING STRATEGIES

If there is one thing that distinguishes skilled writers from less skilled writers, it is that they are more strategic. Specifically, "skilled writers plan more and are better at revising than less-skilled writers" (Graham & Harris, 2012, p. 186). Secondary students who are struggling (or reluctant) writers are generally unable (or unwilling) to plan or revise their writing. Teaching these writers specific strategies for these components of the writing process can improve their writing performance (Graham et al., 2016; Graham & Harris, 2012; Graham & Perin, 2007).

Although the writing process is often presented as a series of linear stages (planning, drafting, revising, editing, and publishing), it is more flexible than that. Skilled writers don't only engage in planning before drafting and revising and editing after the fact. It is more accurate to say that writing is a recursive process that includes multiple components that writers implement simultaneously

(Graham et al., 2016). The components of the writing process are depicted in Figure 8.4. According to theories of the cognitive processes used in writing, writers draw on their knowledge of topic and audience from their long-term memory, while their working memory regulates the processes of planning (generating and organizing ideas), setting goals for writing, drafting (transcribing ideas into text), evaluating what has been written, revising (rewriting the text), and editing the written product (Graham, 2018; Hayes & Flower, 1980). While teaching students how to use the writing process can positively improve their writing, it is more effective to integrate explicit instruction of strategies for two components (planning and revising) when teaching the writing process (Graham & Perin, 2007; Graham & Sandmel, 2011).

So how should writing strategies be taught? One of the most widely used (and most effective) instructional procedures is Self-Regulated Strategy Development (SRSD). Although SRSD was first developed and tested in elementary grades (e.g., Graham, Harris, & Mason, 2005; Harris, Graham, & Mason, 2006), it has more recently been validated in secondary grades (e.g., Kiuhara, O'Neill, Hawken, & Graham, 2012; Ray, Graham, & Liu, 2019). In fact, the CSET strategy for teaching text-based arguments we discussed in Chapter 7 was taught using SRSD when it was initially tested in classrooms (Lewis & Ferretti, 2011). In the SRSD model, writing strategies are taught in six recursive stages representing a gradual release of responsibility from the teacher to students: (1) developing background knowledge for a writing strategy, (2) discussing the strategy, (3) modeling the strategy, (4) memorizing the strategy, (5) teacher-supported use of the strategy, and (6) independent performance (Graham & Harris, 2012).

While some students, especially those who struggle with writing, may need all of the steps of SRSD to learn how to use a strategy, others might not. For whole-class instruction, we suggest following the more streamlined Model–Practice–Reflect cycle that includes modeling how to use a writing strategy,

FIGURE 8.4. Components of the writing process.

supporting students as they practice using the strategy collaboratively or independently, and then having students reflect on their strategy use and writing performance (Graham et al., 2016). This straightforward routine can be used to teach any strategy in any type of writing. Next, we describe exemplar strategies for teaching students how to plan, revise, and edit when producing argumentative, expository, and narrative writing.

Planning Strategies

Imagine (if you have to) that you are a middle school science teacher. If you asked a classroom of students to write a lab report following an experiment, how many do you think would spend any time planning before writing? How many would just start writing straight away? In one study, Keys (2000) asked 16 eighth-grade students to think aloud as they composed their earth science lab reports. She found that only two of the students spent time planning how they would organize their ideas before writing. Five students did not plan at all, essentially writing all of their ideas straight from memory. What about the other nine students? They returned to their data multiple times, planning ideas throughout the writing process.

So how do teachers get students to plan throughout the writing process? Luckily, most secondary students, including those with writing difficulties, can be taught planning strategies that improve the quality of their writing (Graham & Perin, 2007). Planning can take multiple forms, such as taking notes about reading, activating prior knowledge, or brainstorming ideas with others, in order to organize ideas before writing (Graham et al., 2016). In writing this book, for example, we planned by collecting ideas from reading, reflecting on our teaching experiences, and discussing the content and organization of the book with each other. The goal of teaching planning strategies is to give students a window into how more expert writers, like their content-area teachers, organize ideas using genre and disciplinary conventions.

Genre-specific planning strategies focus students on generating ideas based on the "purpose, structure, and elements of a specific type of writing" (Graham et al., 2016, p. 8). Therefore, teaching students how to plan their own writing in a particular genre begins with teaching them the features of that genre. One way to accomplish this is to teach students how to identify the genre elements and organizational structures associated with a type of writing using exemplar texts. Teachers should ultimately use a variety of exemplar texts, including both published work and examples of student writing (Graham et al., 2016). In our work with teachers, we have encouraged them to use the student writing samples available from Achieve the Core. Exemplar texts written by students at each grade level for the three writing types in the CCSS are available on their website.[1] Once you have enough writing samples from your own students, we would encourage

---

[1] Available at *https://achievethecore.org/category/330/student-writing-samples*.

you to use those instead. We hope you find that these exemplar texts will be useful in teaching students how to plan and revise argumentative, expository, and narrative texts.

Argumentative Writing

One of the most effective strategies for planning an argument, DARE, comes from the work of De La Paz and Graham (1997). A graphic organizer to help students use the strategy is represented in Figure 8.5. DARE is a mnemonic that prompts students to take specific actions when planning four parts of a written argument: (1) **D**evelop a topic sentence (or claim) that shows the writer's position, (2) **A**dd ideas (reasons and evidence) that support the position, (3) **R**eject possible arguments that support the opposing position, and (4) **E**nd with a conclusion that restates or summarizes the position (De La Paz, 2001). In studies of the DARE strategy, teachers employed the SRSD model of instruction, showing students how to identify the elements of argumentative writing in sample essays, modeling how to plan and draft an argumentative essay using a graphic organizer like the one in Figure 8.5, and supporting students as they practiced using DARE collaboratively and then independently (De La Paz & Graham, 1997; Kiuhara et al., 2012). In both studies, students spent more time planning and wrote better argumentative essays when using DARE. The utility of the DARE strategy goes beyond planning, as students can also set product goals based on these genre elements (Ferretti, MacArthur, & Dowdy, 2000) and then draft from their completed planning graphic organizer.

Let's consider an example of how John used the DARE strategy in a high school English language arts classroom. After reading Martin Luther King Jr.'s "I Have a Dream" speech, students were asked to write an argument about whether the ideas in the speech are more practical or inspirational (Lewis et al., 2014). To prepare them for writing, John first had his students discuss this question using the Discussion Web activity (see Chapter 6). After students had considered evidence for both positions, he guided them through planning an argument using the DARE graphic organizer in Figure 8.5. Since there is no correct answer for this prompt, students were able to develop a claim for either position, add evidence from the text to support their claim, reject the opposing position of some of their classmates, and end with a conclusion. When drafting, students used the ideas they had generated to expand their claim into an introductory paragraph, their reasons and evidence into two (or more) body paragraphs, their rebuttal into an additional body paragraph, and their ending into a concluding paragraph. This is just one example of how the strategy might be used, but it is important to note that it is flexible enough to be used to write arguments in any content area. To use DARE, teachers and their content-area teams should design prompts that allow students to argue for one of two (or more) positions or prompts that force students to argue in favor of or against a position.

Claim	**D**evelop a topic sentence (or claim) that shows your position.
Reasons/ Evidence	**A**dd ideas (reasons and evidence) that support your position.
	Reject possible arguments that support the opposing position.
Ending	**E**nd with a conclusion that restates or summarizes your position.

FIGURE 8.5. Planning strategy for argumentative writing.

Expository Writing

Writing expository text is more difficult for children and adolescents than other types of writing. One reason is that there are multiple ways to organize expository texts, including compare–contrast, cause–effect, problem–solution, description, and sequence (Meyer, Brandt, & Bluth, 1980). Students need not only learn these text structures to aid in reading comprehension, but they also must learn them to communicate effectively in writing. We find a particular instructional program developed by Raphael and Englert (1990) to be a useful framework for teaching students to compose narrative and expository text. The program, Cognitive Strategy Instruction in Writing (CSIW), has been used to teach upper-elementary and middle school students, including students with learning disabilities, how to compose in four text structures: narrative, explanation (sequence), compare–contrast, and problem–solution (Englert, Raphael, Anderson, Anthony, & Stevens, 1991; Raphael, Englert, & Kirschner, 1989).

In studies of CSIW, students were taught how to write in different text structures through four phases of instruction (Englert et al., 1991). First, the teacher presented exemplars of student writing in each text structure. Students were taught how to analyze texts by focusing on what questions are answered using that structure (e.g., "What is being compared?") and identifying key words that signal text organization (e.g., *alike, different*). Second, teachers modeled how to use genre-specific strategies while composing a whole-class essay, aided by a graphic organizer for each stage of the writing process. Figure 8.6 presents a graphic organizer for planning a compare–contrast essay based on work by Raphael, Kirschner, and Englert (1986). Third, the teacher led students in guided practice for using the graphic organizers to compose a paper using the same text structure, during which time they were encouraged to communicate and collaborate with each other. Finally, students used the graphic organizers when writing independently.

Writing in the compare–contrast structure is particularly challenging for students due to its complex organizational structure. The expectation in compare–contrast writing is to determine important information about two or more topics and then clearly communicate how the two are similar or different (Hammann & Stevens, 2003). This task often includes reading more than one text and making comparisons that are not explicitly stated in either text on its own. For example, students in a social studies class might write about the similarities and differences between two topics after reading different articles about the Gobi and Sahara deserts or about the Stonehenge and Hagar Qim ruins (Hammann & Stevens, 2003). There are a number of different ways to organize this task: writing about one topic and then the other; writing about all the ways the topics are similar and then all the ways they differ; or writing about how each topic is alike and different according to specific aspects. Research with middle school students shows that the third option is the most effective way to organize compare–contrast

Topic	What two things are being compared and/or contrasted?

Ideas/ Details	On what are they being compared and/or contrasted?

How are they alike?	How are they different?

On what are they being compared and/or contrasted?

How are they alike?	How are they different?

On what are they being compared and/or contrasted?

How are they alike?	How are they different?

Ending	End with a conclusion that summarizes your ideas.

FIGURE 8.6. Planning strategy for compare–contrast writing.

writing (Kirkpatrick & Klein, 2009). For example, students in a science class might be expected to compare different minerals such as diamond and bauxite on a number of aspects such as location, formation, and uses, writing a paragraph for how they are alike and different on each aspect (Hammann & Stevens, 2003). The graphic organizer in Figure 8.6 is organized according to this aspect-based structure.

Let's continue our example of John's students who had written an argument about King's "I Have a Dream" speech. Following the next text in their ELA textbook, Nelson Mandela's (1994) "Glory and Hope" speech, John asked his students to compare and contrast the two speeches. After having students read exemplar compare–contrast essays written by former students, he guided them through planning their own compare–contrast essay using the graphic organizer in Figure 8.6. The assigned topic of the essay was to compare the two speakers' use of rhetorical devices to communicate their message. John asked his students to select rhetorical devices, such as repetition, parallelism, and extended metaphors, on which to compare the two speeches. Students identified whether King's and Mandela's speeches were alike or different on each aspect and then summarized their ideas in a concluding section. Like the argumentative essay, John had his students use the completed graphic organizer to draft their compare–contrast essay.

Explanation is another genre of expository writing common in science and social studies classrooms. In general, explanatory essays use a procedural, or sequence, text structure in order to inform readers about how or why a process occurs, such as how rocks are formed, how the human digestive system works, or why a nation was formed from different states (Klein & Kirkpatrick, 2010; Reynolds & Perin, 2009). Scientific explanation papers are particularly challenging for students because they also require explaining cause–effect relationships between ideas, such as the effects of pollutants on an ecosystem or the causes and effects of sickle cell anemia (Chambliss, Christenson, & Parker, 2003; Peker & Wallace, 2009). In the CSIW program, students were taught to plan explanatory texts by answering the questions of what is being explained and what steps are involved in the process, using transition words such as first, next, and last to signal organization (Englert et al., 1988). Explanatory texts should also end with a conclusion that communicates the significance of the process (Klein & Kirkpatrick, 2010). The graphic organizer in Figure 8.7 can be used to teach students to plan explanatory writing.

The final expository text structure taught in the CSIW program is problem–solution. Problem–solution text structure is commonly found in social studies textbook passages, describing the problem that an individual or group faced (e.g., the conditions of westward expansion trails), their attempts to solve the problem (e.g., building transcontinental railroads), and the outcome or results of the solution (e.g., improved transportation; Armbruster, Anderson, & Ostertag, 1987). Studies in which middle grade students were taught how to identify the elements of problem–solution in social studies passages and then use a graphic organizer to

Topic	What is being explained?
Ideas/ Details	What is the first step in the process?
	What are the next steps in the process?
	What is the last step in the process?
Ending	End with a conclusion that summarizes your ideas.

FIGURE 8.7. Planning strategy for explanatory writing.

plan their own problem–solution texts resulted in both more time spent planning and higher writing quality (Armbruster et al., 1987; Guzel-Ozmen, 2006). In the CSIW program, students were taught to answer four questions when planning problem–solution texts: (1) What is the problem?; (2) What are the causes of the problem?; (3) What are the steps to solve the problem?; and (4) What is the outcome? (Guzel-Ozmen, 2006; Raphael et al., 1989). The graphic organizer in Figure 8.8 can be used to teach students to plan problem–solution texts that answer these questions.

Narrative Writing

Both the SRSD and CSIW instructional models have also been used to teach secondary students to write narrative texts, including stories and personal narratives. This type of writing, which primarily occurs during ELA instruction, focuses on teaching students to identify narrative elements in reading and then use those elements to plan their own narratives. For example, middle grade students who were taught how to plan a story by answering questions about story elements using the SRSD model wrote better organized stories than a business-as-usual control group (Sawyer, Graham, & Harris, 1992). In the CSIW program, eighth-grade students were taught to identify narrative elements in short stories before planning their own stories by answering questions about story elements, resulting in more well-developed stories (Simmons et al., 1994). These questions included (1) Who is the story about?; (2) What is the setting of the story?; (3) What problem does the main character face?; (4) How does the main character respond to the problem?; and (5) How does the story end? (Englert et al., 1988). The graphic organizer in Figure 8.9 can be used to teach students to plan narratives based on these questions.

Let's return to the example of John's ninth-grade students who had written an argument and a compare–contrast essay. They also wrote a personal narrative during the same 9-week marking period. After reading an excerpt from Maya Angelou's (1970) autobiography, *I Know Why the Caged Bird Sings,* in their ELA textbook, John asked them to identify examples of narrative techniques that Angelou used to convey experience such as dialogue, figurative language, and sensory details. The excerpt depicts Angelou's relationship with Mrs. Bertha Flowers, a mentor who helps her to find her voice through books after dealing with traumatic experiences as a young woman. John had his students plan their own personal narrative in which they recounted a memorable experience of an important person in their life. Using the graphic organizer in Figure 8.9, students identified the important characters, the setting, the problem, the response to the problem, and the ending in their narrative. Students used their completed graphic organizers to write a draft of their story, adding narrative techniques they had learned about by reading Angelou's autobiography to make their writing more interesting to readers.

Topic	What is the problem?
Ideas/ Details	What are the causes of the problem?
	What are the steps to solve the problem?
	What is the outcome of the solution?
Ending	End with a conclusion that summarizes your ideas.

FIGURE 8.8. Planning strategy for problem–solution writing.

Beginning	Who is the story about?
	What is the setting of the story?
Middle	What problem does the main character face?
	How does the main character respond to the problem?
Ending	How does the story end?

FIGURE 8.9. Planning strategy for narrative writing.

Revising Strategies

While planning strategies can improve students' writing, teaching them how to revise is just as important. Consider the example of the eighth-grade students writing a lab report discussed earlier in this chapter. If you asked them to revise their report after writing, what do you think they would change? According to Keys's (2000) study, most students limited their revisions to superficial changes such as spelling and punctuation. These surface-level changes might be more accurately described as editing. Revision, on the other hand, includes making substantive changes to the content of the text based on self-evaluation or feedback from a peer (Graham et al., 2016). Like planning strategies, secondary students can be taught strategies for revising that result in improved writing quality (Graham & Perin, 2007). However, children and adolescents typically have a great deal of difficulty revising (De La Paz, 1999). Rather than teaching a generic strategy, we recommend that teachers show students how to evaluate and then revise their own writing based on the elements of the genre in which they are writing.

Argumentative Writing

Following the planning and drafting of an argumentative essay using DARE (De La Paz & Graham, 1997), students should be taught how to revise. Students can either be taught how to revise their own work or a peer's. Engaging students in peer-revision activities focused on *evaluating* each other's arguments and then making *revisions* based on peer feedback improves their writing quality, particularly their sense of audience (Wong, Butler, Ficzere, & Kuperis, 1996). In a study conducted by Midgette and Haria (2016), eighth-grade students were taught to identify argumentative elements in exemplar texts (i.e., position, reasons, evidence, opposing position, rebuttal, and conclusion), evaluate the organizational structure of their own argumentative essays, and then revise their writing using a self-evaluation checklist. As a result, their essays were more convincing and demonstrated greater audience awareness.

Blending the revising strategy in the CSIW program (Raphael et al., 1986) with goals for revising arguments (Midgette, Haria, & MacArthur, 2008), we present a strategy for revising arguments in Figure 8.10. We recommend that you teach students to use the strategy to identify, evaluate, and revise argumentative elements in student writing samples before engaging in self- and peer-revision activities. When using this strategy, each student should be paired with a peer. The first step is to *read for content*. Each student pair should read the first partner's argumentative essay, noting what they like best and what parts they think are unclear (Englert et al., 1988). The next step is to *evaluate for organization*. Students should identify argumentative elements in the first essay and rate whether each is clearly stated, responding with a "yes," "sort of," or "no" for each question.

Read for Content	What is one thing you like best about the essay? Why?
	What parts of the essay were unclear? Why?
Evaluate for Organization	What is the writer's claim (or position)? Is it clear?
	What reasons support the writer's position? Are they clear?
	What evidence supports the reasons? Is it clear?
	What is the rebuttal to the opposing position? Is it clear?
	Does the conclusion effectively summarize the position?
Plan for Revision	What could make the essay more convincing to readers?
	What will you do to make the essay easier to follow?

FIGURE 8.10. Revising strategy for argumentative writing.

At this point, students should repeat the first two steps for the second partner's essay. The final step is for each partner to *plan for revision*. Writers should set goals for making their own essay more convincing and easier to follow. Teachers should model and support students as they practice making revisions by adding, deleting, moving, or rewriting parts of their essay (De La Paz, 1999; Englert et al., 1988). Students can make these revisions on the first draft they produced after planning if writing by hand or using a word processor if typing.

Expository Writing

Teaching students to evaluate and revise expository writing after planning and drafting improves the quality of their writing (De La Paz & Graham, 2002). In two studies of the CSIW program, teachers modeled how to use a graphic organizer to revise compare–contrast essays with exemplar texts before students engaged in peer evaluation and self-revision (Englert et al., 1991; Gamelin, 1996). The graphic organizer for revising compare–contrast writing is displayed in Figure 8.11. The strategy steps are the same as described above for revising argumentative essays. Student pairs read for content to identify the strengths and weaknesses in their writing, evaluate the compare–contrast text structure, and make a plan for revising their own writing to make it more interesting and easier to follow (Englert et al., 1988).

Additional graphic organizers for revising explanatory and problem–solution writing are displayed in Figures 8.12 and 8.13, respectively. Although they have not been extensively studied, they are based on graphic organizers used in studies of the CSIW program in which students were taught how to plan, draft, and revise explanatory (Englert et al., 1991) and problem–solution texts (Guzel-Ozmen, 2006). While the strategy is the same for each type of expository writing, the questions used to evaluate for organization are specific to the text structure. Evaluating text structure is the hallmark of effective revision.

Narrative Writing

It should not surprise you that the same strategies used to evaluate and revise argumentative and expository writing are also effective for narratives. For example, middle grade students made more substantive revisions and wrote higher quality stories when they were taught a peer-revising strategy (MacArthur, Schwartz, & Graham, 1991). Eighth-grade students who were taught how to revise their own stories as part of the CSIW program wrote stories with better use of narrative elements (Simmons et al., 1994). A graphic organizer for revising narrative writing is displayed in Figure 8.14. As with other types of writing, the strategy is most effective when teachers model and then support students in peer- and self-revision as they read for content, evaluate for organization, and make plans for revision.

Read for Content	What is one thing you like best about the essay? Why?
	What parts of the essay were unclear? Why?
Evaluate for Organization	What two things are compared and/or contrasted? Is it clear?
	On what are they being compared and/or contrasted? Is it clear?
	How are they alike? How are they different? Is it clear?
	What transitions are used to signal organization? Are they clear?
	Does the conclusion effectively summarize ideas?
Plan for Revision	What could make the essay more interesting to readers?
	What will you do to make the essay easier to follow?

FIGURE 8.11. Revising strategy for compare–contrast writing.

Read for Content	What is one thing you like best about the essay? Why?
	What parts of the essay were unclear? Why?
Evaluate for Organization	What is being explained? Is it clear?
	What are the steps in the process? Are they clear?
	What transitions are used to signal organization? Are they clear?
	Does the conclusion effectively summarize ideas?
Plan for Revision	What could make the essay more interesting to readers?
	What will you do to make the essay easier to follow?

FIGURE 8.12. Revising strategy for explanatory writing.

Read for Content	What is one thing you like best about the essay? Why?
	What parts of the essay were unclear? Why?
Evaluate for Organization	What is the problem? Is it clear?
	What are the causes of the problem? Are they clear?
	What are the steps to solve the problem? Are they clear?
	What is the outcome of the solution? Is it clear?
	What transitions are used to signal organization? Are they clear?
	Does the conclusion effectively summarize ideas?
Plan for Revision	What could make the essay more interesting to readers?
	What will you do to make the essay easier to follow?

FIGURE 8.13. Revising strategy for problem–solution writing.

Read for Content	What is one thing you like best about the story? Why?
	What parts of the story were unclear? Why?
Evaluate for Organization	Who is the story about? Is it clear?
	What is the setting of the story? Is it clear?
	What problem does the main character face? Is it clear?
	How does the main character respond to the problem? Is it clear?
	How does the story end? Is it clear?
	What narrative techniques are used to tell the story? Are they clear?
Plan for Revision	What could make the story more interesting to readers?
	What will you do to make the essay easier to follow?

FIGURE 8.14. Revising strategy for narrative writing.

Editing Strategy: COPS

Unlike planning and revising strategies, we recommend teaching the same strategy for editing regardless of which genre students are writing. As stated earlier, editing includes making changes to the written text based on the conventions of standard written English (Graham et al., 2016). Students can be taught to edit their writing by using a simple strategy using the mnemonic COPS, checking their writing for **C**apitalization, **O**verall appearance, **P**unctuation, and **S**pelling (Schumaker et al., 1981). As with other writing strategies, COPS should be modeled with student writing samples before students practice using it in pairs and independently. Research demonstrates that middle school students made fewer errors in conventions when they were taught how to use the COPS strategy than when they were asked to edit their work without guidance (Reynolds, Hill, Swassing, & Ward, 1988). COPS has also been used successfully in the editing phase of the CSIW program following revision (Gamelin, 1996). See Figure 8.15 for a graphic organizer to help students use the COPS strategy. Like revising strategies, students can answer "yes," "sort of," or "no" when answering the editing questions (Englert et al., 1988). They can either edit their first draft before producing a final draft if they are writing by hand or edit using word processing software if they are typing.

Capitalization	Has the writer capitalized first letters in each sentence and proper nouns?
Overall appearance	How is the overall appearance, including spacing and indentation?
Punctuation	Is the writer's punctuation correct, including commas and end punctuation?
Spelling	Has the writer used correct spelling for all words?

FIGURE 8.15. COPS editing strategy for all writing types.

ASSESSING STUDENT WRITING

Often when we talk with teachers about writing assessment, the conversation turns to how long it takes to grade students' writing. We hear their concerns. No one wants to spend their whole weekend grading 100 essays or more, though secondary school teachers often do, providing extensive feedback on each paper (traditionally in red pen). In fact, middle and high school teachers report that they often use writing to assess student learning and provide written feedback on papers; however, they report less frequently having students assess their own writing or using writing assessment data to inform instruction (Graham et al., 2014; Kiuhara et al., 2009). We argue that it doesn't have to take countless hours to assess students' writing. But given the significant time investment that it does require, it should at least be informative.

How can teachers make their writing assessment more informative? It is important to remember that the purposes of assessing students' writing are to identify strengths and areas of improvement in order to plan targeted instruction and monitor progress (Graham et al., 2016; Olinghouse & Santangelo, 2010). Writing assessment, like writing itself, is a process. Figure 8.16 depicts the writing assessment cycle. To begin, teachers should identify the learning objectives and goals, which are often based on grade-level writing standards such as those in the CCSS (NGA & CCSSO, 2010). These standards tell what types of writing to teach but not how to teach them. Next, teachers should provide targeted writing instruction that incorporates evidence-based practices such as writing strategies for planning, revising, and editing.

Third, teachers should collect writing assessment data. We recommend using on-demand writing prompts at the beginning, middle, and end of the school year to identify strengths and areas of improvement (Olinghouse & Santangelo, 2010; Philippakos & FitzPatrick, 2018). If you don't have state- or district-mandated writing assessments for this purpose, we recommend using the resources from Achieve the Core at the beginning of the school year. On-demand writing prompts for each of the three writing types in the CCSS are available on their website. For example, there is an argumentative writing prompt about whether schools should participate in an initiative to use less technology,[2] an informative/explanatory writing prompt about the effects of the Great Depression on people who lived through it,[3] and a narrative writing prompt about the experience of living through the Dust Bowl.[4]

Once students' writing samples are collected, teachers should assess them. You have probably heard the widely told joke that some teachers accomplish this

---

[2] Available at *https://achievethecore.org/page/1271/argument-opinion-writing-on-demand*.

[3] Available at *https://achievethecore.org/page/454/informative-explanatory-writing-on-demand*.

[4] Available at *https://achievethecore.org/page/1311/narrative-writing-on-demand*.

FIGURE 8.16. The writing assessment cycle.

by using the "staircase method," throwing a stack of essays down the stairs and assigning the highest grade to the papers at the bottom of the stairs (the heaviest and, therefore, the longest) and the lowest grade to those at the top. This "method" of grading is certainly silly, but it is no less silly than writing a letter grade at the top of a paper without providing any feedback whatsoever (something you likely experienced in college). Assessment of students' writing performance should be informative to both you as the teacher and to your students.

Writing assessment is generally accomplished through the use of a rubric. Three types of rubrics are typically used: holistic, analytic, or primary-trait rubrics (Olinghouse & Santangelo, 2010; Philippakos & FitzPatrick, 2018). Holistic rubrics involve assigning a single score to a written product based on a holistic judgment or evaluation of its quality. Since scoring with holistic rubrics is faster than other methods, they are often used in large-scale writing assessments such as Advanced Placement exams. The downside is that they aren't as useful for planning instruction as other types of rubrics (Olinghouse & Santangelo, 2010), nor are they useful as tools for guiding students' revision.

Analytic rubrics involve assigning scores to elements of writing not tied to a specific genre. One of the most widely used analytic rubrics is associated with the *6 + 1 Traits of Writing* program, which scores writing for ideas, organization, voice, word choice, sentence fluency, conventions, and presentation (Culham, 2003). However, there is minimal evidence of the effectiveness of using *6 + 1 Traits* to improve writing instruction (Graham, Hebert, & Harris, 2015). While analytic rubrics are more informative for planning instruction than holistic rubrics, they are not very sensitive to monitoring student progress over time (Olinghouse & Santangelo, 2010). If you are required to use a state- or district-mandated analytic rubric for grading purposes, we would certainly recommend that you continue using it. However, the third type of rubric might prove more useful for day-to-day formative assessment and instructional planning.

Primary-trait rubrics are similar to analytic rubrics, but they involve assigning scores to elements of writing that are assignment- or genre-specific (Olinghouse & Santangelo, 2010). Each element is typically scored on a scale that indicates its presence or absence in students' writing. For example, teachers might choose a 4-point scale from not present (0), to developing (1), competent (2), or effective (3) to evaluate each element (Graham et al., 2016; Olinghouse & Santangelo, 2010). Such evaluations provide teachers and students with more specific information about which genre elements to target in writing instruction (Graham & Perin, 2007). As such, we recommend that you use a primary-trait rubric to analyze students' writing when planning for instruction. Because it is important that the rubric is consistent with the writing strategies that you teach (De La Paz, 2009), we have designed three primary-trait rubrics based on the types of writing in the CCSS (NGA & CCSSO, 2010) for students in grades 6–12.

Our argumentative writing rubric is displayed in Figure 8.17. The primary-trait rubric targets five genre-specific elements based on argumentative structure: claim (or position), reasons, evidence, rebuttal, and conclusion (Midgette, Haria, & MacArthur, 2008). You will notice its similarity to the planning and revising strategies for argumentative essays presented earlier in the chapter. When

		3	2	1	0
Claim	Is the writer's claim (or position) clearly stated?				
Reasons	Are there clear and valid reasons to support the writer's position?				
Evidence	Are the reasons supported with relevant and sufficient evidence?				
Rebuttal	Is the rebuttal to the opposing position (counterargument) clear?				
Conclusion	Does the conclusion summarize the writer's position?				
Scoring: 3 = effective, 2 = competent, 1 = developing, 0 = not present.					

FIGURE 8.17. Argumentative writing rubric.

analyzing students' writing assessment data, you can use this rubric to monitor progress over time, noting improvements in students' scores on each element of argumentative writing.

Our informative/explanatory writing rubric is displayed in Figure 8.18. Instead of making a rubric for each specific text structure, we chose to make one that can be used to assess students' compare–contrast, explanatory, or problem–solution writing. The primary-trait rubric includes five elements of informative writing: topic, organized ideas, elaboration of details, transitions, and conclusion (Olinghouse et al., 2015). Despite not being tied to one text structure, you will notice the rubric's similarity to the expository writing strategies described above.

Our narrative writing rubric is displayed in Figure 8.19. The primary-trait rubric includes five elements of narrative writing: exposition (characters and setting), problem (initiating event), events (attempts to solve the problem), narrative techniques (e.g., dialogue), and conclusion (Fitzgerald & Teasley, 1986; Olinghouse et al., 2015; Simmons et al., 1994). You will notice its similarity to the planning and revising strategies we recommended for narrative writing.

These primary-trait rubrics can help teachers to identify students' writing strengths and plan instruction based on areas of improvement (Graham et al., 2016). For example, a student who receives a 2 or 3 for claim, reasons, and evidence on his argumentative essay while also receiving a 0 or 1 for rebuttal and conclusion might need targeted instruction for those two elements. We urge you to be cautious about converting these evaluations into percentage grades, however. Consider a writer who receives a 2 (competent) on all five elements. Converting a score of 10 out of a possible 15 points would mean that our competent writer earned a 66.67% on his writing assignment. Does that seem like a fair grade for competency? Although primary-trait rubrics are better used for instructional purposes, if you do choose to assign a letter or percentage grade, you should use a conversion table (Arter & Chappuis, 2007). Using the rubric score to percent grade conversion table in Figure 8.20, the student would instead receive the correct grade of 81% or a B– on his argumentative writing assignment.

After students' writing assessments are analyzed, they should receive targeted feedback for how to improve their writing. This phase of the assessment cycle can be accomplished in several ways. Research demonstrates that feedback from teachers, peer feedback, and self-feedback are all effective methods for improving writing quality (Graham et al., 2015, 2016). While teachers should model how to score and communicate constructive feedback, students can also be taught to use primary-trait rubrics for peer evaluation and self-evaluation (Andrade, Du, & Wang, 2008; Philippakos & MacArthur, 2016). Feedback should be used to identify new instructional objectives, returning to the beginning of the writing assessment cycle.

We know that the assessment cycle sounds like a lot of work, but it's important to remember that teaching secondary students to write is a team effort. While students will likely engage in much more argumentative, expository, and narrative

		3	2	1	0
Topic	Does the writer introduce the topic clearly?				
Ideas	Is the topic developed with clear and organized ideas?				
Details	Are the ideas elaborated with relevant and sufficient details?				
Transitions	Does the writer use clear transitions to signal organization?				
Conclusion	Does the conclusion summarize the writer's ideas?				
Scoring: 3 = effective, 2 = competent, 1 = developing, 0 = not present.					

FIGURE 8.18. Informative/explanatory writing rubric.

		3	2	1	0
Exposition	Does the writer clearly introduce the characters and setting?				
Problem	Does the writer establish the central problem or initiating event?				
Events	Is there a sequence of events or attempts to solve the problem?				
Techniques	Does the writer use narrative techniques such as dialogue?				
Conclusion	Does the conclusion follow from and resolve the problem?				
Scoring: 3 = effective, 2 = competent, 1 = developing, 0 = not present.					

FIGURE 8.19. Narrative writing rubric.

Score Average	Letter Grade	Percent Grade
2.9–3.0	A+	100
2.7–2.8	A	95
2.5–2.6	A–	91
2.3–2.4	B+	88
2.1–2.2	B	85
1.9–2.0	B–	81
1.7–1.8	C+	78
1.5–1.6	C	75
1.3–1.4	C–	71
1.1–1.2	D+	68
0.9–1.0	D	65
0.7–0.8	D–	61
0.0–0.6	F	55

FIGURE 8.20. Rubric score to percent grade conversion table.

writing in ELA, they should also learn to write discipline-specific genres in science and social studies. Providing students with multiple opportunities to write in the same genre across a marking period and school year will allow for a continuous cycle of instruction, assessment, feedback, and improvements in writing.

EXTENDED WRITING IN DISCIPLINARY TEXT SETS

To conclude this chapter, we describe how to make writing instruction and assessment work within our quad text set examples. We follow up on the before-, during-, and after-reading strategies with recommendations for extended writing. With so many options from which to choose, we decided to highlight expository writing in ELA and social studies and argumentative writing in science for students to demonstrate understanding of content-area learning.

English Language Arts

Figure 8.21 shows the completed ELA quad text set on *Romeo and Juliet*. Remember that students viewed a video of Act I of *Romeo and Juliet,* and they read an informational text on gender roles in Elizabethan England, Act I of *Romeo and Juliet,* and excerpts from the young adult novel *Eleanor and Park*. Students engaged in a variety of before-, during-, and after-reading activities, including

Instructional Objective(s): Analyze how characters develop over the course of a text, interact with other characters, advance the plot, and develop the theme.		
Visual Text: Video of Act I from contemporary film version of *Romeo and Juliet*		
Instructional Strategies	**Before Reading:** Listen–Read–Discuss	
	During Reading: Collaborative Listening–Viewing Guide	
	After Reading: Questioning the Author	
Informational Text(s): Article on gender roles and power in Elizabethan England		
Instructional Strategies	**Before Reading:** Concept of Definition	
	During Reading: Reciprocal Teaching	
	After Reading: Magnet Summary	
Target Text: Act I of Shakespeare's *Romeo and Juliet*		
Instructional Strategies	**Before Reading:** K-W-L strategy	
	During Reading: Reading Guide	
	After Reading: CSET Strategy	
Accessible Text: Selected chapters from *Eleanor and Park* by Rainbow Rowell		
Instructional Strategies	**Before Reading:** Prereading Plan	
	During Reading: Collaborative Strategic Reading	
	After Reading: Discussion Web	
Extended Writing: Students will write a compare–contrast essay about how gender representations are alike and different in *Romeo and Juliet* and *Eleanor and Park*.		

FIGURE 8.21. ELA quad text set with extended writing.

text-based discussions that turned their attention to the gendered expectations of the characters in the two works of literature. To conclude the quad text set, the teacher asks her students to write a compare–contrast essay examining the theme of gender and how it is developed through the characters and plot of the novel and play.

Although her students have written compare–contrast essays before, this task challenges students by requiring them to synthesize evidence from multiple texts. They won't find direct comparisons being made in any of the texts they read in the quad text set. The teacher shows her students an exemplar compare–contrast essay on two different works of literature that a student in a previous school year had written. She spends the first day of instruction teaching students how to evaluate the organizational structure of compare–contrast essays using the graphic organizer for revising in Figure 8.11. On the second day, the teacher quickly models and then supports students as they plan their own compare–contrast essays on *Romeo and Juliet* and *Eleanor and Park*. Using the planning strategy in Figure 8.6, students identify different aspects of comparison and how the theme of gender is portrayed similarly and differently in the two texts. For instance, students might compare and contrast the female and male characters in the two works, how the authority figures are depicted, and the relative intensity of the title characters' relationships.

On the third day of the week, students write a draft of their compare–contrast essays by hand using their completed graphic organizers. Since students have already used the revising strategy (see Figure 8.11), she has them peer-evaluate their drafts on the fourth day of instruction and use the COPS strategy in Figure 8.15 to check for errors in conventions. On the fifth day, students write a final draft of their compare–contrast essay. The teacher uses the rubric for informative/explanatory texts in Figure 8.18 to analyze their writing and provide feedback. She tells her students that they will write another compare–contrast essay in the next unit and add it to their writing portfolio. The teacher keeps track of students' rubric scores to monitor their progress in composing compare–contrast essays over time.

Social Studies

The completed social studies quad text set on segregation is displayed in Figure 8.22. Students engaged in before-, during-, and after-reading activities to support comprehension and learning from a video, an informational text, a primary-source document, and a digital magazine article about the history of school segregation and attempts at desegregation. Based on the topic and her instructional objectives, the teacher decided to conclude the quad text set by assigning a problem–solution essay about the causes of the problem of school segregation, attempts to solve the problem through legislation, and the outcomes of the attempted solutions.

	Instructional Objective(s): Analyze historical materials to trace the development of an idea over time and explain patterns of continuity and change; determine the central idea of a primary source and accurately summarize the central idea and key details.

Visual Text: "Kids Talk about Segregation" video

Instructional Strategies	**Before Reading:** Prereading Plan
	During Reading: Collaborative Listening–Viewing Guide
	After Reading: Collaborative Reasoning

Informational Text(s): Article on the history of racial segregation in the United States

Instructional Strategies	**Before Reading:** Semantic Feature Analysis
	During Reading: Reciprocal Teaching
	After Reading: Discussion Web

Target Text: *Brown v. Board of Education* decision

Instructional Strategies	**Before Reading:** Listen–Read–Discuss
	During Reading: PALS (Paragraph Shrinking)
	After Reading: Magnet Summary

Accessible Text: Article on racial disparities in modern U.S. public schools

Instructional Strategies	**Before Reading:** Concept of Definition
	During Reading: Reading Guide
	After Reading: CSET Strategy

Extended Writing: Students will write a problem–solution essay about the causes of school segregation, attempts to solve the problem, and outcomes of proposed solutions.

FIGURE 8.22. Social studies quad text set with extended writing.

Because students will all be writing about the same topic, she begins her instruction by leading the class in collaboratively planning a whole-class problem–solution essay using the graphic organizer in Figure 8.8. She guides students in using evidence from the texts in the quad text set to describe the problem of school segregation, its causes (including both *de facto* and *de jure segregation*), the steps to solve the problem (including the *Brown v. Board of Education* decision), and the outcome of the attempted solution (including continued segregation in schools). On the next day, students work independently to write a first draft of the problem–solution essay based on the planning they had done as a class. On the third day, the teacher projects a draft of her own problem–solution essay for the whole class. She leads the class in collaboratively evaluating and making substantive revisions to her essay using the strategy shown in Figure 8.13. On the fourth day, students use the same strategy to self-evaluate, revise their essay, and check for errors in conventions using the COPS strategy (see Figure 8.15). On the last day of the week, students turn in their problem–solution essays, which the teacher evaluates using the rubric for informative/explanatory writing in Figure 8.18 before providing them with written feedback.

Science

The completed science quad text set on climate change is shown in Figure 8.23. You will recall that students engaged in before-, during-, and after-reading activities to help them engage with a video, a digital text with scientific data, a young-adult novel chapter, and an informational article about climate change throughout the unit. Due to his instructional objectives, the teacher chose to assign an argumentative essay to assess student understanding. To give his students an authentic purpose and audience for their writing assignment, he asks them to write an argumentative letter to a local public official on the causes, impacts, and ways to mitigate climate change using evidence from the texts they read in the quad text set.

Because his students have not written in this genre before, he begins his instruction by showing them an example of an argumentative letter that he wrote himself. He also models how to plan an argumentative letter using a graphic organizer representing the DARE strategy (see Figure 8.5) on the first day of instruction. The next day, the teacher supports students as they plan their own argumentative letters in response to his prompt. On the third day, he asks students to compose a first draft using the laptop computers available to him in his department, supporting them as they type their letters. On the fourth day, he assigns students to collaborative pairs to engage in peer revision using the strategy in Figure 8.10. Because their essays are typed, he also shows the student pairs how to use the COPS strategy (see Figure 8.15) to edit their drafts. On the last day of the week, students enact their plans for revision to produce another draft of their argumentative letter. The teacher has students self-evaluate using

	Instructional Objective(s): Construct an argument supported by evidence (e.g., patterns in graphs, charts, and images) for how humans impact Earth's systems; integrate technical information expressed in words in a text with a visual representation of that information.

Visual Text: "Climate Change 101" video with Bill Nye

Instructional Strategies	**Before Reading:** Prereading Plan
	During Reading: Collaborative Listening–Viewing Guide
	After Reading: Magnet Summary

Informational Text(s): "Climate Change: How Do We Know?" website

Instructional Strategies	**Before Reading:** Listen–Read–Discuss
	During Reading: Jigsaw Groups with Reading Guide
	After Reading: Collaborative Reasoning

Accessible Text: Chapter 1 of *Ship Breaker* by Paolo Bacigalupi

Instructional Strategies	**Before Reading:** K-W-L strategy
	During Reading: PALS (Paragraph Shrinking)
	After Reading: Questioning the Author

Target Text: "5 Ways to Curb Climate Change" articles

Instructional Strategies	**Before Reading:** Semantic Feature Analysis
	During Reading: Reciprocal Teaching
	After Reading: Discussion Web

Extended Writing: Students will write an argumentative letter to a public official about the causes, impacts, and ways to mitigate climate change based on scientific evidence.

FIGURE 8.23. Science quad text set with extended writing.

the argumentative writing rubric in Figure 8.17, which he also uses to evaluate their performance. After providing feedback on their letters, students make final revisions before sending their letters to their public official.

FINAL THOUGHTS

In this chapter, we have shown you how to assign different types of writing, teach writing strategies, and assess students' writing. To be frank, this whirlwind of a chapter could easily be expanded into a whole book. We hope that this chapter will at least help you get your feet wet. However, we don't want you to get the false impression that writing is overly formulaic or prescriptive. The key take-away is that students should be taught how to organize their ideas according to conventional text structures and disciplinary norms. We encourage you to start with the graphic organizers and rubrics in this chapter and then adapt them based on the learning objectives for your grade and content area. And we hope that you feel prepared to teach writing!

CHAPTER 9

Inquiry in the Disciplines

In the late 1950s, a group of high school and college teachers attended the Haverford Conference in Advance Standing in English. There the participants discussed guidelines for assigning and teaching the research paper in secondary schools. One of the most interesting outcomes of this conference was the decision to change the name that teachers used for this project from *research paper* to *library paper*. They did this, Burton (1958) explains, because "teachers should not lead students to suppose that they are doing real research when they are in reality doing rather simple reports" (p. 291). In an *English Journal* article 30 years later, another English teacher took up this same theme criticizing what passed for research and inquiry in the classrooms that she observed. Labeling the traditional secondary school research paper as an "exquisite torture" (Dellinger, 1989, p. 31), she called for a more effective and engaging alternative. Dellinger (1989) asked if we could "teach our students how to do *real* research instead of tediously 'clipping and stitching' together meaningless reports of others' research" (p. 32).

Understanding the distinction between *real* research and inquiry and the "clip-and-stitch" report approach that happens in many secondary classrooms is an important one. First, inquiry is highlighted in many states' college and career readiness (CCR) standards for writing as a critically important literacy skill. The authors of the CCSS reinforced the need for all students to "research to build and present knowledge" (NGA & CCSSO, 2010). In fact, three of the ten CCR anchor standards for writing are directly related to conducting inquiry and research to build and present knowledge. These are represented in Figure 9.1.

Second, the centrality of research and inquiry to learning in the disciplines is reflected in the changes that have been made to disciplinary standards. For instance, for some time experts in science education have argued that secondary science instruction should focus on inquiry, critical reasoning, and evidence-based

Research to Build and Present Knowledge		
Writing Standard 7	**Writing Standard 8**	**Writing Standard 9**
Conduct short as well as more sustained research projects based on focused questions, demonstrating understanding of the subject under investigation.	Gather relevant information from multiple print and digital resources, assess the credibility and accuracy of each source, and integrate the information while avoiding plagiarism.	Draw evidence from literary or informational texts to support analysis, reflection, and research.

FIGURE 9.1. CCR anchor standards related to inquiry and research.

argumentation instead of the rote memorization of scientific knowledge (Driver, Newton, & Osborne, 2000; Simon, Erduran, & Osborne, 2006). The Next Generation Science Standards (NGSS; NGSS Lead States, 2013) have responded to this concern by emphasizing that students should engage in scientific inquiry and the practices that are crucial to participation in scientific discourse and the real work of scientists. These include the ability to form hypotheses, collect and evaluate data, transform data into evidence, develop interpretations of evidence, justify evidence based on scientific principles, and effectively communicate findings to others (Sampson, Grooms, & Walker, 2011). As Duschl (2008) argues, science teachers must provide thoughtful instruction and significant opportunities for practice in order for students to gain proficiency in these inquiry-based scientific practices, what the National Institutes of Health sees as the core of "doing science" (Bybee, Bloom, Phillips, & Knapp, 2005, p. 1).

Social studies, too, has a renewed focus on inquiry. In the College, Career, and Civic Life (C3) Framework for Social Studies State Standards (National Council for the Social Studies [NCSS], 2013)—often called the "C3 Framework"—the standards' authors plainly state that "inquiry is at the heart of social studies" (p. 8) and that those who are hoping to become social studies teachers "must understand the fundamental components of disciplinary inquiry including questioning, gathering and evaluating sources, developing claims and using evidence, communicating conclusions, and taking informed action" (p. 13). Research and inquiry cannot be merely "add-ons" for content-area teachers. Rather, they must be central to the way that science and social studies teachers understand teaching, learning, *and doing* in their disciplines.

ELA standards also highlight the role of inquiry in students' learning. In the *Standards for the English Language Arts,* jointly released by the International Reading Association (IRA; now the International Literacy Association) and the National Council of Teachers of English (NCTE) in 1996 and reaffirmed in 2012, two of the twelve standards address research and inquiry. The IRA and NCTE (1996) standards define inquiry as "the learner's desire to look deeply into a question or idea that interests him or her" (p. 27). Further, the authors state, "The ability to identify good topics, to gather information, and to evaluate, assemble, and interpret findings from among the many general and specialized information sources now available to them is one of the most vital skills that students can acquire" (IRA & NCTE, 1996, p. 28). Therefore, inquiry in the ELA classroom is not merely engaging students in topics that they desire to learn about; it is also an essential skill that promotes student agency in posing questions, thinking critically, and communicating effectively about topics and issues that concern them.

The goal of this chapter is to help you to understand how research and inquiry can be used to extend and enhance students' understanding of material in content-area classrooms. However, it is also our goal to help teachers identify and leverage the real tools of inquiry that disciplinary experts use to make sense of the world and to communicate that understanding to others. We begin this chapter by highlighting the inquiry tools that students must use to become effective researchers in our complex and digitally sophisticated world. These include data collection and analysis tools, resource evaluation tools, and the sharing tools that disciplinary experts use to communicate their findings. We then describe discipline-specific inquiry frameworks in science, social studies, and ELA that leverage these tools. We also suggest three possible inquiry projects that can be used to extend student understanding in the quad text sets that we have built across the course of this book. These examples will help you to avoid the pitfalls of the painful and ineffective "clip-and-stitch" approach to research projects and to instead provide a "real" research and inquiry experience that is both motivating for students and effective for reinforcing disciplinary concepts, skills, and practices.

THE REAL TOOLS OF INQUIRY AND RESEARCH

Although we pointed out the limitations of the "library paper" in the introduction to this chapter, we recognize that the Internet, school and community libraries, and media specialists are invaluable resources for engaging in research and inquiry in middle and high schools. In fact, the book you are now holding would never have been written had it not been for the rich resources and talented people available to us online and at our university libraries. That being said, if teachers are to engage students in the types of research and inquiry that will extend their understanding of disciplinary concepts *and* teach them the practices that experts in the field really use, they need to help students think more comprehensively about the data sources, analysis tools, and sharing methods that are available to them. Lewis et al. (2014) identified four categories of these inquiry tools, which are represented in Figure 9.2.

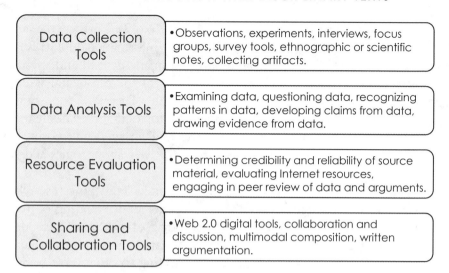

FIGURE 9.2. Tools of inquiry. Adapted with permission from Lewis, Walpole, and McKenna (2014). Copyright © 2014 The Guilford Press.

Data Collection Tools

The first of these inquiry tools are *data collection tools*. Unlike the "clip-and-stitch" data gathering of traditional library papers, teachers must help their students look further than the Internet and hard-copy print resources for the information they will use to answer their research questions (Lewis et al., 2014). Instead of relying only on traditional print and digital media, teachers must also instruct their students in the data collection methods that disciplinary experts use to answer important questions. These include designing and conducting interviews and focus groups, developing paper or online survey instruments, carrying out field observations or experiments, taking detailed ethnographic or scientific notes, and collecting artifacts, to name just a few.

Data Analysis Tools

The second set of inquiry tools, *data analysis tools,* are the skills that students need to analyze data that is collected; to question and look for patterns in the data; and to let their claims and further questions emerge from this analysis. As Hillocks (2011) argues, secondary students are too often asked to develop research questions or claims without first spending time immersed in the data around their topic of inquiry. Figure 9.3 outlines the inquiry process that Hillocks (2011) suggests. It begins with students identifying a research direction and then moving to data collection and analysis. Only after engaging in data analysis do students begin to answer their questions, formulate claims, and back those claims with evidence from their data.

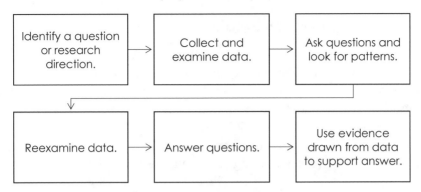

FIGURE 9.3. Hillocks's (2011) suggested research process.

When Bill first taught literary research, for instance, he provided his students with what he felt was a helpful scaffold—a list of 50 thesis topics that students might use for their research paper. These topics ranged from the general (e.g., "music plays an important role in Shakespeare's plays") to thesis statements that were much more specific (e.g., "the ending of *Huckleberry Finn* is significantly flawed"). However, what Bill failed to realize was that by providing these topics first, he was asking his students to commit to a thesis or claim before they ever did any research or collected any data. This is the exact opposite of what inquiry looks like in the real world of the disciplines. Instead of starting with a claim, real inquiry begins by identifying a question and clear research direction, collecting and analyzing data related to that question, and *then* developing a claim from that analysis. Only after these first important steps are taken should the writer move on to support that claim with evidence from the data set (Hillocks, 2011).

Resource Evaluation Tools

Because students are often inundated with information, we also encourage teachers to provide students with *resource evaluation tools* so that they can learn to appraise the credibility and reliability of the information they collect, especially from Internet resources. Increased access to online information is clearly a benefit to students who can draw on a vast array of resources to inform their inquiry and research. However, researchers agree that with greater access to information comes an equally pressing need for the tools to evaluate it (Asselin, 2005).

We recommend, therefore, that students should be taught these evaluation skills (see Figure 9.2) before their inquiry process begins and that teachers should choose inquiry-based instructional strategies and collaborative frameworks that contain a robust data evaluation or peer review component. We will address these resource evaluation tools in greater detail in the discipline-specific examples described later in this chapter.

Sharing and Collaboration Tools

The last set of tools is *sharing and collaboration tools.* Although there is still room for the traditional research paper or report in secondary classroom inquiry, robust state and disciplinary standards require that students do more to develop 21st-century sharing skills that leverage digital tools and that occur in a variety of digital environments (Karchmer-Klein, 2019). The CCR standards for writing acknowledge this reality by requiring students to *use technology* to "produce and publish writing and to interact and collaborate with others" (NGA & CCSSO, 2010). We agree with Dalton (2012), who argues that our digitally oriented society requires teachers to instruct their students how to effectively use technology to design multimedia texts by teaching them how to leverage text, visuals, and sound to convey meaning to others.

Therefore, instead of restricting research products to the traditional paper form, we suggest that teachers encourage their students to use multimodal sharing tools, as well as Web 2.0 tools, to share the products of their inquiry, and to collaborate with others. Web 2.0 is a term used to describe digital tools that not only allow students to share their work with audiences but also allow those audiences to collaborate and respond to what the author produces (Karchmer-Klein, 2019). As Boscolo and Gelati (2013) point out, research and writing in secondary classrooms is often a solitary pursuit carried out by individual students, with the teacher being the only audience. Using Web 2.0 tools allows students to leverage technology to construct meaning with others and to share the fruits of their inquiry with their school community and, quite literally, the world. This kind of collaborative sharing leads to higher-quality written products (Graham & Perin, 2007) and is also more motivating for students (Lapp, Shea, & Wolsey, 2010), more closely mirroring the workplace where most writing takes place in collaboration with others (Bremner, 2010; Perin, 2013). Although today's fast technological pace would quickly make a more detailed discussion of Web 2.0 tools obsolete, later in this chapter we will highlight how discipline-specific inquiry projects might leverage these tools.

PUTTING THE TOOLS OF INQUIRY TO WORK

We have argued that inquiry in content-area classrooms should be guided by four instructional priorities. Students should be provided instruction and practice with the real-life tools of inquiry, which include *data collection, data analysis, resource evaluation,* and *sharing and collaboration* tools. The discipline-specific inquiry examples in this chapter leverage these tools. However, the examples we have chosen also adhere closely to the research methodology that Hillocks (2011) suggests in which students' research questions, claims, and arguments are thoroughly grounded in data collection and analysis. To illustrate how these guidelines can operate in content-area classrooms, we have chosen three research-validated inquiry frameworks, one in science, one in social studies, and one in ELA. We introduce each framework, explain its steps, and provide a specific example of how it can be used to extend student understanding of the content in the disciplinary text sets we have presented in the previous chapters.

Science: Argument-Driven Inquiry

One instructional model that has proven successful for supporting the practices of scientific inquiry and the goals of the NGSS is the Argument-Driven Inquiry (ADI) framework (Sampson et al., 2011; Walker & Sampson, 2013). The ADI framework has eight distinct instructional steps that are grounded in the authentic practices of scientific argumentative discourse. Figure 9.4 outlines the steps of the ADI framework. Importantly, students are not asked to engage in these inquiry activities without exposure to the scientific concepts and content that can inform their research, data collection, and scientific argumentation. In the ADI framework, students participate in targeted lectures, reading, discussion, and collaborative work before being asked to engage in ADI explorations. In this way, inquiry becomes a natural extension of their disciplinary and text-based learning in their science classrooms.

In *step 1* of the ADI framework, the teacher identifies a task that provides the need for students to solve problems or explain a phenomenon. For example, in a chemistry class that is studying osmosis, students might be asked how the concentration of saltwater influences the rate of osmosis. Students who are studying the specific gravity of liquids might be asked how they can predict whether a material will float or sink in water or in alcohol (Grooms, Enderle, & Sampson, 2015). Sampson and colleagues (2011) provide another helpful illustration of an ADI exploration. In a study they conducted in a 10th-grade science class, they first presented students with the candle and the inverted flask demonstration as a way to engage students in inquiry around a natural phenomenon. During this demonstration, a candle is held upright in a pan of water using clay. A graduated cylinder is then placed over the candle until the flame is extinguished and water begins to rise in the cylinder. Students are then asked to conduct inquiry and develop an argument for why the water rises after the candle is extinguished.

In *step 2*, students work in small groups to develop a plan for answering the question and generating the needed data, which they then use to collect the data that will help them solve the problem. In *step 3*, student groups analyze the data they collected and develop a tentative evidence-based argument based on their data analysis. During this step, groups are encouraged to use whiteboards and a specific graphic framework to share their explanation for the phenomenon, the evidence for their explanation, and their rationale for their choice of evidence. In *step 4*, students are provided with significant dialogic support for argumentation when they are asked to engage in an argumentation session. In the argumentation

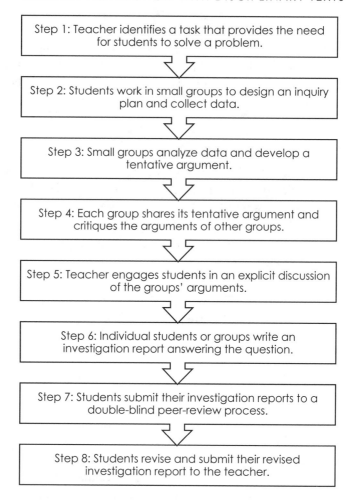

FIGURE 9.4. ADI framework.

session, groups share their tentative arguments. In *step 5,* students' tentative arguments in response to the research question are critiqued by other groups and
subsequently refined through a teacher-led discussion. This step leads to the production of a more formal written argument in *step 6* of the ADI framework.

Like real scientists who must submit their work to the scrutiny of their peers,
in *step 7* students submit their inquiry-based arguments to a double-blind peer-
review process in which small groups of students read the investigative reports
and, using a rubric that indicates specific criteria for judging each section of the
report, provide another round of anonymous critical feedback on the evidence-
based arguments of their peers. Using this feedback, students then revise and
submit a final draft of their inquiry project to the teacher in *step 8.*

The ADI framework has a positive impact on students' ability to engage in
scientific argument and generate and evaluate scientific claims (Sampson et al.,

2011). It also utilizes the real-world tools of inquiry that have guided our instructional choices in this chapter. A summary of how the ADI framework utilizes these tools is presented in Figure 9.5.

First, students are presented with real-world questions that require data to answer them, and then they use experimentation, scientific tools, and observational methods to generate and collect it. Next, students analyze that data to form initial hypotheses and potential answers to the research questions. Although students are not required to evaluate online resources in this framework, their arguments and use of data and evidence are evaluated by their peers two separate times in this instructional method, forcing students to hone their reasoning and make clearer connections between the evidence they select and their proposed solutions to the inquiry questions. Although the research we reviewed on ADI did not include the use of Web 2.0 tools to share results or collaborate with others, sharing and collaboration are a crucial part of this framework, with students first presenting oral arguments that incorporate visuals and then producing formal written reports that meet the standards of scientific discourse. Web 2.0 tools could easily be used in the initial sharing phase of their inquiry (step 3), the double-blind peer review process (step 7), and in the final sharing of their inquiry project (step 8).

Inquiry in a Science Text Set

Our science quad text set focused on the impact of climate change on Earth's systems (see Figure 9.6). Because climate change is complex and multifaceted, teachers will need to focus on a specific aspect of the problem when expanding

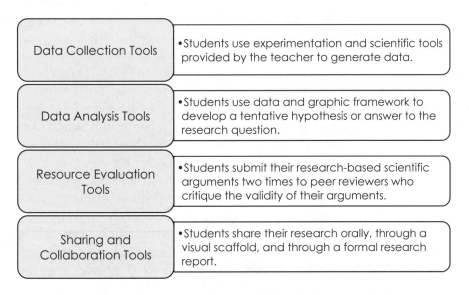

FIGURE 9.5. ADI framework and the tools of inquiry.

Instructional Objective(s): Construct an argument supported by evidence (e.g., patterns in graphs, charts, and images) for how humans impact Earth's systems; integrate technical information expressed in words in a text with a visual representation of that information.	
Visual Text: "Climate Change 101" video with Bill Nye	
Informational Text(s): "Climate Change: How Do We Know?" website	
Accessible Text: Chapter 1 of *Ship Breaker* by Paolo Bacigalupi	
Target Text: "5 Ways to Curb Climate Change" articles	
Inquiry Extension: Exploring how melting freshwater can impact ocean systems	

FIGURE 9.6. Science quad text set with inquiry extension.

student understanding of the topic through inquiry. For example, as an extension of his unit, our science teacher can utilize the ADI framework (Sampson et al., 2011) to expand students' understanding of climate change by researching its impact on the Global Ocean Conveyor (GOC; Science Learning Hub, 2017). As you may know, the GOC is a complex ocean system that moves heat, nutrients, and salt throughout the world's oceans. Although the ocean's surface currents are impacted by wind, deeper currents are primarily impacted by changes in water density. Denser water drops under less dense water, moving nutrients contained in the less dense water closer to the surface. Because warmer global temperatures are leading to significantly more melting of land ice, ice melt can lead to changes in the density and salinity of the ocean and have a significant impact on the complex processes in the GOC. The focus of this project is to engage students in inquiry about the impact of melting freshwater on this critical ocean system.

In step 1 of this ADI-informed inquiry project, our science teacher introduces the problem by explaining the workings of the GOC and asking students to determine how the melting of land ice—and the subsequent addition of more freshwater into the ocean—can impact this earth system. To illustrate the process, the teacher sets up a scientific demonstration. Using two glasses, he fills one glass with 8 ounces of room temperature saltwater and one with an equal amount of room temperature freshwater. Labeling each glass so that his students can clearly see which contains the freshwater and saltwater, he introduces an ice cube—made with freshwater and a few drops of food coloring—into each glass. As the ice cubes melt, students will see that in the freshwater the tinted melting water drops to the bottom, but in the saltwater, the melting water stays on the surface. Students are asked why there is a difference in the way the water reacts in each of the two conditions, and they are instructed to develop a scientific argument for how this demonstration illustrates how melting freshwater due to climate change can disrupt the GOC.

In step 2, students are organized into groups and given access to all the materials that the teacher used in his demonstration, including a scale to weigh the 8 ounces of freshwater and saltwater and digital cameras to record their experiments. In these groups they design an inquiry plan, rerun the experiment, and collect data. In step 3, small groups represent their data on a large whiteboard and begin to analyze it to form a preliminary argument. At this point students should begin to see that the melting freshwater acts differently in the saltwater and freshwater, because freshwater is less dense than the saltwater and, therefore, remains on the surface of the saltwater. Understanding this, students can apply their data-derived knowledge to the question of how increased freshwater melt due to climate change can impact the GOC, which depends on denser, heavier water moving downward, pushing the less dense, lighter water upward.

Students share their preliminary arguments during step 4 in an argumentation session with the other groups during which their peers critique their analysis, followed by step 5 in which the teacher engages students in a discussion of their data analysis and preliminary argument about salinity, density, and the potential impact on the GOC. Although the ADI intervention studies cited in this chapter used traditional whiteboards and markers for these sharing steps, students could just as easily be encouraged to share their preliminary arguments using collaborative web-based whiteboards such as Baiboard or Web Whiteboard.

Using peer and teacher feedback, the student groups advance to step 6 in which they hone their arguments and write formal investigation reports that answer the research questions. These are submitted to a double-blind peer review process in step 7, and then revised and submitted as final reports during step 8, processes that could be facilitated through Google Docs.

Social Studies: Stripling Model of Inquiry

Experts in social studies education have highlighted the similarities between historical and scientific inquiry (Barton & Levstik, 2004). Both scientists and historians pose questions, collect and analyze data, draw conclusions, and communicate their findings to their peers. And both groups of disciplinary experts view inquiry as the essential activity involved in *doing* science and history. Although we understand that history education is only one discipline under the broader social studies umbrella (along with geography, psychology, sociology, and economics), inquiry is critical to learning in these social studies domains and to development of the habits of mind that allow for full, critical participation in democratic life (Barton & Levstik, 2004).

One framework that we have found particularly helpful for inquiry in social studies is the Stripling Model of Inquiry (Stripling, 2008), which is aligned with the Teaching with Primary Sources initiative of the Library of Congress. This framework includes six inquiry phases that are also aligned with the "Inquiry Arc" of the C3 Framework (NCSS, 2013) that requires students to (1) ask questions and plan for inquiry, (2) apply disciplinary tools, (3) evaluate sources and use evidence, and (4) communicate conclusions and take informed action. It is important to note that the Stripling Model of Inquiry is an iterative model in which teachers are encouraged to have their students revisit and repeat stages if they find it is needed to accomplish their research goals. Figure 9.7 displays the six phases in the Stripling Model of Inquiry.

As an illustration of how this model can work in a history classroom, Woyshner (2010) developed a sample inquiry project around the development of the bicycle, a project that focused on the impact of technological change on the social history of the United States. In the first phase of the framework, students were encouraged to *connect* to the topic by reflecting on their own first experiences with learning to ride a bicycle and sharing the feelings they had about this experience with others. Woyshner (2010) points out that in the Stripling

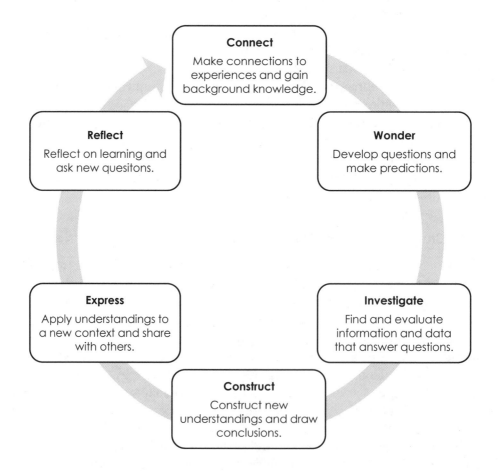

FIGURE 9.7. The Stripling Model of Inquiry. Based on Schlosser and Johnson (2014).

Model of Inquiry, the *connect* phase is crucial for getting students to buy in to the inquiry process.

Following this initial step, students were provided with a series of images in the *wonder* phase, which included photographs and advertisements from the early days of bicycle development, the dates of their creation, and a subtitle for each image that provided context. These images also included a number of advertisements that depicted women enjoying the freedom from domestic responsibility that bicycles represented. It was important to include these pictures during this inquiry phase because technology's impact on social change was the focus of this project; the photographs of women encouraged students to see this thematic pattern and ask pertinent questions to guide their personal inquiry arc. During this phase of the inquiry process, students wrote questions about what they observed and shared those questions with their peers.

After students personally connected to the topic and developed preliminary background knowledge and research questions through the use of primary source visuals, they were ready to engage in the *investigate* phase of the process. In this stage, students were encouraged to chart what they gleaned about the bicycle's impact by revisiting the images, dates, and subtitles and organizing the information into a concept map that included key ideas about bicycle development, its use, and its possible impact on society. This phase serves as a foundation on which further inquiry using primary source documents can be built.

The next phase of inquiry is the *construct* phase in which students read and analyzed primary-source documents that addressed women's use of the bicycle. Woyshner (2010) sees this phase as the most important to disciplinary inquiry since interpretation of primary-source documents is "at the heart of historical inquiry" (p. 41). Additionally, this phase of the inquiry process provides students with the opportunity to practice the discipline-specific analytic skills that historians really use. Wineburg (2010) calls this "thinking like a historian," which includes three key skills: (1) sourcing a document by thinking about the author, the document's creation, purpose, and trustworthiness; (2) contextualizing the document by situating it in its historical and social context; and (3) corroborating the document by looking across multiple resources to see if sources confirm or refute the author's account (Wineburg et al., 2012).

The *express* phase follows students' analysis of the primary-source documents. Students express what they have found in writing and share their findings with their peers. Woyshner (2010) suggests that during this phase of the inquiry cycle, teachers should leverage a variety of writing genres that mimic the media that their students study in the classroom or that are reflected in state social studies standards. For instance, in the inquiry project on the bicycle's impact on social norms, the teacher encouraged students to express their findings in an editorial format as if they were writing in 1895. This genre, an important primary resource for historians, was also a genre that students read during the *construct* phase of the inquiry process.

The last phase in the Stripling Model is *reflect*. Students and teachers not only reflect on what they have learned from their inquiry, but they also determine if there are any gaps in their knowledge and if they need to return to other stages of the inquiry process to fill those gaps.

As you may have noticed, the Stripling Model of Inquiry parallels the quad text set framework that we laid out in Chapter 3. In both instructional models, teachers build critical background knowledge (including the use of strategically chosen visual texts), students read and analyze carefully selected challenging texts and share their understanding with their peers. However, this framework also utilizes the real-life tools of inquiry (see Figure 9.8). Although students are not searching out primary-source documents themselves, they do engage with a variety of primary-source print and visual texts, and they use historical thinking tools (Wineburg, 2010; Wineburg et al., 2012) to analyze and evaluate these resources. Students are also encouraged to use a variety of written genres to share their findings with others and then use their shared research products to evaluate if they were successful in their inquiry.

Inquiry in a Social Studies Text Set

Our social studies quad text set focused on tracing the development of segregation over time and explaining patterns of continuity and change in segregation in American institutions, particularly schools (see Figure 9.9). To extend student understanding of this concept, our teacher has students participate in an inquiry activity following the Stripling Model of Inquiry in which they explore patterns of segregation in an American city. In this way her students can apply what they

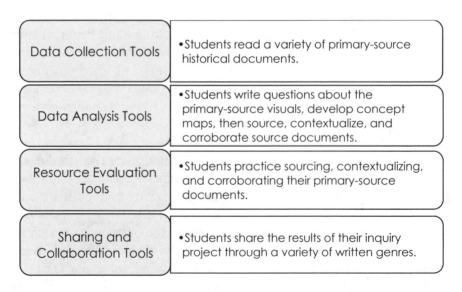

Data Collection Tools	• Students read a variety of primary-source historical documents.
Data Analysis Tools	• Students write questions about the primary-source visuals, develop concept maps, then source, contextualize, and corroborate source documents.
Resource Evaluation Tools	• Students practice sourcing, contextualizing, and corroborating their primary-source documents.
Sharing and Collaboration Tools	• Students share the results of their inquiry project through a variety of written genres.

FIGURE 9.8. The Stripling Model of Inquiry and the tools of inquiry.

Instructional Objective(s): Analyze historical materials to trace the development of an idea over time and explain patterns of continuity and change; determine the central idea of a primary source and accurately summarize the central idea and key details.
Visual Text: "Kids Talk about Segregation" video
Informational Text(s): Article on the history of racial segregation in the United States
Target Text: *Brown v. Board of Education* decision
Accessible Text: Article on racial disparities in modern U.S. public schools
Inquiry Extension: How has public policy impacted segregation in cities, and can we can get involved to create social change around this issue?

FIGURE 9.9. Social studies quad text set with inquiry extension.

have learned about segregation, and they can also come to a more comprehensive understanding of the policies that exacerbated or ameliorated segregation in that location.

As in the previous science example, the teacher organizes students into collaborative small groups for this inquiry project. This collaborative grouping option serves two purposes. It supports students throughout the data collection, analysis, and sharing process. It also allows the teacher to strategically select a smaller subgroup of cities for groups to research where segregation has historically been an issue, where there is robust data on racial segregation available, and where segregation has led to increased tension and contemporary problems.

Because students will already have substantial background knowledge about the topic from their engagement with the quad text set, they will not need to engage in a long *connect* and *wonder* phase of inquiry. That said, students can begin their inquiry project by researching digital maps of racially segregated cities like Chicago, Detroit, Houston, Syracuse, or Pittsburgh, examining the maps for patterns of racial segregation over time, and using these maps to develop important questions that can guide the rest of their inquiry during a brief *investigate* phase.

At this point the teacher can provide students with several primary and secondary source documents related to housing policy and urban renewal projects during the *construct phase* and how these projects have led to significantly more segregation in American urban centers or to the denial of services to racial minorities. Now that students have background knowledge on the types of policies that lead to communities of color being segregated, groups of students can begin to engage in more targeted online research about their choice city, noting specific policies and projects that have a negative or positive impact on the problem of segregation in that city and evaluating the reliability of their online resources.

During the *express phase,* students use a cloud-based platform, such as Glogster, to create an online interactive poster that combines text, images, video, and audio to communicate their findings with peers. After the presentations, the teacher leads her students in the *reflect* phase by examining the patterns in the student-chosen cities, encouraging them to reflect on what they have learned, and deciding whether more information is needed about the topic. She also uses the *reflect* phase to engage students in conversations about how they can become more engaged in their communities and advocate for more just policies. This is one way that she incorporates the C3 Framework's (NCSS, 2013) focus on preparing students to take informed action.

ELA: Critical Inquiry for Constructing Social Worlds

As we noted earlier in this chapter, disciplinary experts in English have been sharply critical of the traditional research paper. One model, the Critical Inquiry for Constructing Social Worlds framework (Beach, 2002; Beach & Myers, 2001), can serve as a robust and flexible alternative for extending students' understanding of literary texts and encouraging them to apply literary knowledge to their broader social worlds through the use of real-world tools of inquiry.

It is important to note that the Constructing Social Worlds model is a comprehensive framework with the expressed purpose of transforming ELA curriculum and instruction in secondary classrooms. For the purposes of this chapter, we distill what we see as the key elements of this framework to provide a succinct and workable outline that can be adapted to extend your students' understanding of disciplinary concepts through targeted inquiry projects. Figure 9.10 depicts the phases and tools of inquiry in this framework (Beach & Myers, 2001).

The initial phase of this inquiry framework begins with students *immersing themselves in a social world.* This social world could either be a fictional world that is represented in literature or media, or it could be a real-life world of a student's family, sports team, or other group that is of interest to students and to which they have access. For example, Beach and Myers (2001) have used this inquiry framework in a middle school girls' book club to explore the medieval world of Karen Cushman's (1994) YA novel *Catherine, Called Birdy,* which details the struggles of an adolescent woman against her controlling father and the patriarchal society of the Middle Ages. They have also used this framework to encourage students to conduct inquiry by immersing themselves in the world of snowboarding, a favorite coffee shop, a church choir, and a group of baseball fans.

During the initial *immersion* phase, students begin preliminary inquiry work, studying specific aspects of their chosen social world, sharing ideas with other classmates, and asking critical questions about what they are learning. In the YA novel project, students began working in pairs to research aspects of the medieval social world in which the main character, Birdy, was embedded. This included preliminary research into the feudal system, the lives of the aristocracy

FIGURE 9.10. Model of Critical Inquiry for Constructing Social Worlds.

and peasants, the medieval church, and educational institutions. Students used this information to question particular aspects of the novel's world, including queries about the morality of using marriage to secure family wealth or about how the father can claim to love Birdy but still use violence to enforce his will on her.

The next phase of inquiry begins when students *identify concerns, issues, and dilemmas*. During this stage of inquiry, students use their preliminary immersion into the social world to delve more deeply into issues that manifest themselves there. Students studying Birdy's medieval social world, for instance, were *concerned* that women in this society were not viewed as intelligent enough to educate, were not able to marry who they wanted, and were subjected to regular physical abuse from men. From these micro-level concerns in the novel, students then identified broader macro-level *issues* operating at the social level of the novel or *dilemmas* that connected Birdy's struggles to those in their own lives. Students identified the institutions, laws, and procedures that subjected women to this treatment, or broader dilemmas that connected Birdy's struggles to those in their own lives. Some students recognized that, like Birdy, they too experienced both loving someone despite their parents' disapproval and attempting to maintain friendships with peers despite not wanting to go along with their peers' illegal activity. The goal of this phase is for students to identify a more specific focus for their inquiry based on the concerns, issues, or dilemmas that are at work in their social world.

In the *contextualizing social worlds* phase, students conduct further inquiry by examining the purposes, roles, rules, beliefs, and history operating in the social world they are exploring. As Beach and Myers (2001) explain, by inquiring into these crucial components of social worlds, students can more effectively "examine and represent that world, how it is constructed, and how it might be transformed" (p. 58). In the girls' book club, students used focused and critical questions to compare and contrast the identities of women in the medieval world with women in the contemporary world, and then expanded their inquiry by contextualizing the social worlds of women in other environments (e.g., women in the military, single-sex classrooms, women's sports teams). In this way students began to move from the social world of the book to the world that they inhabited. See Figure 9.11 for examples of the questions that students might ask for each of these social-world components, whether that world be literary-, media-, or reality-based.

As students build their understanding of these social worlds, Beach and Myers (2001) suggest that students use real-world inquiry tools to collect data and share their developing understanding with others. Figure 9.12 shows how this framework leverages these tools. These include asking questions, making observations of social practices, recording observations in detailed field notes, conducting interviews, and analyzing data. To better understand young women's perception of male and female relationships in the contemporary social world, Beach and Myers (2001) offer the example of a student who organized viewing parties composed of female high school students for two television programs (*Melrose Place* and *Beverly Hills, 90210*). The researcher observed the students' conversations about the conflicts and characters in the show and interviewed them about their perceptions of the program. After collecting these data, the researcher analyzed the observations and interviews using the critical questions in Figure 9.11 to identify the patterns that would help her to contextualize this social world. Not surprisingly, she found that the students would often predict how characters would act based on past behavior and would use the programs' conflicts to vicariously discuss their own male and female relationships. More importantly, she found that the students would often judge characters' behavior based on middle-class values around work, family, and sexual behavior, but they did little critical analysis of their own assumptions about relationships and the consumer-oriented world in which these relationships take place.

Purposes
• Why are people doing what they are doing?
• What are people trying to accomplish?
• What is driving this activity?
• Are multiple or conflicting purposes at work?

Roles
• What roles do participants or characters enact in an activity or a world?
• What practices or language do they employ to enact a role?
• How do they align themselves in relationship to alternative identities within a world?
• What are their feelings about being in a role?

Rules
• What are the rules operating in a social world?
• Who establishes or defines these rules?
• What are the cues or violations of rules suggesting inappropriate behavior in a world?
• What are the consequences for not following these rules?
• How might a rule be both good and bad at the same time?

Beliefs
• What practices define this world?
• How does participants' use of language define one's role in the social world?

History
• What are the traditions of this social world?
• How has the past influenced the values, identities, and relationships of this world?
• How have the meaning of texts or images changed over time because of cultural forces?

FIGURE 9.11. Questions for contextualizing social worlds.

Once students have analyzed what they have collected, they can advance to the next stage of inquiry in which they *represent* their social world using sharing tools. These can include writing, music, video, dramatic performances, art and sculpture, photography, and digital tools. For example, in an inquiry project about a short story that explored the social worlds of peer groups, a high school student represented her social world by creating a video that combined excerpted scenes from the movie *The Breakfast Club* with digital photos she took of teens in her school. She edited these pictures by turning them into grayscale photos and colorizing single aspects of the photos (e.g., clothing, accessories, shoes) that signified membership in a specific teen social group (Beach & Myers, 2001). In

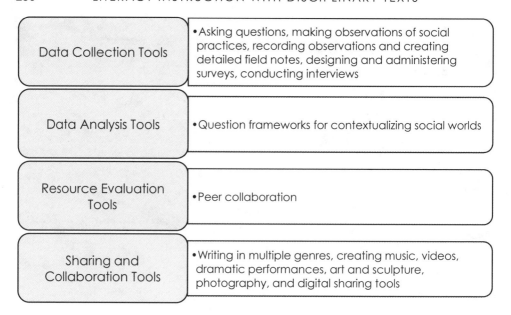

Data Collection Tools	• Asking questions, making observations of social practices, recording observations and creating detailed field notes, designing and administering surveys, conducting interviews
Data Analysis Tools	• Question frameworks for contextualizing social worlds
Resource Evaluation Tools	• Peer collaboration
Sharing and Collaboration Tools	• Writing in multiple genres, creating music, videos, dramatic performances, art and sculpture, photography, and digital sharing tools

FIGURE 9.12. Model of Critical Inquiry for Constructing Social Worlds and the tools of inquiry.

this way, the student was able to move her inquiry from the world of the book into the broader world of competing teen social groups.

One of the most compelling aspects of this framework is the last stage, in which students *critique and transform* the representation of the social world that was the focus of their inquiry. Beach and Myers (2001) suggest that this stage be guided by a seven-step process that not only supports students' critical analysis of the world but also empowers them to develop alternatives to the status quo, addressing the concerns, issues, and dilemmas they identified in their second stage of inquiry. Figure 9.13 represents this process.

For example, after reading Larry Watson's (1993) novel *Montana 1948,* a story about a family torn by a crime against its Native American housekeeper, students decided to study representations of model and conflicted families on contemporary television shows (Beach & Myers, 2001). What the students found through their inquiry was that most of the shows they studied portrayed generally happy and functional families. Using this process, they were able to recognize that the status quo was inadequate and possibly harmful to children whose families do not meet this representational standard and may feel that they are doing something wrong. In response to this critique, students could begin to *transform* the status quo of that social world by creating vlogs, blogs, or videos that address the real messiness of family life and then share those stories with their peers. This could be followed by a reflection and evaluation of the intervention.

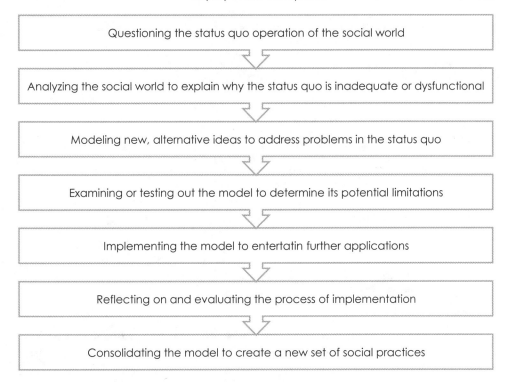

FIGURE 9.13. Process for critiquing and transforming social worlds.

Inquiry in an ELA Text Set

As you will recall, our ELA quad text set was focused on the impact of gendered expectations on the characters in the play *Romeo and Juliet,* as well as how those expectations impacted the plot and theme (see Figure 9.14). Using the Model of Critical Inquiry for Constructing Social Worlds framework (Beach & Myers, 2001), the teacher has students begin *immersing themselves* in the world of Renaissance Italy by working in small groups to begin preliminary research into the aristocracy, the Renaissance church, codes of conduct around marriage, or the legal system. Students develop questions about particular aspects of Romeo and Juliet's world, such as the morality of marrying for wealth and power instead of love or why violence is so prevalent among members of the aristocracy.

In the immersion stage, students begin to *identify concerns, issues, and dilemmas,* which can serve as a focus for the rest of their inquiry. They might identify the concern that Juliet has little choice in determining a life partner, and then they go on to identify the broader societal issue that legal and religious institutions allowed aristocratic families to treat female children like property. Alternatively, students might connect to an essential dilemma for Juliet: follow the rational will of her family or give into the overpowering and destructive force of her emotions.

Instructional Objective(s): Analyze how characters develop over the course of a text, interact with other characters, advance the plot, and develop the theme.	
Visual Text: Video of Act I from contemporary film version of *Romeo and Juliet*	
Informational Text(s): Article on gender roles and power in Elizabethan England	
Target Text: Act I of Shakespeare's *Romeo and Juliet*	
Accessible Text: Selected chapters from *Eleanor and Park* by Rainbow Rowell	
Inquiry Extension: How do gender, family, religion, and class impact young adults' ability to control their own lives?	

FIGURE 9.14. ELA quad text set with inquiry extension.

Next, students advance to the *contextualizing social worlds* phase of the project. They can begin asking critical questions (see Figure 9.11) about the purposes, roles, rules, beliefs, and history of the social world of *Romeo and Juliet,* and then connect the world of Renaissance Italy to their own social world. For example, students might begin to expand their inquiry to compare the control Juliet's family had over her life to the kinds of control parents assert on their female and male children today, including whether the gender of the child impacts parental decision making. Other groups might decide to connect Juliet's passion-driven relationship with Romeo to unhealthy relationships between romantic partners in their peer groups or to what they see in social media. Using data collection tools, students might observe romantic partners in their school environment and take detailed field notes. Other students might design a survey that asks questions about respondents' gender, whether they have siblings of the same or different gender, how their parents allowed them to exercise responsibility as they moved from childhood into adolescence, and whether gender impacted their parents' decision making.

Once they have contextualized these worlds and collected and analyzed their data, the teacher has her students share the products of their inquiry as they represent their social worlds to others. Utilizing an interactive tool like Voki (*www.voki.com*), small groups of students might choose to represent their social worlds through video presentations that allow them to create speaking avatars and choose backgrounds, illustrations, and text to share what they found about the impact of gender on their ability to control decision making. Other groups might choose to construct collages that represent specific aspects of the peer relationships they see in their school and the healthy—and not so healthy—behaviors associated with these relationships.

After the representation phase, the teacher has her students end their inquiry cycle by *critiquing and transforming* the social world they represented. Students who were researching the impact of gender on parents' willingness to give their children adult privileges and responsibilities might recognize that male children are often given more agency to make decisions, they are provided greater opportunities to take responsibility outside the home, and they are able to gain privileges at a younger age than female children. Recognizing the injustice of the status quo to female children and the limits it represents to their opportunities, this group might seek out additional research on the differences in maturity between female and male adolescents, insurance statistics that demonstrate that males are more likely than females to engage in risky behavior with an automobile, and develop public service announcements that challenge the perceptions of parents and the gendered limits their social world places on them.

FINAL THOUGHTS

As you can see, these three inquiry frameworks are very different from each other and from the mechanistic and formulaic library paper that we described at the beginning of this chapter. The projects we highlight encourage students to immerse themselves in data, to collect data with tools that disciplinary experts actually use, to collaborate with their peers, to evaluate the validity of their data sources and data-based arguments, and to share their findings with a broad audience that goes beyond their classroom teacher. By studying these examples and utilizing these frameworks, we hope that you can extend student understanding of important disciplinary concepts while building what Einstein called "the holy curiosity of inquiry."

C H A P T E R   1 0

Putting It All Together

In this book we have presented a specific vision for literacy instruction in secondary grades. We started from the understanding that there is not nearly enough reading and writing in middle and high school classrooms (Applebee & Langer, 2011; Swanson et al., 2016). We argued that the current state of adolescent literacy achievement will not improve unless all students are expected to engage in reading and writing activities with challenging texts in every content area every day. To that end, we described how to analyze texts for their complexity and design sets of connected texts built around a challenging disciplinary text in Chapters 2 and 3.

We also operated from the understanding that adolescents are able to comprehend and learn from challenging texts when provided with instructional support (Lupo et al., 2019). We wrote this book to show teachers what that support can look like using a B-D-A reading framework. We suggested instructional strategies for building background knowledge before reading, supporting comprehension during reading, conducting discussions after reading, and teaching text-based writing in Chapters 4–7. We also described how to teach extended writing and inquiry for students to demonstrate and extend their understanding of challenging content-area material in Chapters 8 and 9.

In this chapter, we first provide a bird's-eye view of what must happen on a schoolwide level to improve literacy instruction and achievement in secondary grades. We summarize the recommendations in several widely cited reports written about this topic. Then we provide a ground-level view of what steps content-area teachers can take on a daily basis to accomplish these goals. We provide specific guidance for planning weekly and daily instruction to fit within traditional class periods and extended block periods typical of secondary school schedules. We conclude with suggestions for where else to look for guidance beyond the pages of this book.

IMPROVING SECONDARY LITERACY INSTRUCTION

The last 20 years have seen an explosion in attention to the literacy needs of adolescents. While there has been substantial research on elementary literacy instruction for decades, studies of adolescent literacy instruction are a relatively recent phenomenon (Sedita, 2011). One of the first major reports on improving literacy instruction in secondary schools was the Carnegie Corporation's *Reading Next* report (Biancarosa & Snow, 2006). In their report, the authors identified 15 elements of effective adolescent literacy programs, nine of which detail necessary instructional improvements and six that suggest improvements to infrastructure.

Biancarosa and Snow's (2006) nine recommendations for improving adolescent literacy instruction are displayed in Figure 10.1. Some of these can be accomplished in tandem by implementing the instructional strategies we have described in this book. For example, supporting students' reading of content-area texts through RT (Palincsar & Brown, 1986), which we described in Chapter 5, constitutes explicit comprehension strategies instruction, instructional principles embedded in content, and self-directed learning. Conducting discussions about narrative and informational texts using strategies such as QtA (McKeown et al., 1993), which is illustrated in Chapter 6, is an example of both text-based collaborative learning and providing students with diverse texts. PALS (Fuchs et al., 1999), which is also described in Chapter 5, addresses each of these recommendations as well as the need to provide individualized, strategic tutoring from peers. Finally, teaching strategies for the writing process through CSIW (Raphael & Englert, 1990), which is detailed in Chapter 8, provides students with intensive writing that can be easily paired with technology and ongoing formative assessment. The point is that implementing research-validated instructional strategies across content-area classrooms will be necessary to improve student achievement.

While these instructional improvements will certainly impact students' literacy and content learning in individual classrooms, they are unlikely to lead

- Direct, explicit comprehension instruction
- Effective instructional principles embedded in content
- Motivation and self-directed learning
- Text-based collaborative learning
- Strategic tutoring
- Diverse texts
- Intensive writing
- A technology component
- Ongoing formative assessment of students

FIGURE 10.1. Instructional improvements for adolescent literacy.

to widespread growth in achievement without also improving infrastructure (Biancarosa & Snow, 2006). Figure 10.2 shows the six elements of school infrastructure that will need to be changed. Many of these will require a coordinated effort on behalf of teachers, instructional coaches, and school administrators to enact. However, we feel that the most immediately actionable of these recommendations is providing extended time for literacy. Biancarosa and Snow (2006) suggest that middle and high school students should receive between *2 and 4 hours* of literacy learning per day. In no way can this be accomplished in ELA classes alone. Students must have opportunities to read and write in social studies, science, and other content areas.

Our own professional development (PD) work in schools suggests that ongoing coaching, curriculum development, and collaboration in professional learning communities (PLCs) will also be necessary to improve achievement (Walpole et al., 2018). All school leaders and interdisciplinary grade-level teams of teachers will have to participate in PD and PLCs for them to be effective. Finally, schools will have to design a comprehensive and coordinated literacy program that utilizes summative assessment data to continually inform and improve instruction. As two of our school district partners indicated in the foreword to this book, this is often referred to as a school's *instructional brand*. In the highest-performing schools where we have worked, it is common to see every teacher implementing research-validated instructional strategies, as well as every student engaging in connected reading and writing, every day. It is unlikely that this would have happened without each of these infrastructural elements in place.

While the recommendations in the *Reading Next* report (Biancarosa & Snow, 2006) represent a large-scale vision that will be difficult for many schools to realize without significant effort, other reports provide suggestions for improving instruction at the level of the classroom. The Institute of Education Sciences (IES) Practice Guide entitled *Improving Adolescent Literacy: Effective Classroom and Intervention Practices* (Kamil et al., 2008) consolidated the best evidence at the time to provide five recommendations for secondary classroom teachers. These recommendations are summarized in Figure 10.3. You will see that the

- Extended time for literacy
- Professional development
- Ongoing summative assessment of students and programs
- Teacher teams
- Leadership
- A comprehensive and coordinated literacy program

FIGURE 10.2. Infrastructure improvements for adolescent literacy.

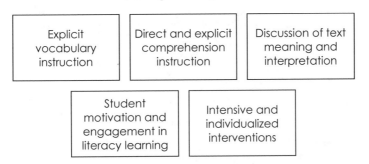

FIGURE 10.3. Effective practices for improving adolescent literacy.

three recommendations in the top row mirror the B-D-A reading framework we have used to organize this book.

Based in part on the IES Practice Guide, we have suggested explicitly teaching key vocabulary before reading, providing explicit comprehension strategies instruction and support during reading, and conducting text-based discussions after reading (Kamil et al., 2008). The research evidence is clear that these are best practices that should be included in all content-area classrooms. You will recall that we also suggested six classroom practices for motivating students to read in Chapter 1, including content goals, real-world interactions, interesting texts, student choice, strategy instruction, and collaboration support (Guthrie & Davis, 2003). We hope you agree that these targets will be easily met by integrating the quad text set framework and the B-D-A instructional strategies described in this book. The last recommendation is to provide intensive and individualized interventions for students with reading difficulties delivered by trained professionals (Kamil et al., 2008). While nearly all of the instructional strategies in this book were developed for students with reading difficulties, we have been mostly silent until this point on what to do during the intervention period that many secondary schools set aside for addressing significant reading difficulties. We break our silence on this issue later in this chapter.

Recent research has shown that while the *Reading Next* report and IES Practice Guide are valuable, they do not represent the most up-to-date information (Baye et al., 2019; Reynolds, 2020). A report recently published by the United Kingdom's Education Endowment Foundation, *Improving Literacy in Secondary Schools* (Quigley & Coleman, 2019), provides seven recommendations for secondary literacy instruction compiled from the best available international evidence (see Figure 10.4). We hope you notice how these recommendations also resemble the chapters in this book. In fact, this book is based on the premise that secondary literacy instruction must prioritize teaching students how to read and write with complex texts in each discipline, for which we have argued the use of the quad text set framework. We have also argued for targeted instruction of

- Prioritize disciplinary literacy across the curriculum.
- Provide targeted vocabulary instruction in every subject.
- Develop students' ability to read complex academic texts.
- Provide opportunities for structured discussion.
- Combine writing instruction with reading in every subject.
- Break down complex writing tasks.
- Provide high-quality literacy interventions for struggling students.

FIGURE 10.4. Guidance for improving secondary literacy instruction.

general academic and discipline-specific vocabulary words before reading, supporting students' ability to read complex texts with comprehension strategies during reading, and providing opportunities for high-quality discussions about texts after reading. We have described strategies for teaching students how to write both summaries and text-based arguments to promote reading comprehension. Finally, we have presented how to break down complex writing tasks by teaching students how to use strategies for planning, revising, and editing, as well as how to use the tools of inquiry to conduct real research.

For the students who need additional support beyond what we just described, we suggest possible interventions later in this chapter. However, we want to be clear up front that no amount of intervention will ever make up for weak whole-class instruction. That is why we put most of our eggs into the ELA, social studies, and science baskets instead of intervention. We hope that this big-picture view of what it will take to transform classroom literacy instruction has been reaffirming. Next, we take you down into the view from the classroom on Monday morning and what it will take for you to schedule your weekly and daily calendar to meet these goals.

SCHEDULING SECONDARY LITERACY INSTRUCTION

Earlier in this chapter we stated that secondary students will need between 2 and 4 hours of literacy instruction each day to make significant growth in achievement (Biancarosa & Snow, 2006). Think about how much time that really is. Two to 4 hours means somewhere between 120 and 240 minutes of literacy instruction during each school day. That amounts to 10 to 24 hours of connected reading and writing activities per week. Given the limited amount of instructional time each day and week, that is not going to happen in a single class period. If secondary schools are going to provide students with the amount of literacy instruction that experts recommend, it will have to occur across all content areas on a daily basis.

In addition to releasing practice guides, IES regularly reports the amount of instructional time spent in different content areas in public and private schools. The most recent report tracked the amount of time spent in ELA/reading, mathematics, science, and social studies in elementary and middle grades (Hoyer & Sparks, 2017). The data from public middle schools are shown in Figure 10.5, but private schools were not significantly different. The first main finding of this report is that middle school students spend, on average, 33.8 hours per week in school. Between 10 and 20 hours devoted to reading and writing amounts to around 30–60% of the school week. The second main finding is that students spend more time in ELA/reading than any other content area, close to 20% of the school week. If we are to assume that nearly all of the time spent in ELA will involve literacy-related instruction (a big assumption), that leaves 10–40% of the school week unexplained. Try adding up the percentage of time middle school students spend in mathematics, science, and social studies combined. Are you surprised that it's exactly 40%? We were! The reality is that meeting these targets, mathematically speaking, will require some to all of students' time spent in content-area classes devoted to reading and writing of texts.

Now that we've established that secondary school schedules must account for literacy instruction across content areas, the question remains as to how to schedule those precious minutes of instruction. Based on our work in secondary schools, and as former high school teachers ourselves, we understand that most middle and high schools operate on a traditional class period or a block schedule. A report by Hanover Research (2014) found neither type of schedule to be associated with higher achievement, but it did note the benefits and drawbacks of each model. Traditional class periods last between 45 and 55 minutes, with the benefit of having students attend class every day but the drawback being relatively little instructional time. Block periods tend to alternate by day or semester and typically last between 85 and 100 minutes, with the drawback of having students not attend class every day. The benefit of additional instructional time also means that teachers will have to carefully plan their lessons to maximize efficiency and minimize fatigue.

Content Area	Minutes per Day	Hours per Week	Percentage
ELA/Reading	78.0	6.5	19.4
Mathematics	60.0	5.0	14.8
Science	51.6	4.3	12.7
Social Studies	50.4	4.2	12.5
Other	165.6	13.8	40.6
Total	405.6	33.8	100.0

FIGURE 10.5. Time spent in each content area in middle school.

We are not going to recommend that schools adopt one scheduling model or another. Instead, we will provide recommendations for how content-area teachers should spend their weekly and daily instructional time in order to provide opportunities for literacy instruction.

Weekly Schedule

Whether a school has traditional class periods or a block schedule, we think it makes sense to consider instruction in 5-day cycles. If the class meets every day, that's one full week without days off from school, pep rallies, assemblies, fire drills, or other interruptions to instructional time. If the class meets every other day, five class periods will be 2 weeks.

In Figure 10.6 we present a possible plan for scheduling instruction that includes reading and text-based writing activities as well as a plan for teaching extended writing across a 5-day cycle. It is not meant to be a rigid structure but rather a flexible one in which the moving parts can be adjusted as needed. If the instructional focus is reading and text-based writing to learn content, the 5-day cycle follows our quad text set framework (see Chapter 3). On the first day of the cycle, students will view a visual text to activate background knowledge. On the next day they will read an informational text to build additional knowledge. Next, you might choose to chunk the target text, especially if it is long or difficult, to be read across two class periods on days three and four. On the final day of the cycle, students will read the accessible text. On each of these days, you should employ B-D-A instructional strategies to support comprehension. We address those strategies later in our sample daily instructional schedules.

If the teacher's instructional focus is extended writing to demonstrate understanding, the 5-day cycle follows the writing process (see Chapter 8). Based on our experiences, it takes many students, especially those with writing difficulties, at least this much class time to produce multiparagraph compositions. On the first day of the cycle, students should begin planning and setting goals for their writing. On the second day, most students will either continue planning or begin drafting from their completed plan. On the third day, most students should finish

Instructional Focus	Day 1	Day 2	Day 3	Day 4	Day 5
Reading and Text-Based Writing	Visual Text	Informational Text	Target Text	Target Text	Accessible Text
Extended Writing	Planning and Goal Setting	Planning and Drafting	Drafting	Evaluating and Revising	Revising and Editing

FIGURE 10.6. Sample weekly instructional schedule for reading and writing lessons.

the first draft of their composition. On the fourth day, students should engage in peer-evaluation and peer-revising activities. On the final day, students should finish revising and editing in order to produce their final draft. As we noted in Chapter 8, the writing process is more flexible than it is a set of linear stages (Graham et al., 2016). However, secondary teachers must often balance their limited instructional time and large number of students. Therefore, we think it is important to plan for the writing schedule in Figure 10.6 in an ideal world and accept the reality that many students will move back and forth through the stages of the writing process throughout the week.

We don't mean to suggest that teachers should alternate between reading and text-based writing and teaching extended writing on a week-by-week basis. That couldn't be further from our recommendation. It is likely the case that most weeks in a 9-week marking period will be spent reading to learn new content, with fewer weeks spent demonstrating understanding through extended writing. An instructional unit might contain two or three quad text sets, for example, with students completing an extended writing assignment after the final text set in the unit. Again, the schedule we are proposing here is meant to be more of a suggestion than a directive.

The weekly schedules we have outlined were also designed with CCR standards in mind. You will recall from Chapter 1 that the CCSS (NGA & CCSSO, 2010) delineate the percentage of instructional time that should be devoted to each text type for reading and writing (see Figure 10.7). The CCSS suggest that middle school students should read 55% informational texts and 45% literature; in high school it is 70% informational and 30% literary text. If two or three texts in each quad text set are informational, middle and high school teachers should have no problem meeting these goals. The CCSS suggest equal percentages of argumentative and informative/explanatory writing in middle school (35%) and high school (40%), with less time devoted to narrative writing. Let's say that in one 9-week marking period students write three extended compositions in ELA, one in science, and one in social studies. To meet these targets, students would have to write an argumentative and an informative/explanatory composition between science and social studies. In ELA, they would have to write one argumentative, one informative/explanatory, and one narrative composition. Again,

Grade	Reading		Writing		
	Literature	Informational	Argumentative	Informative	Narrative
Fourth	50%	50%	30%	35%	35%
Eighth	45%	55%	35%	35%	30%
Twelfth	30%	70%	40%	40%	20%

FIGURE 10.7. Distribution of reading and writing by text type.

we don't mean that our example should be taken as prescriptive. Our purpose is to illustrate that students must write across content areas, and they must write a lot. And interdisciplinary grade-level teams will have to plan their weekly schedules accordingly.

Daily Schedule

Mapping out your weekly schedules across a marking period is a regular part of your work as a teacher. You are also responsible for planning daily lessons, which will obviously vary depending on whether you teach in a traditional class period or a block schedule. In Figure 10.8 we present examples of daily schedules for teaching reading and text-based writing and for teaching extended writing in an 80-minute block period. Our decisions about time were made to provide the maximum amount of time allowable for connected reading and writing activities, while also making time for effective instructional practices. The timing will have to be adjusted if you have less or more instructional time in your school's schedule.

If the instructional focus is teaching content through reading and text-based writing, the lesson begins with about 10 minutes for before-reading activities, including building background knowledge or teaching key vocabulary (see Chapter 4). Ten minutes is not a hard and fast rule, but before-reading activities are meant to be brief. We once saw a teacher spend a whole class period on a Friday building background knowledge for the text students were going to read on Monday. That was not an effective use of time. In a block period, we recommend at least 45 minutes for during-reading activities that support comprehension of content-area texts (see Chapter 5). This will allow enough time for students to read a sizeable text selection and engage in the full protocol for timed reading frameworks such as PALS (Fuchs et al., 1999). After reading, we suggest

Minutes	Reading and Text-Based Writing	Minutes	Extended Writing
10	Build background knowledge or teach key vocabulary.	10	Analyze exemplar texts or student writing samples.
45	Support reading of complex content-area texts.	15	Teach and model how to use genre-specific writing strategy.
15	Provide opportunities for classroom discussion.	45	Provide opportunities for guided and/or independent practice of genre-specific writing strategy.
10	Teach or practice strategies for text-based writing.	10	Provide opportunities for reflection on strategy use.

FIGURE 10.8. Sample daily instructional schedule for reading and writing in an 80-minute block.

around 15 minutes for classroom discussion (see Chapter 6) and 10 minutes for text-based written responses such as arguments and summaries (see Chapter 7). Again, these suggestions are meant to be variable based on the needs of the students, as well as the difficulty of the text, the demands of the task, and the amount of time in a teacher's schedule.

When the focus is teaching extended writing, a typical lesson follows a Model–Practice–Reflect cycle (Graham et al., 2016), which we described in Chapter 8. When teaching a new genre or text structure, teachers should begin by analyzing an exemplar text or a writing sample written by a student or the teacher for genre elements (Englert et al., 1991). This 10-minute activity could be delivered through modeling or guided practice depending on level of scaffolding students require. Next, the teacher should explicitly teach and model how to use a genre-specific strategy for planning or revising. We anticipate that this might take 15 minutes, but the timing is totally variable based on the needs of the students and the difficulty of the task. Next, teachers should devote most of the class period, around 45 minutes, to supporting students as they apply the strategy collaboratively or independently through writing. The lesson should conclude with around 10 minutes for students to evaluate they writing they produced and reflect on the effectiveness of the strategy (Graham et al., 2016).

In Figure 10.9 we present sample schedules for teaching reading and text-based writing and for teaching extended writing in a 50-minute class period. You will notice two differences in the daily schedule for reading and text-based writing. First, while the amount of time devoted to before-reading activities remains the same, we reduced the amount of time spent reading to 30 minutes. This means that the texts students read will have to be chunked into smaller segments. We do not suggest selecting shorter texts due to time constraints. Again, we made this decision in order to leave the maximum time allowable for reading while also leaving enough time to use the full protocol for PALS (Fuchs et al., 1999). The second difference is that teachers will likely have time for only discussion or text-based writing, not both. Given that both activities

Minutes	Reading and Text-Based Writing	Minutes	Extended Writing
10	Build background knowledge or teach key vocabulary.	10	Analyze exemplar texts or student writing samples.
30	Support reading of complex content-area texts.	10	Teach and model how to use genre-specific writing strategy.
10	Provide opportunities for classroom discussion or teach strategies for text-based writing.	30	Provide opportunities for guided and/or independent practice of writing strategy and reflection.

FIGURE 10.9. Sample daily instructional schedule for reading and writing in a 50-minute period.

support comprehension after reading, albeit in different ways, we feel comfortable suggesting that teachers decide which is more appropriate each day based on students' needs and the text.

In the daily schedule for teaching extending writing, the changes are less drastic. We still suggest beginning with about 10 minutes for analyzing exemplar texts or writing samples. In addition, we have reduced the amount of explicit teaching and modeling from 15 minutes to 10. Of course, we recommend that teachers use their professional judgment to allow less or more time for modeling based on the level of support their students need and the task difficulty. Finally, we suggest providing at least 30 minutes for guided or independent practice in which students apply the strategy in the context of writing. The trade-off in this schedule is that you will also have to use some of that time for students to reflect on the effectiveness of their strategy use.

To make it abundantly clear, we will once again state that the time allotments in our sample schedules are suggestions. They are not empirically validated. Teachers will likely have to adapt these schedules to fit their students and their school context. That said, we do feel that at least one of our suggestions should be heeded. Based on the advice of literacy experts, students must receive between 2 and 4 hours of literacy instruction daily, including at least 1 hour of writing (Biancarosa & Snow, 2006; Graham et al., 2012). Therefore, teachers should leave the maximum amount of time possible for connected reading and writing activities each day.

There is one more piece of the daily schedule puzzle that we have not yet addressed in this chapter. We firmly believe that *all* of the instructional strategies that teachers employ should be based on, if not validated by, research. In this book we have presented a relatively small number of instructional strategies that we think should be used schoolwide across content areas. They are represented in Figure 10.10. We know many teachers might feel constrained by having to select from a short list of instructional strategies when planning their lessons, but we feel quite the opposite. Instead of spending your planning time designing a new instructional activity each day, you can devote your effort to deciding on the best instructional strategy to use each day based on the needs of your students, the text, and your instructional objectives.

Our thinking on this issue has been heavily influenced by our work with Sharon Walpole and Michael McKenna (e.g., Lewis et al., 2014; Walpole, McKenna, Philippakos, & Strong, 2020). Their curriculum, *Bookworms K–5 Reading and Writing* (Open Up Resources, 2018), employs a small number of instructional strategies each day, leading teachers and students to become familiar with the strategies and leaving room for them to wrestle with a new selection of challenging text each day (Walpole, McKenna, Amendum, Pasquarella, & Strong, 2017). Think about how much different a lesson would be if your students already knew how to use the K-W-L strategy (Ogle, 1986) before reading, RT (Palincsar & Brown, 1986) during reading, Discussion Web (Alvermann, 1991) after reading,

Before Reading	• Concept of Definition • Semantic Feature Analysis • Listen–Read–Discuss • Prereading Plan • K-W-L strategy
During Reading	• Collaborative Strategic Reading • Reciprocal Teaching • Peer-Assisted Learning Strategies • Reading Guides • Collaborative Listening–Viewing Guide
After Reading	• Quality Talk • Reciprocal Questioning • Questioning the Author • Collaborative Reasoning • Discussion Web
Text-Based Writing	• Magnet Summaries • Somebody Wanted But So • RAFT strategy • CSET strategy
Extended Writing	• Planning strategies • Revising strategies • Editing strategy: COPS
Research and Inquiry	• Argument-Driven Inquiry • Stripling Model of Inquiry • Critical Inquiry for Constructing Social Worlds

FIGURE 10.10. Schoolwide instructional strategies for secondary grades.

and the CSET strategy (Lewis & Ferretti, 2011) for text-based writing. There would be little to no instructional time wasted explaining (and re-explaining) directions or reviewing procedures. There would only be more time to engage in reading and writing challenging text and learning about content.

As pragmatists, however, we realize that there will be times when you will need to engage your students in activities beyond the instructional strategies suggested in Figure 10.11. The instructional strategies in this book do not represent the full range of research-validated practices. There is always more that teachers (and we include ourselves) can learn about instruction. As a result, we have compiled a list of 10 trusted resources to learn more about adolescent literacy and help you with your instructional planning. Half of these websites (AdLit, the Center on Instruction, the International Literacy Association, ReadWriteThink, and the What Works Clearinghouse) are places to go to look for research-validated instructional strategies instead of scouring Google, Pinterest, or Teachers Pay Teachers. The other half (CommonLit, Newsela, ReadWorks, Science News for Students, and the Smithsonian Tween Tribune) are websites that will help you start finding texts for your quad text sets.

AdLit: www.adlit.org/strategy_library

Center on Instruction: www.centeroninstruction.org

CommonLit: www.commonlit.org/en/texts

International Literacy Association: www.literacyworldwide.org/get-resources

Newsela: https://newsela.com

ReadWorks: www.readworks.org/find-content

ReadWriteThink: www.readwritethink.org/classroom-resources/lesson-plans

Science News for Students: www.sciencenewsforstudents.org

Smithsonian Tween Tribune: www.tweentribune.com

What Works Clearinghouse: https://ies.ed.gov/ncee/wwc/practiceguides

FIGURE 10.11. Resources for planning adolescent literacy instruction.

PROVIDING SECONDARY LITERACY INTERVENTIONS

Even with the best planned whole-class literacy instruction, there will be students who require additional intervention outside the classroom. In secondary grades, this will often occur during a reading intervention or reading support class or from instruction delivered by a special education teacher. Two reports from the Center on Instruction indicate that adolescents with reading difficulties can benefit from word- and text-level interventions; however, most will not need instruction in foundational skills such as phonemic awareness and phonics (Boardman et al., 2008; Scammacca et al., 2007). Instead, Boardman and colleagues (2008) suggest that they benefit from interventions in five areas: word study (including decoding multisyllabic words), fluency, vocabulary, comprehension, and motivation. To this list we would also add writing.

Because we feel that teachers should invest most of their time and effort in planning effective literacy *instruction,* we will keep our suggestions for providing literacy *interventions* decidedly brief. Many commercially available programs address each of these areas through multicomponent interventions. Some of them have been empirically studied. We encourage you to visit the What Works Clearinghouse (*https://ies.ed.gov/ncee/wwc*) to examine the evidence for yourself before selecting an intervention program for your students.

You may not be surprised to learn that many of the instructional strategies we have described in this book have been tested in intervention settings. Evidence of their effectiveness is available from the What Works Clearinghouse. We have also used many of them in our own work with schools to support students requiring additional support during reading intervention periods. Figure 10.12 presents intervention options for different areas of literacy and online modules to learn more about them. Although we cannot guarantee that they will be effective

Areas	Interventions
Reading Comprehension	Collaborative Strategic Reading *https://iris.peabody.vanderbilt.edu/module/csr*
Fluency and Comprehension	Peer-Assisted Learning Strategies *https://iris.peabody.vanderbilt.edu/module/palshs*
Vocabulary and Comprehension	Explicit Vocabulary Instruction *https://iris.peabody.vanderbilt.edu/module/sec-rdng*
Motivation and Comprehension	Concept-Oriented Reading Instruction *www.cori.umd.edu/professional-development*
Writing Competence	Self-Regulated Strategy Development *https://iris.peabody.vanderbilt.edu/module/srs*

FIGURE 10.12. Effective adolescent literacy interventions.

for all students, the research evidence suggests that these interventions can be easily implemented and will meet the needs of many adolescent students with reading and writing difficulties.

FINAL THOUGHTS: THE ROAD AHEAD

In this chapter, we have given you guidance for putting all of our recommendations in this book together. We want you to keep the big picture in focus while remembering the details in your daily and weekly instruction. The road ahead to effective secondary literacy instruction across disciplines will be long and bumpy. We can't pretend that it will be easy, but we can tell you about how some of the teachers with whom we have worked have traveled this road.

John recently spent a full school year providing ongoing professional learning in a rural middle school in Georgia. In the spring, he had spoken with the principal and an instructional coach about working with sixth-, seventh-, and eighth-grade ELA, social studies, and science teachers during the following school year. In the summer, he provided a full-day institute explicitly teaching and modeling the quad text set and B-D-A frameworks. After the school year started and the dust had settled, he worked with interdisciplinary, grade-level PLCs to design quad text sets for teachers to implement later in the school year. They spent the next 2 months learning and practicing before-, during-, and after-reading and text-based writing strategies in their weekly PLC meetings. For the remainder of the school year, teachers implemented the quad text sets they had designed and the instructional strategies they had learned and practiced. John visited classrooms and PLCs to provide ongoing coaching, modeling, and feedback.

Midway through the year, the reading intervention teacher resigned. A young woman with no prior teaching experience, eager to help the neediest students, was hired to fill the vacancy. She and John met often, selecting texts and planning lessons that alternated between practicing reading with PALS and teaching writing with SRSD.

Were all of these efforts successful? In short, yes and no. Teachers implemented many of the instructional strategies with success. Students engaged in more connected reading and writing across their classes. However, there is still a long way to go from planning quad text sets, implementing instructional strategies, and changing classroom reading and writing practices to seeing widespread improvements in students' literacy achievement. The teachers we have worked with refer to these efforts as "working on the work." The work isn't easy, but we hope it's worth it.

References

Afflerbach, P., & Harrison, C. (2017). What is engagement, how is it different from motivation, and how can I promote it? *Journal of Adolescent and Adult Literacy, 61*(2), 217–220.

Alexander, P. A., & Fox, E. (2011). Adolescents as readers. In M. L. Kamil, P. D. Pearson, E. B. Moje, & P. P. Afflerbach (Eds.), *Handbook of reading research* (Vol. 4, pp. 157–176). New York: Routledge.

Alexander, P. A., Kulikowich, J. M., & Jetton, T. L. (1994). The role of subject-matter knowledge and interest in the processing of linear and nonlinear texts. *Review of Educational Research, 64*(2), 201–252.

Alfassi, M. (1998). Reading for meaning: The efficacy of reciprocal teaching in fostering reading comprehension in high school students in remedial reading classes. *American Educational Research Journal, 35*(2), 309–332.

Alozie, N. M., Moje, E. B., & Krajcik, J. S. (2010). An analysis of the supports and constraints for scientific discussion in high school project-based science. *Science Education, 94*(3), 395–427.

Alvermann, D. E. (1981). The compensatory effect of graphic organizers on descriptive text. *Journal of Educational Research, 75*(1), 44–48.

Alvermann, D. E. (1991). The discussion web: A graphic aid for learning across the curriculum. *The Reading Teacher, 45*(2), 92–99.

Alvermann, D. E., Hynd, C., & Qian, G. (1995). Effects of interactive discussion and text type on learning counterintuitive science concepts. *Journal of Educational Research, 88*, 146–154.

Alvermann, D. E., O'Brien, D. G., & Dillon, D. R. (1990). What teachers do when they say they're having discussions of content area reading assignments: A qualitative analysis. *Reading Research Quarterly, 25*, 296–322.

Amendum, S. J., Conradi, K., & Hiebert, E. (2018). Does text complexity matter in the elementary grades?: A research synthesis of text difficulty and elementary students' reading fluency and comprehension. *Educational Psychology Review, 30*(1), 121–151.

AmericanCivilWar.com. (n.d.). Confederate and Union Civil War song lyrics. Retrieved from *www.americancivilwar.com/Civil_War_Music/song_lyrics*.

Anders, P. L., & Bos, C. S. (1986). Semantic feature analysis: An interactive strategy for vocabulary development and text comprehension. *Journal of Reading, 29*(7), 610–616.

Anderson, R. C., Wilson, P. T., & Fielding, L. G. (1988). Growth in reading and how children spend their time outside of school. *Reading Research Quarterly, 23,* 285–303.

Andrade, H. L., Du, Y., & Wang, X. (2008). Putting rubrics to the test: The effect of a model, criteria generation, and rubric-referenced self-assessment on elementary school students' writing. *Educational Measurement: Issues and Practice, 27*(2), 3–13.

Angelou, M. (1970). *I know why the caged bird sings.* New York: Random House.

Applebee, A. N., & Langer, J. A. (2011). A snapshot of writing instruction in middle schools and high schools. *English Journal, 100*(6), 14–27.

Applebee, A. N., Langer, J. A., Nystrand, M., & Gamoran, A. (2003). Discussion-based approaches to developing understanding: Classroom instruction and student performance in middle and high school English. *American Educational Research Journal, 40*(3), 685–730.

Appleman, D. (2015). *Critical encounters in secondary English: Teaching literary theory to adolescents* (3rd ed.). New York: Teachers College Press.

Apthorp, H. S. (2006). Effects of a supplemental vocabulary program in third-grade reading/language arts. *Journal of Educational Research, 100*(2), 67–79.

Armbruster, B. B., Anderson, T. H., & Ostertag, J. (1987). Does text structure/summarization instruction facilitate learning from expository text? *Reading Research Quarterly, 22,* 331–346.

Arter, J., & Chappuis, J. (2007). *Creating and recognizing quality rubrics.* Upper Saddle River, NJ: Pearson Education.

Arya, D. J., Hiebert, E. H., & Pearson, P. D. (2011). The effects of syntactic and lexical complexity on the comprehension of elementary science texts. *International Electronic Journal of Elementary Education, 4*(1), 107–125.

Asaro-Saddler, K., Muir-Knox, H., & Meredith, H. (2018). The effects of a summary writing strategy on the literacy skills of adolescents with disabilities. *Exceptionality, 26,* 106–118.

Ash, G. E., Kuhn, M. R., & Walpole, S. (2009). Analyzing "inconsistencies" in practice: Teachers' continued use of round robin reading. *Reading and Writing Quarterly, 25*(1), 87–103.

Asselin, M. (2005). Teaching information skills in the information age: An examination of trends in the middle grades. *School Libraries Worldwide, 11*(1), 17–36.

Bacigalupi, P. (2010). *Ship breaker.* New York: Little, Brown.

Barton, K. C., & Levstik, L. S. (2004). *Teaching history for the common good.* Mahwah, NJ: Erlbaum.

Baye, A., Inns, A., Lake, C., & Slavin, R. E. (2019). A synthesis of quantitative research on reading programs for secondary students. *Reading Research Quarterly, 54*(2), 133–166.

Bazerman, C., Applebee, A. N., Berninger, V. W., Brandt, D., Graham, S., Matsuda, P. K., . . . Schleppegrell, M. (2017). Taking the long view on writing development. *Research in the Teaching of English, 51*(3), 351–360.

Beach, R. (2002). Critical inquiry strategies for responding to social worlds portrayed in literature. In J. Holden & J. S. Schmit (Eds.), *Inquiry and the literary text: Constructing discussions in the English classroom* (pp. 123–137). Urbana, IL: National Council of Teachers of English.

Beach, R., & Myers, J. (2001). *Inquiry-based English instruction: Engaging students in life and literature*. New York: Teachers College Press.

Beck, I. L., & McKeown, M. G. (2001). Inviting students into the pursuit of meaning. *Educational Psychology Review, 13*(3), 225–241.

Beck, I. L., McKeown, M. G., Hamilton, R. L., & Kucan, L. (1997). *Questioning the Author: An approach for enhancing student engagement with text*. Newark, DE: International Reading Association.

Beck, I. L., McKeown, M. G., & Kucan, L. (2013). *Bringing words to life: Robust vocabulary instruction* (2nd ed.). New York: Guilford Press.

Beck, I. L., McKeown, M. G., & Sandora, C. (2021). *Robust comprehension instruction with Questioning the Author: 15 years smarter*. New York: Guilford Press.

Beck, I. L., McKeown, M. G., Sandora, C., Kucan, L., & Worthy, J. (1996). Questioning the Author: A yearlong classroom implementation to engage students with text. *Elementary School Journal, 96*, 385–414.

Beck, I. L., Perfetti, C. A., & McKeown, M. G. (1982). Effects of long-term vocabulary instruction on lexical access and reading comprehension. *Journal of Educational Psychology, 74*(4), 506–521.

Beers, G. K., & Probst, R. E. (2012). *Notice and note: Strategies for close reading*. Portsmouth, NH: Heinemann.

Berkeley, S., King-Sears, M. E., Hott, B. L., & Bradley-Black, K. (2014). Are history textbooks more "considerate" after 20 years? *Journal of Special Education, 47*(4), 217–230.

Berninger, V. W., Vaughan, K., Abbott, R. D., Begay, K., Byrd Coleman, K., Curtin, G., . . . Graham, S. (2002). Teaching spelling and composition alone and together: implications for the simple view of writing. *Journal of Educational Psychology, 94*(2), 291–304.

Best, R. M., Floyd, R. G., & McNamara, D. S. (2008). Differential competencies contributing to children's comprehension of narrative and expository texts. *Reading Psychology, 29*(2), 137–164.

Biancarosa, C., & Snow, C. E. (2006). *Reading next: A vision for action and research in middle and high school literacy—A report to Carnegie Corporation of New York* (2nd ed.). Washington, DC: Alliance for Excellent Education.

Bickford, J. H., III. (2013). Examining historical (mis)representations of Christopher Columbus within children's literature. *Social Studies Research and Practice, 8*(2), 1–24.

Blachowicz, C., & Ogle, D. (2008). *Reading comprehension: Strategies for independent learners* (2nd ed.). New York: Guilford Press.

Boardman, A. G., Klingner, J. K., Buckley, P., Annamma, S., & Lasser, C. S. (2015). The efficacy of collaborative strategic reading in middle school science and social studies classes. *Reading and Writing, 28*(9), 1257–1283.

Boardman, A. G., Roberts, G., Vaughn, S., Wexler, J., Murray, C. S., & Kosanovich, M. (2008). *Effective instruction for adolescent struggling readers: A practice brief*. Portsmouth, NH: RMC Research Corporation, Center on Instruction.

Boardman, A. G., Vaughn, S., Buckley, P., Reutebuch, C., Roberts, G., & Klingner, J. (2016). Collaborative strategic reading for students with learning disabilities in upper elementary classrooms. *Exceptional Children, 82*(4), 409–427.

Boscolo, P., & Gelati, C. (2013). Best practices in promoting motivation for writing. In S. Graham, C. A. MacArthur, & J. Fitzgerald (Eds.), *Best practices in writing instruction* (2nd ed., pp. 284–308). New York: Guilford Press.

Bossone, R. M. (1962). Every secondary teacher a teacher of reading. *High School Journal, 46,* 74–77.

Bransford, J. D., & Johnson, M. K. (1973). Considerations of some problems of comprehension. In W. Chase (Ed.), *Visual information processing* (pp. 383–438). New York: Academic Press.

Bremner, S. (2010). Collaborative writing: Bridging the gap between the textbook and the workplace. *English for Specific Purposes, 29*(2), 121–132.

Brooks, W. (2003). Accentuating, preserving, and unpacking: Exploring interpretations of family relationships with African-American adolescents. *Journal of Children's Literature, 29*(2), 78–84.

Brown, A. L., & Day, J. D. (1983). Macrorules for summarizing texts: The development of expertise. *Journal of Verbal Learning and Verbal Behavior, 22,* 1–14.

Brozo, W. G., Schmelzer, R. V., & Spires, H. A. (1983). Beneficial effect of chunking on good readers' comprehension of expository prose. *Journal of Reading, 26,* 442–445.

Buehl, D. (1993). Magnetized: Students are drawn to technique that identifies key words. *WEAC News and Views, 29*(4), 13.

Buehl, D. (2014). *Classroom strategies for interactive learning* (4th ed.). Portsmouth, NH: Stenhouse.

Burton, K. (1958). Some further thoughts on research papers. *English Journal, 47*(5), 291–292.

Bybee, R. W., Bloom, M., Phillips, J., & Knapp, N. (2005). *Doing science: The process of scientific inquiry.* Bethesda, MD: National Institute of General Medical Sciences.

Cain, K., Oakhill, J., & Bryant, P. (2004). Children's reading comprehension ability: Concurrent prediction by working memory, verbal ability, and component skills. *Journal of Educational Psychology, 96*(1), 31–42.

Cappello, M. (2017). Considering visual text complexity: A guide for teachers. *The Reading Teacher, 70*(6), 733–739.

Carr, E., & Ogle, D. (1987). KWL Plus: A strategy for comprehension and summarization. *Journal of Reading, 30*(7), 626–631.

Catts, H. W., Tomblin, J. B., Compton, D., & Bridges, M. S. (2012). Prevalence and nature of late-emerging poor readers. *Journal of Educational Psychology, 104*(1), 166–181.

Cazden, C. (1988). *Classroom discourse: The language of teaching and learning.* Portsmouth, NH: Heinemann.

CBS Evening News. (2017, August 4). Why Florida has become the lightning capital of the country [Video file]. Retrieved from *www.youtube.com/watch?v=NCR8hBjwSWA.*

Chall, J. S. (1996). *Stages of reading development* (2nd ed). Fort Worth, TX: Harcourt Brace.

Chambliss, M. J., Christenson, L. A., & Parker, C. (2003). Fourth graders composing scientific explanations about the effects of pollutants. *Written Communication, 20*(4), 426–454.

Chinn, C. A., Anderson, R. C., & Waggoner, M. A. (2001). Patterns of discourse in two kinds of literature discussion. *Reading Research Quarterly, 36*(4), 378–411.

Clark, A.-M., Anderson, R. C., & Kuo, L. (2003). Collaborative reasoning: Expanding ways for children to talk and think in school. *Educational Psychology Review, 15*(2), 181–198.

Coker, D. L., Jr., & Erwin, E. (2011). Teaching academic argument in an urban middle school: A case study of two approaches. *Urban Education, 46*(2), 120–140.

College Board. (2019). *2019 SAT suite of assessments annual report*. New York: Author.

College Board. (n.d.). Sample questions: Essay example 1 of 2. Retrieved from *https://collegereadiness.collegeboard.org/sample-questions/essay/1.*

Compton, D. L., Miller, A. C., Elleman, A. M., & Steacy, L. M. (2014). Have we forsaken reading theory in the name of "quick fix" interventions for children with reading disability? *Scientific Studies of Reading, 18*(1), 55–73.

Connell, R. E. (1957). *The most dangerous game and other stories of adventure*. New York: Berkley.

Conrad, J. (1902). *Youth: A narrative, and two other stories*. London: Thomas Nelson & Sons.

Conradi, K., Jang, B. G., Bryant, C., Craft, A., & McKenna, M. C. (2013). Measuring adolescents' attitudes toward reading: A classroom survey. *Journal of Adolescent and Adult Literacy, 56*(7), 565–576.

Council of Chief State School Officers. (2012, January 26). The Common Core State Standards: Supporting districts and teachers with text complexity. Retrieved from *http://programs.ccsso.org/projects/common%20core%20resources.*

Council of Chief State School Officers & National Governors Association. (2012). Supplemental information for Appendix A of the Common Core State Standards for English language arts and literacy: New research on text complexity. Retrieved from *www.corestandards.org/assets/E0813_Appendix_A_New_Research_on_Text_Complexity.pdf.*

Crafton, L. K. (1982). Comprehension before, during, and after reading. *The Reading Teacher, 36,* 293–297.

Culham, R. (2003). *6 + 1 traits of writing: The complete guide, grades 3 and up*. New York: Scholastic.

Cunningham, A. E., & Stanovich, K. E. (1997). Early reading acquisition and its relation to reading experience and ability 10 years later. *Developmental Psychology, 33*(6), 934–945.

Cunningham, A. E., & Stanovich, K. E. (1998). What reading does for the mind. *American Educator, 22*(1), 8–15.

Cunningham, J. W., Hiebert, E. H., & Mesmer, H. A. (2018). Investigating the validity of two widely used quantitative text tools. *Reading and Writing, 31*(4), 813–833.

Cunningham, J. W., & Mesmer, H. A. (2014). Quantitative measurement of text difficulty: What's the use? *Elementary School Journal, 115*(2), 255–269.

Cushman, K. (1994). *Catherine, called Birdy*. New York: Houghton Mifflin Harcourt.

Dalton, K. M. (2012). Bridging the digital divide and guiding the millennial generation's research and analysis. *Barry Law Review, 18,* 167.

Daniels, H. (2002). *Literature circles: Voice and choice in book clubs and reading groups* (2nd ed.). Portland, ME: Stenhouse.

Daniels, H., & Zemelman, S. (2003/2004). Out with textbooks, in with learning. *Educational Leadership, 61*(4), 36–40.

De La Paz, S. (1999). Teaching writing strategies and self-regulation procedures to middle school students with learning disabilities. *Focus on Exceptional Children, 31*(5), 1–16.

De La Paz, S. (2001). Stop and dare: A persuasive writing strategy. *Intervention in School and Clinic, 36*(4), 234–243.

De La Paz, S. (2009). Rubrics: Heuristics for developing writing strategies. *Assessment for Effective Intervention, 34*(3), 134–146.

De La Paz, S., & Graham, S. (1997). Effects of dictation and advanced planning instruction on the composing of students with writing and learning problems. *Journal of Educational Psychology, 89*(2), 203–222.

De La Paz, S., & Graham, S. (2002). Explicitly teaching strategies, skills, and knowledge: Writing instruction in middle school classrooms. *Journal of Educational Psychology, 94*(4), 687–698.

Delaware Department of Education. (2018). Social studies standards—history. Retrieved from *www.doe.k12.de.us/Page/2548*.

Dellinger, D. G. (1989). Alternatives to clip and stitch: Real research and writing in the classroom. *English Journal, 78*(5), 31–38.

Douglass, F. (1845). *Narrative of the life of Frederick Douglass, an American slave*. Boston: Anti-Slavery Office.

Dreher, M. J., & Guthrie, J. T. (1990). Cognitive processes in textbook chapter search tasks. *Reading Research Quarterly, 25*, 323–339.

Drew, S. V., Olinghouse, N. G., Faggella-Luby, M., & Welsh, M. E. (2017). Framework for disciplinary writing in science grades 6–12: A national survey. *Journal of Educational Psychology, 109*(7), 935–955.

Driver, R., Newton, P., & Osborne, J. (2000). Establishing the norms of scientific argumentation in classrooms. *Science Education, 84*(3), 287–312.

Duffy, T. M., Higgins, L., Mehlenbacher, B., Cochran, C., Wallace, D., Hill, C., . . . Smith, S. (1989). Models for the design of instructional text. *Reading Research Quarterly, 24*, 434–457.

Duschl, R. (2008). Science education in three-part harmony: Balancing conceptual, epistemic, and social learning goals. *Review of Research in Education, 32*(1), 268–291.

Dweck, C. S. (1986). Motivational processes affecting learning. *American Psychologist, 41*, 1040–1048.

Elizabethi.org. (1998–2019). Elizabethan women: Women in Tudor history. Retrieved from *www.elizabethi.org/contents/women*.

Englert, C. S., & Hiebert, E. H. (1984). Children's developing awareness of text structures in expository materials. *Journal of Educational Psychology, 76*, 65–74.

Englert, C. S., Raphael, T. E., Anderson, L. M., Anthony, H. M., Fear, K. L., & Gregg, S. L. (1988). A case for writing intervention: Strategies for writing informational text. *Learning Disabilities Focus, 3*(2), 98–113.

Englert, C. S., Raphael, T. E., Anderson, L. M., Anthony, H. M., & Stevens, D. D. (1991). Making strategies and self-talk visible: Writing instruction in regular and special education classrooms. *American Educational Research Journal, 28*(2), 337–372.

Fahnestock, J., & Secor, M. (1991). The rhetoric of literary criticism. In C. Bazerman & J. Paradis (Eds.), *Textual dynamics of the professions: Historical and contemporary studies of writing in professional communities* (pp. 77–96). Madison: University of Wisconsin Press.

Fang, Z. (2014). Preparing content area teachers for disciplinary literacy instruction. *Journal of Adolescent and Adult Literacy, 57*(6), 444–448.

Ferretti, R. P., & De La Paz, S. (2011). On the comprehension and production of written texts: Instructional activities that support content-area literacy. In R. O'Connor & P. Vadasy (Eds.), *Handbook of reading interventions* (pp. 326–355). New York: Guilford Press.

Ferretti, R. P., & Graham, S. (2019). Argumentative writing: Theory, assessment and instruction. *Reading and Writing, 32,* 1345–1356.

Ferretti, R. P., & Lewis, W. E. (2019). Discourse knowledge and writing goals predict the quality of children's persuasive writing. *Reading and Writing. 32*(6), 1411–1430.

Ferretti, R. P., MacArthur, C. A., & Dowdy, N. S. (2000). The effects of an elaborated goal on the persuasive writing of students with learning disabilities and their normally achieving peers. *Journal of Educational Psychology, 92*(4), 694–702.

Firetto, C. M., Murphy, P. K., Greene, J. A., Li, M., Wei, L., Montalbano, C., . . . Croninger, R. M. V. (2019). Bolstering students' written argumentation by refining an effective discourse intervention: Negotiating the fine line between flexibility and fidelity. *Instructional Science, 47*(2), 181–214.

Fisher, D., & Frey, N. (2003). Writing instruction for struggling adolescent readers: A gradual release model. *Journal of Adolescent and Adult Literacy, 46,* 396–405.

Fisher, D., & Frey, N. (2014a). Addressing CCSS anchor standard 10: Text complexity. *Language Arts, 91*(4), 236–250.

Fisher, D., & Frey, N. (2014b). Speaking and listening in content area learning. *The Reading Teacher, 68*(1), 64–69.

Fisher, D., & Frey, N. (2015). Selecting texts and tasks for content area reading and learning. *The Reading Teacher, 68*(7), 524–529.

Fisher, D., Frey, N., & Lapp, D. (2011). Coaching middle-level teachers to think aloud improves comprehension instruction and student reading achievement. *Teacher Educator, 46*(3), 231–243.

Fisher, D., Frey, N., & Lapp, D. (2012). Building and activating students' background knowledge: It's what they already know that counts: Teachers must assess and build on the background knowledge students possess. *Middle School Journal, 43*(3), 22–31.

Fisher, D., & Ivey, G. (2005). Literacy and language as learning in content-area classes: A departure from "every teacher a teacher of reading." *Action in Teacher Education, 27*(2), 3–11.

Fitzgerald, F. S. (1925). *The great Gatsby.* New York: Scribner's.

Fitzgerald, J., & Shanahan, T. (2000). Reading and writing relations and their development. *Educational Psychologist, 35*(1), 39–50.

Fitzgerald, J., & Teasley, A. B. (1986). Effects of instruction in narrative structure on children's writing. *Journal of Educational Psychology, 78,* 424–432.

Flaherty, S. E., & Chisholm, J. S. (2015). An analysis of text complexity in young adult literature. *Kentucky English Bulletin, 64*(2), 5–13.

Flanigan, K., & Greenwood, S. C. (2007). Effective content vocabulary instruction in the middle: Matching students, purposes, words, and strategies. *Journal of Adolescent and Adult Literacy, 51*(3), 226–238.

Frey, N., & Fisher, D. (2011). Task complexity. *Principal Leadership, 11*(7), 56–58.

Friedberg, S., Barone, D., Belding, J., Chen, A., Dixon, L., Fennell, F., . . . Shanahan, T. (2018). *The state of state standards post-Common Core.* Washington, DC: Thomas B. Fordham Institute.

Fuchs, D., Fuchs, L. S., Mathes, P. G., & Simmons, D. C. (1997). Peer-assisted learning strategies: Making classrooms more responsive to diversity. *American Educational Research Journal, 34,* 174–206.

Fuchs, D., Fuchs, L. S., Thompson, A., Svenson, E., Yen, L., Al Otaiba, S., . . . Saenz, L. (2001). Peer-assisted learning strategies in reading: Extensions for kindergarten, first grade, and high school. *Remedial and Special Education, 22*(1), 15–21.

Fuchs, L. S., Fuchs, D., & Kazdan, S. (1999). Effects of peer-assisted learning strategies on high school students with serious reading problems. *Remedial and Special Education, 20*(5), 309–318.

Gamelin, Y. M. A. (1996). *The effects of Cognitive Strategy Instruction in Writing (CSIW) on the writing skills of severely learning disabled students and their peers in an inclusive classroom.* Unpublished master's thesis, Simon Fraser University, Burnaby, British Columbia, Canada.

Gillespie, A., Graham, S., Kiuhara, S., & Hebert, M. (2014). High school teachers use of writing to support students' learning: A national survey. *Reading and Writing, 27*(6), 1043–1072.

Glaus, M. (2014). Text complexity and young adult literature. *Journal of Adolescent and Adult Literacy, 57*(5), 407–416.

Goldman, S. R., & Lee, C. D. (2014). Text complexity: State of the art and the conundrums it raises. *Elementary School Journal, 115*(2), 290–300.

Gordon, T. (1980). Parent effectiveness training: A preventive program and its effects on families. In M. J. Fine (Ed.), *Handbook on parent education* (pp. 101–121). New York: Academic Press.

Gough, P. B., & Tunmer, W. E. (1986). Decoding, reading, and reading disability. *Remedial and Special Education, 7,* 6–10.

Graesser, A. C., McNamara, D. S., Cai, Z., Conley, M., Li, H., & Pennebaker, J. (2014). Coh-Metrix measures text characteristics at multiple levels of language and discourse. *Elementary School Journal, 115*(2), 211–229.

Graff, G. (2008). *Clueless in academe: How schooling obscures the life of the mind.* New Haven, CT: Yale University Press.

Graham, S. (2018). A revised writer(s)-within-community model of writing. *Educational Psychologist, 53*(4), 258–279.

Graham, S. (2019). Changing how writing is taught. *Review of Research in Education, 43*(1), 277–303.

Graham, S., Bollinger, A., Booth Olson, C., D'Aoust, C., MacArthur, C., McCutchen, D., & Olinghouse, N. (2012). *Teaching elementary school students to be effective writers: A practice guide* (NCEE 2012-4058). Washington, DC: National Center for Education Evaluation and Regional Assistance, Institute of Education Sciences, U.S. Department of Education.

Graham, S., Bruch, J., Fitzgerald, J., Friedrich, L., Furgeson, J., Greene, K., . . . Smither Wulsin, C. (2016). *Teaching secondary students to write effectively* (NCEE 2017-4002). Washington, DC: National Center for Education Evaluation and Regional Assistance (NCEE), Institute of Education Sciences, U.S. Department of Education.

Graham, S., Capizzi, A., Harris, K., Hebert, M., & Morphy, P. (2014). Teaching writing to middle school students: A national survey. *Reading and Writing, 27*(6), 1015–1042.

Graham, S., & Harris, K. R. (2012). The role of strategies, knowledge, will, and skills in a 30 year program of research (with homage to Hayes, Fayol, and Boscolo). In V. Berninger (Ed.), *Past, present, and future contributions of cognitive writing research to cognitive psychology* (pp. 177–196). London: Psychology Press.

Graham, S., Harris, K. R., & Mason, L. (2005). Improving the writing performance, knowledge, and self-efficacy of struggling young writers: The effects of self-regulated strategy development. *Contemporary Educational Psychology, 30*(2), 207–241.

Graham, S., & Hebert, M. A. (2010). *Writing to read: Evidence for how writing can improve reading. A Carnegie Corporation Time to Act Report.* Washington, DC: Alliance for Excellent Education.

Graham, S., Hebert, M., & Harris, K. R. (2015). Formative assessment and writing: A meta-analysis. *Elementary School Journal, 115*(4), 523–547.

Graham, S., Liu, X., Aitken, A., Ng, C., Bartlett, B., Harris, K. R., & Holzapfel, J. (2018). Effectiveness of literacy programs balancing reading and writing instruction: A meta-analysis. *Reading Research Quarterly, 53*(3), 279–304.

Graham, S., & Perin, D. (2007). *Writing next: Effective strategies to improve writing of adolescents in middle and high schools—A report to Carnegie Corporation of New York.* Washington, DC: Alliance for Excellent Education.

Graham, S., & Sandmel, K. (2011). The process writing approach: A meta-analysis. *Journal of Educational Research, 104*(6), 396–407.

Graves, M. F., Baumann, J. F., Blachowicz, C. L., Manyak, P., Bates, A., Cieply, C., . . ., Von Gunten, H. (2014). Words, words everywhere, but which ones do we teach? *The Reading Teacher, 67*(5), 333–346.

Green, J. [CrashCourse]. (2014, May 8). Race, class, and gender in *To Kill a Mockingbird* [Video file]. Retrieved from *www.youtube.com/watch?v=mDS32LEe1Ss.*

Griffith, D., & Duffett, A. M. (2018). *Reading and writing instruction in America's schools.* Washington, DC: Thomas B. Fordham Institute.

Gritter, K. (2011). Promoting lively literature discussion. *The Reading Teacher, 64*(6), 445–449.

Grooms, J., Enderle, P., & Sampson, V. (2015). Coordinating scientific argumentation and the Next Generation Science Standards through argument driven inquiry. *Science Educator, 24*(1), 45–50.

Guthrie, J. T., & Davis, M. H. (2003). Motivating struggling readers in middle school through an engagement model of classroom practice. *Reading and Writing Quarterly, 19*(1), 59.

Guthrie, J. T., Hoa, A. L. W., Wigfield, A., Tonks, S. M., Humenick, N. M., & Littles, E. (2007). Reading motivation and reading comprehension growth in the later elementary years. *Contemporary Educational Psychology, 32*(3), 282–313.

Guthrie, J. T., & Wigfield, A. (2000). Engagement and motivation in reading. In M. L. Kamil, P. B. Mosenthal, P. D. Pearson, & R. Barr (Eds.), *Handbook of reading research* (Vol. 3, pp. 403–422). Mahwah, NJ: Erlbaum.

Guzel-Ozmen, R. (2006). The effectiveness of modified cognitive strategy instruction in writing with mildly mentally retarded Turkish students. *Exceptional Children, 72*(3), 281–297.

Hacker, D. J., & Tenent, A. (2002). Implementing reciprocal teaching in the classroom: Overcoming obstacles and making modifications. *Journal of Educational Psychology, 94*(4), 699–718.

Hammann, L. A., & Stevens, R. J. (2003). Instructional approaches to improving students' writing of compare–contrast essays: An experimental study. *Journal of Literacy Research, 35*(2), 731–756.

Hanover Research. (2014). *Optimal scheduling for secondary school students.* Arlington, VA: Author.

Harris, K. R., Graham, S., & Mason, L. H. (2006). Improving the writing, knowledge, and motivation of struggling young writers: Effects of self-regulated strategy development with and without peer support. *American Educational Research Journal, 43*(2), 295–340.

Hart, E. R., & Speece, D. L. (1998). Reciprocal teaching goes to college: Effects for post-secondary students at risk for academic failure. *Journal of Educational Psychology, 90*(4), 670–681.

Hart, J. M. (1996). The effect of personalized word problems. *Teaching Children Mathematics, 2*(8), 504–505.

Hart, J., & Stebick, D. (2016). Making the invisible visible: RtI and reading comprehension. *New England Reading Association Journal, 51*(2), 43–56.

Hattan, C. (2019). Prompting rural students' use of background knowledge and experience to support comprehension of unfamiliar content. *Reading Research Quarterly, 54*(4), 451–455.

Hawkins, R. O., Musti-Rao, S., Hale, A. D., McGuire, S., & Hailley, J. (2010). Examining listening previewing as a classwide strategy to promote reading comprehension and vocabulary. *Psychology in the Schools, 47*(9), 903–916.

Hayes, J. R., & Flower, L. (1980). Identifying the organization of writing processes. In L. W. Gregg & E. R. Steinberg (Eds.), *Cognitive processes in writing: An interdisciplinary approach* (pp. 3–30). Hillsdale, NJ: Erlbaum.

Hebert, M., Kearns, D. M., Hayes, J. B., Bazis, P., & Cooper, S. (2018). Why children with dyslexia struggle with writing and how to help them. *Language, Speech and Hearing Services in Schools, 49*(4), 843–863.

Hemingway, E. (1926). *The sun also rises.* New York Scribner's.

Heron-Hruby, A., Trent, B., Haas, S., & Allen, Z. C. (2018). The potential for using small-group literature discussions in intervention-focused high school English. *Reading and Writing Quarterly, 34*(5), 379–395.

Hiebert, E. H. (2011). Beyond single readability measures: Using multiple sources of information in establishing text complexity. *Journal of Education, 191*(2), 33–42.

Hiebert, E. H. (2013). Supporting students' movement up the staircase of text complexity. *The Reading Teacher, 66*(6), 459–468.

Hiebert, E. H. (2017). The text of literacy instruction: Obstacles to or opportunities for educational equity? *Literacy Research: Theory, Method, and Practice, 66,* 117–134.

Hiebert, E. H., & Mesmer, H. A. E. (2013). Upping the ante of text complexity in the Common Core State Standards: Examining its potential impact on young readers. *Educational Researcher, 42*(1), 44–51.

Hiebert, E. H., & Pearson, P. D. (2014). Understanding text complexity: Introduction to the special issue. *Elementary School Journal, 115*(2), 153–160.

Hillocks, G., Jr. (2011). *Teaching argument writing, grades 6–12: Supporting claims with relevant evidence and clear reasoning.* Portsmouth, NH: Heinemann.

Holmes, B. C. (1985). The effect of four different modes of reading on comprehension. *Reading Research Quarterly, 20,* 575–585.

Hoyer, K. M., & Sparks, D. (2017). *Instructional time for third- and eighth-graders in public and private schools: School year 2011–12.* Washington, DC: National Center for Education Statistics, U.S. Department of Education.

International Literacy Association. (2017). Content area and disciplinary literacy: Strategies and frameworks [Literacy leadership brief]. Newark, DE: Author.

International Reading Association. (2012). *Adolescent literacy: A position statement of the International Reading Association*. Newark, DE: Author.

International Reading Association & National Council of Teachers of English. (1996). *Standards for the English language arts*. Urbana, IL: Authors.

Ivey, G. (1999). A multicase study in the middle school: Complexities among young adolescent readers. *Reading Research Quarterly, 34*(2), 172–192.

Ivey, G., & Broaddus, K. (2001). "Just plain reading": A survey of what makes students want to read in middle school classrooms. *Reading Research Quarterly, 36*(4), 350–377.

Juel, C. (1988). Learning to read and write: A longitudinal study of 54 children from first through fourth grades. *Journal of Educational Psychology, 80*, 437–447.

Kamil, M. L., Borman, G. D., Dole, J., Kral, C. C., Salinger, T., & Torgesen, J. (2008). *Improving adolescent literacy: Effective classroom and intervention practices* (NCEE 2008-4027). Washington, DC: National Center for Education Evaluation and Regional Assistance, Institute of Education Sciences, U.S. Department of Education.

Karchmer-Klein, R. (2019). Writing with digital tools. In S. Graham, C. A. MacArthur, & J. Fitzgerald (Eds.), *Best practices in writing instruction* (3rd ed., pp. 135–161). New York: Guilford Press.

Karsten, E. E. (1965). Thematic structure in "The Pearl." *English Journal, 54*, 1–7.

Kay, L. H., Young, J. L., & Mottley, R. R. (1986). Using Manzo's ReQuest model with delinquent adolescents. *Journal of Reading, 29*, 506–510.

Keys, C. W. (2000). Investigating the thinking processes of eighth grade writers during the composition of a scientific laboratory report. *Journal of Research in Science Teaching, 37*(7), 676–690.

King, A. (1990). Enhancing peer interaction and learning in the classroom through reciprocal questioning. *American Educational Research Journal, 27*, 664–687.

King, A. (1994). Guiding knowledge construction in the classroom: Effects of teaching children how to question and how to explain. *American Educational Research Journal, 31*, 338–368.

King, A., & Rosenshine, B. (1993). Effects of guided cooperative questioning on children's knowledge construction. *Journal of Experimental Education, 61*, 127–148.

King, M. L. (1963). *I have a dream*. New York: Scholastic.

Kintsch, W. (1988). The role of knowledge in discourse comprehension: A construction–integration model. *Psychological Review, 95*, 163–182.

Kintsch, W. (2013). Revisiting the construction–integration model of text comprehension and its implications for instruction. In D. E. Alvermann, N. J. Unrau, & R. B. Ruddel (Eds.), *Theoretical models and processes of reading* (6th ed., pp. 807–839). Newark, DE: International Reading Association.

Kirkpatrick, L. C., & Klein, P. D. (2009). Planning text structure as a way to improve students' writing from sources in the compare–contrast genre. *Learning and Instruction, 19*(4), 309–321.

Kiuhara, S. A., Graham, S., & Hawken, L. S. (2009). Teaching writing to high school students: A national survey. *Journal of Educational Psychology, 101*(1), 136–160.

Kiuhara, S. A., O'Neill, R. E., Hawken, L. S., & Graham, S. (2012). The effectiveness of teaching 10th-grade students STOP, AIMS, and DARE for planning and drafting persuasive text. *Exceptional Children, 78*(3), 335–355.

Klein, P. D., & Kirkpatrick, L. C. (2010). A framework for content area writing: Mediators and moderators. *Journal of Writing Research, 2*(1), 1–46.

Klingner, J. K., Vaughn, S., & Schumm, J. S. (1998). Collaborative strategic reading during social studies in heterogeneous fourth-grade classrooms. *Elementary School Journal, 99*(1), 3–22.

Koeller, S. (1982). Expository writing: A vital skill in science. *Science and Children, 20,* 12–15.

Kuhn, M. R. (2014, May 7). What's really wrong with round robin reading? Retrieved from *www.literacyworldwide.org/blog/literacy-daily/2014/05/07/what's-really-wrong-with-round-robin-reading.*

Langer, J. A. (1981). From theory to practice: A prereading plan. *Journal of Reading, 25,* 152–156.

Langer, J. A. (1984). Examining background knowledge and text comprehension. *Reading Research Quarterly, 19,* 468–481.

Lapp, D., Shea, A., & Wolsey, T. D. (2010). Blogging and audience awareness. *Journal of Education, 191*(1), 33–44.

Laverick, C. (2002). B-D-A strategy: Reinventing the wheel can be a good thing. *Journal of Adolescent and Adult Literacy, 46*(2), 144–147.

Lawrence, J. F., & Snow, C. E. (2011). Oral discourse and reading. In M. L. Kamil, P. D. Pearson, E. B. Moje, & P. P. Afflerbach (Eds.), *Handbook of reading research* (Vol. 4, pp. 320–337). New York: Routledge.

Lee, H. (1960). *To kill a mockingbird*. Philadelphia: Lippincott.

Lewis, W. E., & Ferretti, R. P. (2009). Defending interpretations of literary texts: The effects of topoi instruction on the literary arguments of high school students. *Reading and Writing Quarterly, 25*(4), 250–270.

Lewis, W. E., & Ferretti, R. P. (2011). Topoi and literary interpretation: The effects of a critical reading and writing intervention on high school students' analytic literary essays. *Contemporary Educational Psychology, 36*(4), 334–354.

Lewis, W., & Flynn, J. E. (2017). Below the surface level of social justice: Using quad text sets to plan equity-oriented instruction. *ALAN Review, 45*(1), 22–31.

Lewis, W. E., & Walpole, S. (2016). Designing your own text sets: A four-text framework to build content knowledge in content area classrooms. *Literacy Today, 33*(4), 34–35.

Lewis, W. E., Walpole, S., & McKenna, M. C. (2014). *Cracking the Common Core: Choosing and using texts in grades 6–12*. New York: Guilford Press.

Li, M., Murphy, P. K., Wang, J., Mason, L. H., Firetto, C. M., Wei, L., & Chung, K. S. (2016). Promoting reading comprehension and critical–analytic thinking: A comparison of three approaches with fourth and fifth graders. *Contemporary Educational Psychology, 46,* 101–115.

Liebfreund, M. D., & Conradi, K. (2016). Component skills affecting elementary students' informational text comprehension. *Reading and Writing, 29*(6), 1141–1160.

Lovette, G. E. (2013). Reading preparation of secondary ELA teachers. *Journal of Adolescent and Adult Literacy, 57*(3), 193–203.

Lupo, S. M., Strong, J. Z., & Conradi Smith, K. (2019). Struggle is not a bad word: Misconceptions and recommendations about readers struggling with difficult texts. *Journal of Adolescent and Adult Literacy, 62*(5), 551–560.

Lupo, S. M., Strong, J. Z., Lewis, W., Walpole, S., & McKenna, M. C. (2018). Building background knowledge through reading: Rethinking text sets. *Journal of Adolescent and Adult Literacy, 61*(4), 433–444.

Lupo, S. M., Tortorelli, L., Invernizzi, M., Ryoo, J. H., & Strong, J. Z. (2019). An exploration of text difficulty and knowledge support on adolescents' comprehension. *Reading Research Quarterly, 54*(4), 457–479.

Lysynchuk, L. M., Pressley, M., & Vye, N. J. (1990). Reciprocal teaching improves standardized reading-comprehension performance in poor comprehenders. *Elementary School Journal, 90,* 470–484.

MacArthur, C., Schwartz, S., & Graham, S. (1991). Effects of a reciprocal peer revision strategy in special education classrooms. *Learning Disability Research and Practice, 6,* 201–210.

Mackey, M., Vermeer, L., Storie, D., & DeBlois, E. (2012). The constancy of the school "canon": A survey of texts used in grade 10 English language Arts in 2006 and 1996. *Language and Literacy: A Canadian Educational E-Journal, 14*(1), 26–58.

Macon, J. M., Bewell, D., & Vogt, M. (1991). *Responses to literature: Grades K–8.* Newark, DE: International Reading Association.

Maloch, B. (2002). Scaffolding student talk: One teacher's role in literature discussion groups. *Reading Research Quarterly, 37*(1), 94–112.

Mandela, N. (1994). Nelson Mandela's address to the people of Cape Town, Grand Parade, on the occasion of his inauguration as state president, 9th May 1994. *The Black Scholar, 24*(3), 2–6.

Manzo, A. V. (1969). ReQuest procedure. *Journal of Reading, 13,* 123–126.

Manzo, A. V. (1973). CONPASS: English: A demonstration project. *Journal of Reading, 16,* 539–545.

Manzo, A. V. (1985). Expansion modules for the ReQuest, CAT, GRP, and REAP reading/study procedures. *Journal of Reading, 28,* 498–502.

Manzo, A. V., & Casale, U. P. (1985). Listen–read–discuss: A content reading heuristic. *Journal of Reading, 28*(8), 732–734.

Marshall, J. C. (2006). *The effects of participation in literature circles on reading comprehension.* Unpublished doctoral dissertation, University of Miami, Coral Gables, FL.

Martinelli, G. (Producer), & Luhrmann, B. (Producer and Director). (1996). *William Shakespeare's Romeo and Juliet* [Motion picture]. United States: 20th Century Fox.

Marzano, R. J. (2012). The many uses of exit slips. *Educational Leadership, 70*(2), 80–81.

Mason, L. H., Kubina, R. M., Valasa, L. L., & Cramer, A. M. (2010). Evaluating effective writing instruction for adolescent students in an emotional and behavior support setting. *Behavioral Disorders, 35,* 140–156.

McGlynn, K., & Kelly, J. (2019). Supplementing the textbook effectively to encourage student growth. *Science Scope, 42*(5), 36–41.

McKenna, M. C., Conradi, K., Lawrence, C., Jang, B. G., & Meyer, J. P. (2012). Reading attitudes of middle school students: Results of a U.S. survey. *Reading Research Quarterly, 47*(3), 283–306.

McKenna, M. C., Franks, S., Conradi, K., & Lovette, G. (2011). Using reading guides with struggling readers in grades 3 and above. In R. L. McCormick & J. R. Paratore (Eds.), *After early intervention, then what?: Teaching struggling readers in grades 3 and beyond* (2nd ed., pp. 207–220). Newark, DE: International Reading Association.

McKenna, M. C., Kear, D. J., & Ellsworth, R. A. (1995). Children's attitudes toward reading: A national survey. *Reading Research Quarterly, 30,* 934–956.

McKeown, M. G., Beck, I. L., Omanson, R. C., & Pople, M. C. (1985). Some effects of the
nature and frequency of vocabulary instruction on the knowledge and use of words.
Reading Research Quarterly, 20(5), 522–535.

McKeown, M. G., Beck, I. L., & Worthy, M. J. (1993). Grappling with text ideas: Questioning the author. *The Reading Teacher, 46,* 560–566.

McNamara, D. S., Ozuru, Y., & Floyd, R. G. (2011). Comprehension challenges in the fourth
grade: The roles of text cohesion, text genre, and readers' prior knowledge. *International
Electronic Journal of Elementary Education, 4*(1), 229–257.

Mehan, H. (1979). *Learning lessons.* Cambridge, MA: Harvard University Press.

Meier, D. (2002). *In schools we trust: Creating communities of learning in an era of testing and
standardization.* Boston: Beacon Press.

Meyer, B. J. F., Brandt, D. M., & Bluth, G. J. (1980). Use of top-level structure in text: Key
for reading comprehension of ninth-grade students. *Reading Research Quarterly, 16*(1),
72–103.

Meyer, C. K. (2013). The literacy needs of adolescents: What do content-area teachers know?
Action in Teacher Education, 35(1), 56–71.

Myers, W. D. (1988). *Scorpions.* New York: Harper & Row.

Midgette, E., & Haria, P. (2016). Planning and revising written arguments: The effects of
two text structure-based interventions on persuasiveness of 8th-grade students' essays.
Reading Psychology, 37(7), 1043–1075.

Midgette, E., Haria, P., & MacArthur, C. (2008). The effects of content and audience awareness goals for revision on the persuasive essays of fifth- and eighth-grade students. *Reading and Writing, 21*(1/2), 131–151.

Miller, A. (1953). *The crucible: Text and criticism* (G. C. Weales, Ed.). New York: Viking Press.

Monte-Sano, C., & Allen, A. (2019). Historical argument writing: The role of interpretive
work, argument type, and classroom instruction. *Reading and Writing, 32*(6), 1383–
1410.

Morris, J. A., Miller, B. W., Anderson, R. C., Nguyen-Jahiel, K. T., Lin, T.-J. L., Scott, T., . . .
Ma, S. (2018). Instructional discourse and argumentative writing. *International Journal
of Educational Research, 90,* 234–247.

Mosenthal, P., & Na, T. J. (1980). Quality of children's recall under two classroom testing tasks: Towards a socio-psycholinguistic model of reading comprehension. *Reading
Research Quarterly, 16*(4), 504–528.

Murphy, P. K., Firetto, C. M., Li, M., Wei, L., Croninger, R. M. V., Greene, J. A., . . . Duke,
R. F. (2017). Exploring the influence of homogeneous versus heterogeneous grouping
on students' text-based discussions and comprehension. *Contemporary Educational Psychology, 51,* 336–355.

Murphy, P. K., Greene, J. A., Allen, E., Baszczewski, S., Swearingen, A., Wei, L., & Butler,
A. M. (2018a). Fostering high school students' conceptual understanding and argumentation performance in science through Quality Talk discussions. *Science Education,
102*(6), 1239–1264.

Murphy, P. K., Greene, J. A., Firetto, C. M., Hendrick, B. D., Li, M., Montalbano, C., &
Wei, L. (2018b). Quality Talk: Developing students' discourse to promote high-level
comprehension. *American Educational Research Journal, 55*(5), 1113–1160.

Murphy, P. K., Wilkinson, I. A. G., Soter, A. O., Hennessey, M. N., & Alexander, J. F. (2009). Examining the effects of classroom discussion on students' comprehension of text: A meta-analysis. *Journal of Educational Psychology, 101*(3), 740–764.

Nagy, W. E. (1988). *Teaching vocabulary to improve reading comprehension.* Urbana, IL: National Council of Teachers of English.

National Aeronautics and Space Administration. (2019). Climate change: How do we know? Retrieved from *https://climate.nasa.gov/evidence.*

National Assessment Governing Board. (2017). *Writing framework for the 2017 national assessment of educational progress.* Washington, DC: U.S. Department of Education.

National Assessment Governing Board. (2019). *Reading framework for the 2019 national assessment of educational progress.* Washington, DC: U.S. Department of Education.

National Center for Education Statistics. (2012). *The nation's report card: Writing 2011: National assessment of educational progress at grades 8 and 12.* Washington, DC: Institute of Education Sciences.

National Center for Education Statistics. (2019). *NAEP report card: 2019 NAEP reading assessment: Highlighted results at grades 4 and 8 for the nation, states, and districts.* Washington, DC: Institute of Education Sciences.

National Commission on Writing. (2003). The neglected "R": The need for a writing revolution. Retrieved from *www.nwp.org/cs/public/print/resource/2523.*

National Council for the Social Studies. (2013). *College, career, and civic life (C3) framework for social studies state standards: Guidance for enhancing the rigor of K–12 civics, economics, geography, and history.* Silver Spring, MD: Author.

National Council of Teachers of English. (2012). *NCTE/NCATE standards for initial preparation of teachers of secondary English language arts, grades 7–12.* Urbana, IL: Author.

National Geographic. (2015, December 2). Climate change 101 with Bill Nye [Video file]. Retrieved from *www.youtube.com/watch?v=EtW2rrLHs08.*

National Geographic Partners. (2015–2019). 5 ways to curb climate change. Retrieved from *www.nationalgeographic.com/climate-change/how-to-fix-it/index.html.*

National Governors Association Center for Best Practices & Council of Chief State School Officers. (2010). *Common Core State Standards for English language arts and literacy in history/social studies, science, and technical subjects.* Washington, DC: Authors.

Nelson, J., Perfetti, C., Liben, D., & Liben, M. (2012). *Measures of text difficulty: Testing their predictive value for grade levels and student performance.* New York: Student Achievement Partners.

Neumann, E. (2019). myPhysicsLab roller coaster. Retrieved from *www.myphysicslab.com/roller/roller-single-en.html.*

Newell, G. E., Bloome, D., Kim, M.-Y., & Goff, B. (2019). Shifting epistemologies during instructional conversations about "good" argumentative writing in a high school English language arts classroom. *Reading and Writing, 32*(6), 1359–1382.

Newkirk, T. (1987). The non-narrative writing of young children. *Research in the Teaching of English, 21,* 121–144.

NGSS Lead States. (2013). *Next Generation Science Standards: For states, by states.* Washington, DC: National Academies Press.

Nodjimbadem, K. (2017, May 30). The racial segregation of American cities was anything but accidental. Retrieved from *www.smithsonianmag.com/history/how-federal-government-intentionally-racially-segregated-american-cities-180963494.*

Northrop, L., & Kelly, S. (2019). Who gets to read what?: Tracking, instructional practices, and text complexity for middle school struggling readers. *Reading Research Quarterly, 54*(3), 339–361.

Norton, J. H. (1967). Teaching expository writing using skill levels. *English Journal, 56,* 1015.

Ogle, D. M. (1986). KWL: A teaching model that develops active reading of expository text. *The Reading Teacher, 39*(6), 564–570.

Ogle, D. M. (1992). KWL in action: Secondary teachers find applications that work. In E. K. Dishner, T. W. Bean, & J. E. Readence (Eds.), *Reading in the content areas: Improving classroom instruction* (3rd ed., pp. 270–281). Dubuque, IA: Kendall/Hunt.

Olinghouse, N. G., Graham, S., & Gillespie, A. (2015). The relationship of discourse and topic knowledge to fifth graders' writing performance. *Journal of Educational Psychology, 107*(2), 391–406.

Olinghouse, N. G., & Santangelo, T. (2010). Assessing the writing of struggling learners. *Focus on Exceptional Children, 43*(4), 1–27.

Open Up Resources. (2018). Bookworms K–5 Reading and Writing. Retrieved from *https://openupresources.org/bookworms-k-5-reading-writing-curriculum.*

Palincsar, A. S., & Brown, A. L. (1984). Reciprocal teaching of comprehension-fostering and comprehension–monitoring activities. *Cognition and Instruction, 1*(2), 117–175.

Palincsar, A. S., & Brown, A. L. (1986). Interactive teaching to promote independent learning from text. *The Reading Teacher, 39,* 771–777.

Pearson, P. D., & Gallagher, M. C. (1983). The instruction of reading comprehension. *Contemporary Educational Psychology, 8,* 317–344.

Pearson, P. D., & Hiebert, E. H. (2014). The state of the field: Qualitative analyses of text complexity. *Elementary School Journal, 115*(2), 161–183.

Peker, D., & Wallace, C. (2011). Characterizing high school students' written explanations in biology laboratories. *Research in Science Education, 41*(2), 169–191.

Penhale, R. R. (1939). Every teacher a teacher of reading. *Journal of Education, 122,* 85–87.

Perin, D. (2013). Best practices in teaching writing for college and career readiness. In S. Graham, C. A. MacArthur, & J. Fitzgerald (Eds.), *Best practices in writing instruction* (2nd ed., pp. 48–70). New York: Guilford Press.

Philippakos, Z. A. T., & FitzPatrick, E. (2018). A proposed tiered model of assessment in writing instruction: Supporting all student-writers. *Insights on Learning Disabilities, 15*(2), 149–173.

Philippakos, Z. A., & MacArthur, C. A. (2016). The effects of giving feedback on the persuasive writing of fourth- and fifth-grade students. *Reading Research Quarterly, 51*(4), 419–433.

Pitcher, S. M., Albright, L. K., DeLaney, C. J., Walker, N. T., Seunarinesingh, K., Mogge, S., . . . Dunston, P. J. (2007). Assessing adolescents' motivation to read. *Journal of Adolescent and Adult Literacy, 50*(5), 378–396.

Poe, E. A. (1845). The pit and the pendulum. *Broadway Journal (1845–1846), 1*(20), 307.

Poindexter, C. C. (1994). Classroom strategies that convinced content area teachers they could teach reading, too. *Journal of Reading, 38*(2), 134.

Quigley, A., & Coleman, R. (2019). *Improving literacy in secondary schools: Guidance report.* London: Education Endowment Foundation.

Rabinowitz, P. J., & Smith, M. W. (1998). *Authorizing readers: Resistance and respect in the teaching of literature.* New York: Teachers College Press

Raphael, T. E. (1986). Teaching question answer relationships, revisited. *The Reading Teacher, 39,* 516–522.

Raphael, T. E., & Au, K. H. (2005). QAR: Enhancing comprehension and test taking across grades and content areas. *The Reading Teacher, 59*(3), 206–221.

Raphael, T. E., & Englert, C. S. (1990). Writing and reading: Partners in constructing meaning. *The Reading Teacher, 43*(6), 388–400.

Raphael, T. E., Englert, C. S., & Kirschner, B. W. (1989). Students' metacognitive knowledge about writing. *Research in the Teaching of English, 23,* 343–379.

Raphael, T. E., Kirschner, B. W., & Englert, C. S. (1986). *Text structure instruction within process-writing classrooms: A manual for instruction.* East Lansing, MI: Institute for Research on Teaching.

Raphael, T. E., Kirschner, B. W., & Englert, C. S. (1988). Expository writing program: Making connections between reading and writing. *The Reading Teacher, 41,* 790–795.

Raphael, T. E., & McMahon, S. I. (1994). Book club: An alternative framework for reading instruction. *The Reading Teacher, 48,* 102–116.

Ray, A. B., Graham, S., Houston, J. D., & Harris, K. R. (2016). Teachers' use of writing to support students' learning in middle school: A national survey in the United States. *Reading and Writing, 29*(5), 1039–1068.

Ray, A. B., Graham, S., & Liu, X. (2019). Effects of SRSD college entrance essay exam instruction for high school students with disabilities or at-risk for writing difficulties. *Reading and Writing, 32*(6), 1507–1529.

ReadWorks. (2013). Lightning and fire. Retrieved from *www.readworks.org/article/Lightning-and-Fire/8954495d-9162-49f4-841b-2b2ec4e9bff9#!articleTab:content.*

Recht, D. R., & Leslie, L. (1988). Effect of prior knowledge on good and poor readers' memory of text. *Journal of Educational Psychology, 80*(1), 16.

Reisman, A. (2015). Entering the historical problem space: Whole-class text-based discussion in history class. *Teachers College Record, 117*(2), 1–44.

Reisman, A. (2017). How to facilitate discussions in history. *Educational Leadership, 74*(5), 30–34.

Reynolds, C. J., Hill, D. S., Swassing, R. H., & Ward, M. E. (1988). The effects of revision strategy instruction on the writing performance of students with learning disabilities. *Journal of Learning Disabilities, 21,* 540–545.

Reynolds, D. (2020). Of research reviews and practice guides: Translating rapidly growing research on adolescent literacy into updated practice recommendations. *Reading Research Quarterly.* [Epub ahead of print]

Reynolds, G., & Perin, D. (2009). A comparison of text structure and self-regulated writing strategies for composing from sources by middle school students. *Reading Psychology, 30*(3), 265–300.

Reznitskaya, A., Anderson, R. C., McNurlen, B., Nguyen-Jahiel, K., Archodidou, A., & Kim, S. (2001). Influence of oral discussion on written argument. *Discourse Processes, 32*(2/3), 155–175.

Rinehart, S. D., Stahl, S. A., & Erickson, L. G. (1986). Some effects of summarization training on reading and studying. *Reading Research Quarterly, 21*(4), 422–438.

Romine, B. G. C., McKenna, M. C., & Robinson, R. D. (1996). Reading coursework requirements for middle and high school content area teachers: A U.S. survey. *Journal of Adolescent and Adult Literacy, 40,* 194–198.

Rosenblatt, L. M. (1978). *The reader, the text, and the poem: The transactional theory of the literary work.* Carbondale: Southern Illinois University Press.

Rowell, R. (2012). *Eleanor and Park.* New York: St. Martin's Press.

Rupley, W. H., & Slough, S. (2010). Building prior knowledge and vocabulary in science in the intermediate grades: Creating hooks for learning. *Literacy Research and Instruction, 49*(2), 99–112.

Saddler, B. (2012). *Teacher's guide to effective sentence writing.* New York: Guilford Press.

Sampson, V., Enderle, P., Grooms, J., & Witte, S. (2013). Writing to learn by learning to write during the school science laboratory: Helping middle and high school students develop argumentative writing skills as they learn core ideas. *Science Education, 97*(5), 643–670.

Sampson, V., Grooms, J., & Walker, J. P. (2011). Argument-driven inquiry as a way to help students learn how to participate in scientific argumentation and craft written arguments: An exploratory study. *Science Education, 95*(2), 217–257.

Sandora, C., Beck, I., & McKeown, M. (1999). A comparison of two discussion strategies on students' comprehension and interpretation of complex literature. *Reading Psychology, 20*(3), 177–212.

Santa, C. M. (1988). *Content reading including study systems.* Dubuque, IA: Kendall/Hunt.

Santa, C. M., Havens, L. T., & Valdes, B. J. (2004). *Project CRISS: Creating independence through student-owned strategies.* Dubuque, IA: Kendall/Hunt.

Sawyer, R. J., Graham, S., & Harris, K. R. (1992). Direct teaching, strategy instruction, and strategy instruction with explicit self-regulation: Effects on the composition skills and self-efficacy of students with learning disabilities. *Journal of Educational Psychology, 84,* 340–352.

Scammacca, N., Roberts, G., Vaughn. S., Edmonds, M., Wexler, J., Reutebuch, C. K., & Torgesen, J. K. (2007). *Interventions for adolescent struggling readers: A meta-analysis with implications for practice.* Portsmouth, NH: RMC Research Corporation, Center on Instruction.

Schaefer, J. (1953). *The canyon.* Boston: Houghton Mifflin.

Schlosser, M., & Johnson, B. (2014). Integrating the arts through inquiry in the library media program. *Library Media Connection, 32*(6), 8–10.

Schumaker, J. B., Deshler, D. D., Nolan, S., Clark, F. L., Alley, G. R., & Warner, M. M. (1981). *Error monitoring: A learning strategy for improving academic performance of LD adolescents.* Lawrence, KS: Institute for Research in Learning Disabilities.

Schwartz, R. M. (1988). Learning to learn vocabulary in content area textbooks. *Journal of Reading, 32*(2), 108–118.

Schwartz, R. M., & Raphael, T. E. (1985). Concept of definition: A key to improving students' vocabulary. *The Reading Teacher, 39,* 198–205.

Science Learning Hub. (2017). Temperature, salinity and water density. Retrieved from *www.sciencelearn.org.nz/resources/2280-temperature-salinity-and-water-density.*

Sedita, J. (2011). Adolescent literacy: Addressing the needs of students in grades 4–12. In J. R. Birsh (Ed.), *Multisensory teaching of basic language skills* (3rd ed., pp. 517–548). Baltimore: Brookes.

Sewell, W. C. (2013). Preservice teachers' literacy strategies preferences: Results of a two-year study of content area literacy students. *Journal of Content Area Reading, 10*(1), 121–149.

Shanahan, T. (2015). What teachers should know about Common Core. *The Reading Teacher, 68*(8), 583–588.

Shanahan, T. (2016). Relationships between reading and writing development. In C. MacArthur, S. Graham, & J. Fitzgerald (Eds.), *Handbook of writing research* (2nd ed., pp. 194–207). New York: Guilford Press.

Shanahan, T., Fisher, D., & Frey, N. (2012). The challenge of challenging text. *Educational Leadership, 69*(6), 58–62.

Shanahan, T., & Shanahan, C. (2008). Teaching disciplinary literacy to adolescents: Rethinking content-area literacy. *Harvard Educational Review, 78,* 40–59.

Shanahan, T., & Shanahan, C. (2012). What is disciplinary literacy and why does it matter? *Topics in Language Disorders, 32,* 7–18.

Sheehan, K. M. (2015). Aligning TextEvaluator scores with the accelerated text complexity guidelines specified in the Common Core State Standards. *ETS Research Reports Series, 2015*(2), 1–20.

Sheehan, K. M. (2017). Validating automated measures of text complexity. *Educational Measurement: Issues and Practice, 36*(4), 35–43.

Simmons, D. C., Kameenui, E. J., Dickson, S., Chard, D., Gunn, B., & Baker, S. (1994). Integrating narrative reading comprehension and writing instruction for all learners. In D. J. Leu & C. K. Kinzer (Eds.), *Multidimensional aspects of literacy research, theory, and practice: 43rd yearbook of the National Reading Conference* (pp. 572–582). Chicago: National Reading Conference.

Simon, S., Erduran, S., & Osborne, J. (2006). Learning to teach argumentation: Research and development in the science classroom. *International Journal of Science Education, 28*(2), 235–260.

Smith, H. K. (1967). The responses of good and poor readers when asked to read for different purposes. *Reading Research Quarterly, 3*(1), 53–83.

Smith, P. L., & Friend, M. (1986). Training learning disabled adolescents in a strategy for using text structure to aid recall of instructional prose. *Learning Disabilities Research, 2*(1), 38–44.

Snow, C. E. (2002). *Reading for understanding: Toward an R&D program in reading comprehension.* Santa Monica, CA: RAND.

Snow, C. E., Burns, M. S., & Griffin, P. (1998). *Preventing reading difficulties in young children.* Washington, DC: National Academy Press.

Sparks, R. R., Patton, J., & Murdoch, A. (2014). Early reading success and its relationship to reading achievement and reading volume: Replication of "10 years later." *Reading and Writing, 27*(1), 189–211.

Stahl, S. (1983). Differential word knowledge and reading comprehension. *Journal of Reading Behavior, 15*(4), 33–47.

Stahl, S. A., Hare, V. C., Sinatra, R., & Gregory, J. F. (1991). Defining the role of prior knowledge and vocabulary in reading comprehension: The retiring of number 41. *Journal of Reading Behavior, 23*(4), 487–508.

Stahl, S. A., Jacobson, M. G., Davis, C. E., & Davis, R. L. (1989). Prior knowledge and difficult vocabulary in the comprehension of unfamiliar text. *Reading Research Quarterly, 24*(1), 27–43.

Stanovich, K. E. (1986). Matthew effects in reading: Some consequences of individual differences in the acquisition of literacy. *Reading Research Quarterly, 21*(3), 360–407.

Steinbeck, J. (1947). *The pearl.* New York: Viking Press.

Stenner, A. J., Burdick, H., Sanford, E. E., & Burdick, D. S. (2007). *The Lexile Framework for Reading technical report.* Durham, NC: MetaMetrics.

Stenner, A. J., Sanford-Moore, E., & Williamson, G. L. (2012). *The Lexile Framework for Reading quantifies the reading ability needed for "college and career readiness"* (MetaMetrics Research Brief). Durham, NC: MetaMetrics.

Stripling, B. (2008). Inquiry: Inquiring minds want to know. *School Library Media Activities Monthly, 25*(1), 50–52.

Strong, J. Z., Amendum, S. J., & Conradi Smith, K. (2018). Supporting elementary students' reading of difficult texts. *The Reading Teacher, 72*(2), 201–212.

Swanborn, M. S. L., & de Glopper, K. (1999). Incidental word learning while reading: A meta-analysis. *Review of Educational Research, 69*(3), 261–286.

Swanson, E., Wanzek, J., McCulley, L., Stillman-Spisak, S., Vaughn, S., Simmons, D., . . . Hairrell, A. (2016). Literacy and text reading in middle and high school social studies and English language arts classrooms. *Reading and Writing Quarterly, 32*(3), 199–222.

Tarchi, C. (2010). Reading comprehension of informative texts in secondary school: A focus on direct and indirect effects of reader's prior knowledge. *Learning and Individual Differences, 20*(5), 415–420.

Tatum, A. [AlfredTatum]. (2017, September 17). Leveled texts lead to leveled lives. AWT [Tweet]. Retrieved from *https://twitter.com/alfredtatum/status/909563807525216256*.

Taylor, K. K. (1986). Summary writing by young children. *Reading Research Quarterly, 21*, 193–208.

The Aesop for children. (1919). Chicago: Rand, McNally. Retrieved from *www.read.gov/aesop/001.html*.

Thoreau, H. D. (1849). Resistance to civil government. In E. P. Peabody (Ed.), *Aesthetic papers* (pp. 189–211). Boston and New York: The Editor and G. P. Putnam.

Toste, J., Didion, L., Peng, P., Filderman, M., & McClelland, A. (2020). A meta-analytic review of the relations between motivation and reading achievement for K–12 students. *Review of Educational Research, 90*(3), 420–456.

Toulmin, S. E. (1958). *The uses of argument.* Cambridge, UK: Cambridge University Press.

Troia, G. (2014). Evidence-based practices for writing instruction (Document No. IC-5). Retrieved from *http://ceedar.education.ufl.edu/tools/innovation-configuration*.

Tschida, C. M., & Buchanan, L. B. (2015). Tackling controversial topics: Developing thematic text sets for elementary social studies. *Social Studies Research and Practice, 10*(3), 40–56.

Tytler, R., & Aranda, G. (2015). Expert teachers' discursive moves in science classroom interactive talk. *International Journal of Science and Mathematics Education, 13*(2), 425–446.

UIC College of Education. (2013, May 22). Alfred Tatum on literacy education for African American and Latino students [Video file]. Retrieved from *www.youtube.com/watch?v=DwSKB-mg-mU*.

United States Geological Survey. (n.d.). What are tsunamis? Retrieved from *www.usgs.gov/faqs/what-are-tsunamis*.

Valencia, S. W., Wixson, K. K., & Pearson, P. D. (2014). Putting text complexity in context: Refocusing on comprehension of complex text. *Elementary School Journal, 115*(2), 270–289.

Vaughn, S., Klingner, J. K., & Bryant, D. P. (2001). Collaborative strategic reading as a means to enhance peer-mediated instruction for reading comprehension and content-area learning. *Remedial and Special Education, 22*(2), 66–74.

Vaughn, S., Klingner, J. K., Swanson, E. A., Boardman, A. G., Roberts, G., Mohammed,

S. S., & Stillman-Spisak, S. J. (2011). Efficacy of collaborative strategic reading with middle school students. *American Educational Research Journal, 48*(4), 938–964.

Vonnegut, K. (1969). *Slaughterhouse-five, or, the children's crusade: A duty-dance with death.* New York: Dial Press.

Waggoner, M. A., Chinn, C. A., & Yi, H. (1995). Collaborative reasoning about stories. *Language Arts, 72,* 582–589.

Walker, J. P., & Sampson, V. (2013). Learning to argue and arguing to learn: Argument-driven inquiry as a way to help undergraduate chemistry students learn how to construct arguments and engage in argumentation during a laboratory course. *Journal of Research in Science Teaching, 50*(5), 561–596.

Walpole, S., McKenna, M. C., Amendum, S., Pasquarella, A., & Strong, J. Z. (2017). The promise of a literacy reform effort in the upper elementary grades. *Elementary School Journal, 118*(2), 257–280.

Walpole, S., McKenna, M. C., Philippakos, Z. A., & Strong, J. Z. (2020). *Differentiated literacy instruction in grades 4 and 5: Strategies and resources* (2nd ed.). New York: Guilford Press.

Walpole, S., Strong, J. Z., & Riches, C. B. (2018). Best practices in professional learning for improving literacy instruction in schools. In L. B. Gambrell & L. B. Morrow (Eds.), *Best practices in literacy instruction* (6th ed., pp. 429–446). New York: Guilford Press.

Warren, E., & Supreme Court of the United States. (1953). U.S. Reports: *Brown v. Board of Education, 347 U.S. 483* [Periodical]. Retrieved from the Library of Congress, *www.loc.gov/item/usrep347483.*

Watson, L. (1993). *Montana 1948.* New York: Washington Square Press.

Webb, S., Massey, D., Goggans, M., & Flajole, K. (2019). Thirty-five years of the gradual release of responsibility: Scaffolding toward complex and responsive teaching. *The Reading Teacher, 73*(1), 75–83.

Wei, H., Cromwell, A. M., & McClarty, K. L. (2016). Career readiness: An analysis of text complexity for occupational reading materials. *Journal of Educational Research, 109*(3), 266–274.

Wei, L., Firetto, C. M., Murphy, P. K., Li, M., Greene, J. A., & Croninger, R. M. V. (2019). Facilitating fourth-grade students' written argumentation: The use of an argumentation graphic organizer. *Journal of Educational Research, 112*(5), 627–639.

Wei, L., Murphy, P. K., & Firetto, C. M. (2018). How can teachers facilitate productive small-group talk?: An integrated taxonomy of teacher discourse moves. *Elementary School Journal, 118*(4), 578–609.

Weir, K. (2016). Inequality at school: What's behind the racial disparity in our education system? *Monitor on Psychology, 47*(10). Retrieved from *www.apa.org/monitor/2016/11/cover-inequality-school.*

Wells, J., & Batchelor, K. E. (2017). Incorporating multivoiced texts to investigate the glorification and condemnation of war through a social justice linked text set. *Ohio Journal of English Language Arts, 57*(1), 51–57.

Welton, D. A. (1982). Expository writing, pseudowriting, and social studies. *Social Education, 46,* 444–448.

Wexler, J., Mitchell, M. A., Clancy, E. E., & Silverman, R. D. (2017). An investigation of literacy practices in high school science classrooms. *Reading and Writing Quarterly, 33*(3), 258–277.

Wiesel, E. (1960). *Night*. New York: Hill & Wang.

Wilder, L. (2002). Get comfortable with uncertainty: A study of the conventional values of literary analysis in an undergraduate literature course. *Written Communication, 19*(1), 175.

Wilkinson, I. A. G., & Son, E. H. (2011). A dialogic turn in research on learning and teaching to comprehend. In M. L. Kamil, P. D. Pearson, E. B. Moje, & P. P. Afflerbach (Eds.), *Handbook of reading research* (Vol. 4, pp. 359–387). New York: Routledge.

Williamson, G. L., Fitzgerald, J., & Stenner, A. J. (2013). The Common Core State Standards' quantitative text-complexity trajectory: Figuring out how much complexity is enough. *Educational Researcher, 42*, 59–69.

Williamson, G. L., Fitzgerald, J., & Stenner, A. J. (2014). Student reading growth illuminates the Common Core text-complexity standard: Raising both bars. *Elementary School Journal, 115*(2), 230–254.

Wineburg, S. (2001). *Historical thinking and other unnatural acts: Charting the future of teaching the past*. Philadelphia: Temple University Press.

Wineburg, S. (2010). Thinking like a historian. *Teaching with Primary Sources Quarterly, 3*(1), 2–5.

Wineburg, S., Martin, D., & Monte-Sano, C. (2012). *Reading like a historian: Teaching literacy in middle and high school history classrooms*. New York: Teachers College Press.

Winograd, P. N. (1984). Strategic difficulties in summarizing texts. *Reading Research Quarterly, 19*, 404–425.

WNYC. (2016, May 19). Kids talk about segregation [Video file]. Retrieved from *www.youtube.com/watch?v=Sff2N8rez_8*.

Wolf, S. A., & Gearhart, M. (1994). Writing what you read: Narrative assessment as a learning event. *Language Arts, 71*, 425–444.

Wong, B. Y. L., Butler, D. L., Ficzere, S. A., & Kuperis, S. (1996). Teaching low achievers and students with learning disabilities to plan, write, and revise opinion essays. *Journal of Learning Disabilities, 29*(2), 197–212.

Wood, K. D. (1990). The collaborative listening-viewing guide: An aid for notetaking. *Middle School Journal, 22*, 53–56.

Wood, K. D. (2011). Bridging print literacies and digital literacies using strategy guides. *Journal of Adolescent and Adult Literacy, 55*(3), 248–252.

Wood, K. D., & Mraz, M. (2005). *Teaching literacy in sixth grade*. New York: Guilford Press.

Worthy, M. J., Moorman, M., & Turner, M. (1999). What Johnny likes to read is hard to find in school. *Reading Research Quarterly, 34*(1), 12–27.

Woyshner, C. (2010). Inquiry teaching with primary source documents: An iterative approach. *Social Studies Research and Practice (Board of Trustees of the University of Alabama), 5*(3), 36–45.

Wright, T. S., & Cervetti, G. N. (2017). A systematic review of the research on vocabulary instruction that impacts text comprehension. *Reading Research Quarterly, 52*(2), 203–226.

Zhang, J., & Dougherty Stahl, K. A. (2011). Collaborative reasoning: Language-rich discussions for English learners. *The Reading Teacher, 65*(4), 257–260.

Index

Note. *f* following a page number indicates a figure.